Focus Units in Literature

Focus Units in Literature

A Handbook for Elementary School Teachers

Joy F. Moss

Harley School and University of Rochester, Rochester,
New York

National Council of Teachers of English
1111 Kenyon Road, Urbana, IL 61801

Grateful acknowledgment is made for permission to reprint the following material. "Everyone is asleep" by Seifu-jo and "The harvest moon is so bright!" by Sodō. From *Don't Tell the Scarecrow and Other Japanese Poems by Issa, Yayū, Kikaku and Other Japanese Poets*. Copyright © 1969 by Scholastic Magazines, Inc., a division of Scholastic, Inc. "The Night" from *Whispers and Other Poems* by Myra Cohn Livingston (Harcourt, Brace and World). Copyright © 1958 by Myra Cohn Livingston. Reprinted by permission of Marian Reiner for the author. "In Bed" from *River Winding: Poems by Charlotte Zolotow* (Thomas Y. Crowell Co.). Text copyright © 1970 by Charlotte Zolotow. Reprinted by permission of Harper & Row, Publishers, Inc. Curtis Brown, Ltd. for "Charlie's Bedtime" by Lee Bennett Hopkins. Copyright © 1972 by Lee Bennett Hopkins. "Night Comes" from *A Bunch of Poems and Verses by Beatrice Schenk de Regniers*. Text copyright © 1977 by Beatrice Schenk de Regniers. Reprinted by permission of Ticknor & Fields/Clarion Books, a Houghton Mifflin Company. Acknowledgment is also made to *The Reading Teacher* for permission to incorporate material from the author's articles in *The Reading Teacher* (March 1982 and April 1983) in the chapters on Jay Williams, folktale patterns, and friendship.

Book Design: Tom Kovacs for TGK Design

NCTE Stock Number 17562

© 1984 by the National Council of Teachers of English.
All rights reserved. Printed in the United States of America.

Library of Congress Cataloging in Publication Data

Moss, Joy F.
    Focus units in literature.

    Bibliography: 8 p.
    1. Children—Books and reading. 2. Children's
literature—Study and teaching (Elementary). 3. Language
arts (Elementary). I. Title.
Z1037.A1M883   1984   372.6   84-14820
ISBN 0-8141-1756-2

Contents

Themes

Fantastic Characters

Dedicated to Arthur, Kathy, Debbie, and David

Introduction

As a teacher of young children for over a decade, I have had the good fortune to observe them in the process of learning to read and write. I discovered that many of the children who were successful in this process had been given a head start by adults who had introduced them to the pleasure and delight associated with books and reading. These children had developed the habit of exploring the world of books, a habit which played a significant role in their approach to learning and their growth as readers. They had discovered the purpose of reading and its relevance to their own individual interests. As a result, they were intrinsically motivated to engage in the process of learning to read and to become readers.

It seems to me that the success of a reading program should be measured in terms of the number of students who eventually establish the habit of reading for personal enjoyment, independent learning, and continued growth. Broad exposure to and meaningful experiences with books at all stages of the process of becoming a reader help to build a background from which children can develop personal preferences and special interests and the motivation to pursue these interests on their own. As the range of reading interests expands, the child discovers new possibilities for reading enjoyment and, in the process, is stimulated to read (or listen to) more books. This continued involvement with books provides the linguistic and conceptual input which is so important for reading growth. So the cycle continues . . . as the child gains experience, competence, and confidence and develops the motivation necessary for the reading habit to become firmly established. This cycle can be set into motion by parents and teachers who provide a rich literary environment for their children and instill in them a love for reading, a lasting treasure and probably one of the finest gifts we can offer our children.

To this end, I designed an instructional model through which children from kindergarten through sixth grade would be given every opportunity to learn about the world of books and to derive pleasure and meaning from their reading experiences. The purpose of this book is to describe this instructional model, which I developed for and with my students and which I have used as a framework for building a literature curriculum.

The first chapter defines the instructional model and introduces its distinguishing features. The second chapter focuses on the theoretical foundations on which this model was constructed. The third chapter outlines categories of questions and suggests sample questions in each category. Subsequent chapters offer examples of the instructional model and suggestions for using it to assist elementary schoolchildren in the process of learning to comprehend, produce, and enjoy written language.

This instructional model is translated into classroom practice through diverse literature units designed to expose children to various literary selections, to promote growth of reading, writing, and thinking skills, and to expand reading interests. Although each literature unit is planned as a separate entity, it would be related to other units which might be implemented in a particular classroom or grade level or as part of a total language arts curriculum for kindergarten through grade six. That is, each discrete literature unit would become an integral part of a long-term, cumulative plan for exploring literature. Each new unit would add to the children's growing literary background and store of comprehension skills and, in the process, would enhance the quality of their response to literature.

Each of these literature units is structured around a central theme or focus. This feature prompted the formulation of the term *Focus Unit* to identify this model of instruction. Subsequent chapters in this book describe Focus Units which have been used in elementary school classrooms to bring literature into the lives of children. By sharing some of my own experiences with children encountering literature, I hope to encourage the readers of this book to try some of the ideas offered and to discover for themselves some of the joys of exploring literature with children.

This instructional model is *not* a method for teaching reading. It was created as a catalyst and vehicle for bringing literature into the classroom. As such, it is an essential ingredient in a language arts program in which instruction in decoding and in the mechanics of reading is integrated with instruction in the comprehension and production of meaningful and relevant written and oral language. The Focus Unit is an instructional sequence in which literature is used as a rich natural resource for developing language and thinking skills and is the starting point for diverse reading and writing experiences. The ultimate goal of each Focus Unit is to contribute to children's literary awareness and appreciation and to their capacity to enjoy reading. If the goal of reading is comprehension and the goal of reading instruction is to produce students with the ability to read for meaning and the motivation to read independently, then a reading program is not complete unless literature is incorporated as an integral component.

Why This Book Was Written

The idea for this book originally came from teachers who had been introduced to the Focus Unit model and had used it in their own class-rooms. They requested some sort of guidebook to assist them in preparing and implementing specific literature units or in developing a more long-term literature program. Through numerous inservice courses and work-shops which I have conducted for elementary school teachers over the years, I have had the opportunity to share this model with a great many teachers from public and private schools in rural, urban, inner-city, and suburban areas. Not long ago I carried out an informal follow-up survey to discover how and to what extent the Focus Unit model had actually been used by participants in these courses. Some of the feedback provided by the teachers may be of interest at this point.

A second-grade teacher explained that she had initially shared several Focus Units with her top reading group and then decided to incorporate a series of units into a literature program designed for the whole class. The children responded to each unit with great excitement, and most of them were stimulated to explore the books in the Focus Unit collection on their own. Over the course of the school year the teacher observed evidence of increased interest and involvement in reading and a definite improvement in the students' ability to discuss books in depth. Other teachers commented on their students' growing capacity to generate signif-icant questions in the analysis of stories and to compare themes, charac-ters, and narrative patterns.

These teachers also noted that the literature experiences afforded by the Focus Units complemented the skill instruction in their reading pro-grams. They witnessed growth in attention span, comprehension skills, vocabulary, and critical thinking.

A few of these teachers related that after they had used the Focus Unit model with first one reading group, and then a second one, and, finally, with the entire class, they began to see possibilities for its use in other curricular areas as well. As one teacher put it, "Literature has become an integral part of every day and every subject area in my first-grade class-room!" However, the majority of the teachers expressed a genuine sense of regret that after introducing one or two units to their students, they were unable to develop additional units as part of an ongoing literature program. They explained that in spite of their own enthusiasm for the model and the enthusiastic feedback from their students, they did not feel they had the time or literary background to do the preparation necessary for creating units "from scratch." One after another, these teachers asked me to develop some type of "Teachers' Guide" which would

provide them with lists of appropriate books and suggestions for questions
and follow-up activities which could be used to develop various Focus
Units. One teacher described the type of format she would find useful:
"I'd like to have a set of outlines or lesson plans for a number of different
kinds of units. Then I could select from this collection the particular units
which will fit best in my classroom." It was this request for assistance
from classroom teachers which prompted me to write this book. It consists
of a series of examples of Focus Units which have actually been used
with children, and it is intended to be used as a guide for planning either
a single unit or a total literature program. This book is written for and
dedicated to all teachers interested in bringing literature into the lives of
children.

Joy F. Moss
Rochester, New York

I Background

1 Literature in the Classroom: Using the Focus Unit to Create a Context for Literacy

An essential dimension of the language arts program in an elementary school classroom is exposure to the world of books. A rich literary environment serves as the context within which literacy is developed. Learning how to read is only a preliminary step in the process of becoming a thoughtful and motivated reader who enjoys books and uses them to promote personal growth. Mature reading involves a dynamic interaction of language, thought, and motivation. Carefully planned experiences with literature within the language arts program can provide much of the linguistic, conceptual, and experiential background the child needs to read with understanding and to read creatively and critically. A literary environment which fosters strong positive attitudes about reading is a critical factor in developing the motivation necessary to learn how to read and to become a reader.

This book presents an instructional model, called the *Focus Unit*, which was designed as a basic framework for planning literary experiences for elementary school classrooms. The Focus Unit is an instructional sequence structured around literature and used to expand comprehension skills and literary interests. The Focus Unit was created as a vehicle for introducing children to the world of literature: a rich world of language, ideas, and human experience in the form of poetry, fable, myth, legend, folktale, contemporary realism, historical fiction, modern fantasy, mystery, adventure, and so on.

This first chapter describes the basic components of the Focus Unit model. Chapter 2 identifies the theoretical foundations of this model, Chapter 3 presents seven categories of questions used in the Focus Units to guide comprehension and composition of narrative, and the remaining chapters provide examples of the Focus Unit model as translated into actual classroom practice. Each of these chapters includes a lesson plan for developing a Focus Unit, a description of its implementation, and a bibliography of the texts used in its preparation and implementation. The chapter titles indicate the focus for each unit and the grade level for which it was designed. These units can be reproduced or modified to fit the needs of individual teachers in terms of classroom setting, scheduling factors, curriculum, and student population. Each unit is presented as a discrete instructional sequence which can be used in the classroom alone or in conjunction with other units to develop a more long-term, cumulative program of literary experience.

Goals and Objectives of the Focus Unit

The first step in planning a Focus Unit is to establish a set of goals and objectives. Ultimately, each unit should bring children closer to becoming motivated, thoughtful readers who view reading as a significant dimension of their total life experience. However, each individual unit is also designed to realize more specific and immediate objectives. These objectives depend on the age, learning needs, background, and interests of the students, the nature of the curriculum, and the instructional goals of the teacher. For example, a major objective for one teacher might be to help students discover the basic literary elements of plot, characterization, setting, theme, and style. Another teacher might designate the development of discussion skills as an important objective. Additional objectives might be the promotion of creative writing skills, the discovery of the literary techniques or style of a particular author, or an understanding of traditional genres such as the fable, myth, or folktale. The next step of the planning phase is to select a focus for the unit, such as survival tales or dragon tales. In the chapters which follow, the objectives for each unit are included in the lesson plan. A survey of the chapter headings will give the reader an idea of the nature and diversity of the themes and topics used as the focus for these units.

Once the objectives are formulated and the focus chosen, the teacher is ready to gather together the books which will serve as the core of the unit. This collection will include books to be read aloud and discussed during group story sessions as well as books for independent reading. Excellent resources are available to assist teachers in their search for background information and appropriate books for a particular unit. (See the Appendix for a list of resources and reference materials.)

The Story Sessions

At the heart of the implementation phase of each unit are the story sessions, which are established as a regular feature of the classroom routine. During each session, the teacher reads aloud one or more selections and then introduces questions to generate group discussion. This discussion or dialogue is a critical feature of the Focus Unit model, and its quality is largely determined by the quality of the teacher's questions. Thus, developing significant questions becomes an important part of the process of planning for each unit. The sample questions which are provided were designed to assist comprehension, to focus attention on important ideas, concepts, and themes, and, in general, to guide the search for meaning.

These regularly scheduled sessions provide a basic structure for the study of literature as a cumulative process through which children can build the literary and linguistic background necessary for critical and creative reading. The regularity of the sessions is intended to suggest their value to the children—to highlight story time as a priority and an integral part of the total curriculum.

Comparing Stories and Developing Concepts

The cumulative nature of the discussions is another characteristic of the Focus Unit model. The stories are introduced to the group in a carefully planned sequence so that each new story is discussed in terms of those read previously. A series of questions is introduced to guide this comparative study of diverse tales and to foster the discovery of significant relationships, recurring patterns, and distinguishing characteristics. Such discoveries serve as the context for forming concepts, making inferences, and developing principles which can be used in subsequent experiences with literature.

George Henry, in his book *Teaching Reading as Concept Development* (1974), observes that reading involves two basic modes of thinking: analysis and synthesis. He sees concept development as a form of synthesis and defines it as "a joining or a relating of things seemingly existing separately—and a discovery of the nature of that relation" (p. 9). Benjamin Bloom, in *Taxonomy of Educational Objectives* (1956), defines synthesis as "the putting together of elements and parts so as to form a whole. . . . In synthesis, the student must draw upon elements from many sources and put these together into a structure or pattern not clearly there before" (p. 162). Synthesis is, thus, a creative process. According to Henry, concept development consists of two basic elements: the discovery of relation and the invention of structure (i.e., a set of discovered relations) (p. 13). He suggests that reading for concept development should be a major goal in reading instruction and language arts programs. To this end, he recommends that children be given ample opportunity and encouragement to relate several works into a "lattice or pattern" (p. 3).

The Focus Unit is designed to provide just such opportunities for exploring a series of stories and forming concepts which unify these separate stories into a cohesive structure. The cumulative discussions elicited by a sequence of questions provide a framework for the creative process of synthesis.

Ultimately, however, these questioning strategies are productive only to the extent that the children internalize the questioning procedures and learn to ask their own questions to initiate the search for meaning. As such autonomy emerges, it is reflected in changes in the nature of the discussions. The children become less dependent upon the teacher as the source of ideas and begin to generate their own questions to guide their search for meaning. Through these explorations, they discover for themselves how each separate tale becomes intricately bound to the others in the collection and how all become woven into an integrated web of literary experience.

Learning to ask significant questions is a critical dimension of the process of becoming a mature reader. Reading comprehension results from an active search for meaning guided by implicit questions which the reader brings to a particular passage, book, or poem. For example, the reader may want to know about the qualities of a character in a novel, how a mystery will be solved, the symbolic meaning of specific words, the author's style or craft, how a villain will be punished, and so on. There is no limit to the possibilities for questions used in the process of exploring written material. However, the quality and complexity of these questions will determine the nature and level of the understanding achieved by the reader.

Independent Reading

In addition to the books read aloud during the group sessions, each Focus Unit suggests books for independent reading. These vary in terms of readability level to meet the diverse reading needs of individual children in each classroom. A silent reading period is scheduled into the daily routine to allow for independent reading and the pursuit of personal interests. Again, the regularity of these free-reading periods suggests to children that reading is valued as a private, personal experience. Thus, the children are provided with selected books for independent reading as well as a quiet time for the solitary enjoyment of those books.

The children are invited to share their personal reading experiences during the group story sessions. Their ideas and insights enrich the discussions; and as the children share their enthusiasm about a particular book, others are stimulated to read it.

Creative Writing

In the context of the Focus Unit model, literature provides a background for creative writing experiences. As children listen to and read stories, they become acquainted with the complex vocabulary and syntax of written language as well as the diversity of style and content in written materials. Children's capacity to compose prose or poetry depends largely on their experience with the language and structure of literature. Through the carefully planned literary experiences of the Focus Unit, teachers can help their students gradually discover the basic literary elements of plot, characterization, setting, style, and theme. These discoveries then become the tools for producing narratives. Thus, listening to, reading, and discussing literature serve as the preparation for the creative writing process. The goal is to help children develop effective writing skills and to expand their capacity to express themselves creatively through written language.

The oral discussions in the story sessions function as the link between the reading and writing experiences in the Focus Unit model. The children are encouraged to reflect on what they have heard or read and to express their thoughts orally. The teacher's questions are designed to assist the comprehension of meaning, to help clarify ideas encountered in the written material, and to focus attention on narrative elements and literary patterns. Through the cumulative discussions, the children gradually build a knowledge of literature which becomes the basis of their own stories. Children cannot create stories in a vacuum; stories evolve out of experience, the mind, and the imagination. In the context of the Focus Unit, a program of guided reading and discussion assists children in the process of story production by building their literary experience and stretching their minds and imaginations. In turn, the production of narrative tends to reinforce their knowledge of written language and thus contributes to their growth as readers.

This connection between reading and writing was made especially clear for one class at Hatley School in Rochester, New York. Soon after the completion of the Sea Focus Unit, the class had the rare privilege of meeting author Scott O'Dell. Many of the children had read two of his books about the sea, *The Black Pearl* and *Island of the Blue Dolphins,* and had numerous questions for him. One child asked how he had learned to be a writer. O'Dell replied, "All writers are readers. . . . The only way to learn to write is to read."

Creative Expression

The Focus Unit model provides other opportunities for creative expression through art, drama, dance, and music. These creative activities enrich the children's involvement with the literary selections and concepts explored during the story sessions. Some of these activities are intended for total class involvement and are designed to reinforce specific concepts developed during the group story sessions. Other activities are optional to allow children to select and pursue areas of special interest. These optional activities or suggested projects for small groups or individuals serve an important function in the heterogeneous classroom by providing a wide range of valid learning experiences for children with diverse learning needs and styles, talents, and experiential backgrounds. Examples of these creative experiences are included in each Focus Unit description.

Summary

The Focus Unit functions as a vehicle for incorporating literature into the elementary school curriculum. Each unit is carefully planned to expose children to literature and to promote the growth of literary appreciation and taste. Children become active participants in the process of exploring language and literature, and they gradually expand their capacity to comprehend narrative and to read and write critically and creatively. The ultimate goal of the Focus Unit model is to provide children with rich and enjoyable literary experiences. These pleasurable experiences will enhance the quality of children's response to literature and will foster positive feelings about reading so that it will become a lifelong habit.

References

Bloom, Benjamin. *Taxonomy of Educational Objectives.* New York: Longman, Green, 1956.
Henry, George. *Teaching Reading as Concept Development.* New York: Holt, Rinehart and Winston, 1972.

2 Theory into Practice

Various studies have yielded impressive evidence that positive and meaningful experiences with books and written language play a critical role in the development of literacy skills. Dolores Durkin (1961), for example, studied children who learned to read before entering first grade. These children were heterogeneous in terms of IQ, mental age, and socioeconomic level. However, Durkin found that all the early readers had been read to regularly at home and that their families had a high regard for books and reading (p. 164).

Margaret Clark, in her book *Young Fluent Readers: What Can They Teach Us?* (1976), recorded similar findings about the home environments of thirty-two children who had learned to read at home without formal instruction. "These homes were providing rich and exciting experiences within which books were indeed an integral part" (p. 45). Books were an important part of the life of the family and its shared experiences. Many of the parents were avid readers and enjoyed reading to their children. They also encouraged their children to select and explore books on their own. "The important role played by the local library in catering for and in stimulating the interest of these children is certainly one striking feature of the study. For most of these children the stimulus to use the library came initially from the parents though it was clear that the children themselves later found it a valuable source of information and enjoyment" (p. 103).

Dorothy Cohen (1968) studied 580 "academically retarded" second-grade children in New York City schools. She found that those who were given the opportunity to listen to carefully selected books which were read aloud every day of the school year made significantly higher gains on tests of Word Knowledge and Reading Comprehension (Metropolitan Reading Achievement Test) than those children who did not have this regular exposure to literature. Cohen's concluding statements about this study highlight some of the factors associated with this improvement in reading scores.

> Continued exposure in early childhood to stories read aloud apparently affects basic, beginning stages of the transition that must take place in growth from comprehension of oral language to the final use of symbols in reading. . . .

The slower the children are in academic progress, the more difficult it is for them to deal with words in isolation, unrelated to a
totally meaningful experience. Vocabulary thus appears to be learned
best by young children in a context of emotional and intellectual
meaning. (P. 213)

Levels of competency in comprehension, oral language, and reading are interrelated, but facility in the last, i.e., the use of symbols,
seems to be dependent on facility in the first two, i.e., oral language
and comprehension. This would imply that comprehension of meaning is basic to growth in the language arts.

Continued and regular listening to story books chosen for their
emotional appeal and ease of conceptualization seems to aid facility
in listening, attention span, narrative sense, recall of stretches of
verbalization, and the recognition of newly learned words as they
appear in other contexts. (P. 217)

Carol Chomsky's study (1972) of the language development of children
from six to ten indicates that language learning continues as an active
process throughout the school years and that a strong correlation exists
between reading exposure and linguistic growth. She explains, "The written language is potentially of a more complex nature than speech, both in
vocabulary and syntax. The child who reads (or listens to) a variety of
rich and complex materials benefits from a range of linguistic inputs that
is unavailable to the non-literary child" (p. 23). Chomsky concludes her
report with the suggestion that "perhaps the best thing that we might do
for [the child] in terms of encouraging this learning would be to make
more of it possible, by exposing him to a rich variety of language inputs
in interesting, stimulating situations" (p. 33).

These and other studies of young readers have served to underscore
the importance of rich and meaningful experiences with books for the
growing child. Such research also served to corroborate my own informal
observations as a teacher and my growing conviction that the quality and
extent of a child's literary background and his or her exposure to written
language are major determinants in the child's response to the challenge
of learning to read and write.

It would be difficult to separate the motivational forces from these
early literary experiences which apparently form a foundation for developing reading and writing skills. A literary environment promoting favor-
able associations with the world of books also tends to motivate the child
to learn to read and to become a reader.

The Reading Process

Reading is a cognitive process. A critical reader draws upon his or her
experiential and conceptual background and language competence and
applies thinking skills to process the information on the page and to

reconstruct what the author has constructed. The reader makes sense of new information by relating it to what is already known. According to Frank Smith, "Reading is not a matter of decoding but consists of bringing meaning to print" (1980, p. 416). Kenneth Goodman's view (1973) of the reading process is similar: "The extent to which a reader can get meaning from written language depends on how much related meaning he brings to it" (p. 9).

Smith uses the term *cognitive structure* to refer to knowledge that is structured or organized, thus making it available for retrieval during the reading process (1975, p. 11). Carol Chomsky's studies of linguistic development highlight the crucial role of language competence in the reading process. If comprehension is the goal of reading instruction, the reading program must include learning experiences designed to build children's store of cognitive structures and language competence. The Focus Unit model incorporates such learning experiences into the elementary school curriculum. The core of the model is literature, used as a resource for developing children's literary background as well as their store of cognitive structures and language competence.

Story Comprehension Research

Research in story comprehension has provided significant insights about the development of cognitive structures underlying children's narrative competence. Of particular interest is a model of narrative comprehension which involves the concept of a *story schema* or cognitive structure influencing the comprehension process. The story schema is based on the assumption that stories have an inner structure or "grammar" made up of a network of categories and the logical relationships between them (Stein and Glenn 1979, p. 58). Nancy Stein (1978) used this story grammar approach in her investigations of children's understanding of stories. She demonstrated that children use their implicit knowledge about story grammar in comprehending and producing narratives. According to Stein, children acquire the story schema as they listen to and read a variety of narratives (p. 7). The Focus Unit, designed as a vehicle for exposing children to a wide range and variety of literature, provides the context for the development of the story schema which children use to make sense of the literary world. In addition, the series of questions used to generate reflection and discussion during the group sessions provides further assistance in the development of story schema: specific questions are introduced to help children discover narrative components and the logical relationships among them. Questions are designed to help children understand and enjoy each story in its own right as well as to evolve a conceptual framework for understanding stories in general.

Questioning and the Discussion Process

The question has been used for centuries as an effective teaching technique to facilitate and evaluate comprehension. In recent years, investigators interested in the comprehension of written language have focused on the role of questioning in molding the quality of thinking done by students as they read or listen to written discourse (Carroll and Freedle 1972; Rothkopf 1970; Frase 1967; Ausubel 1960). Various guidelines have been developed to help formulate questions which stimulate increasingly higher levels of thinking, from simple recognition and recall to inferential thinking, interpretation, analysis, and eventually toward synthesis, evaluation, and application (see, for example, Sanders 1966; Taba 1965; Pearson and Johnson 1978).

Hilda Taba (1965) has stressed that the proper business of the school is to help students become autonomous, creative, and productive thinkers. If the teaching of thinking is to be accomplished, then teaching strategies must be specifically designed to affect the development of cognitive skills. Taba's study of the interaction of teaching and the development of cognitive processes highlights the art of asking questions and its crucial role in the teaching of thinking. She identified three cognitive tasks which would become the primary focus in the formulation of questions: (1) concept formation, (2) the development of generalizations and inferences through interpretation of raw data, and (3) the explanation and prediction of new phenomena by applying known principles and facts (p. 536).

Questioning, as a strategy for teaching thinking, is granted priority status in the Focus Unit model. Chapter 3 describes the categories of questions and provides guidelines and sample questions. Specific questions used to promote reflective thinking are suggested in each of the Focus Units described in the following chapters. Reading is essentially a thinking process; comprehension is its goal. Each Focus Unit is designed to promote reading comprehension skills through questioning. The ultimate objective of these questions is to help children learn to ask their own questions in order to initiate their search for meaning as they engage in the process of comprehending written language.

Writing

Frank Smith, in his book *Writing and the Writer* (1982), distinguishes between two broad aspects of writing: *composition,* "what is said in writing," and *transcription,* "what has to be done to say it, . . . the conventions of spelling, punctuation, grammar, and neatness" (p. 2). According to Smith, "composition and transcription can interfere with each other," especially for the beginning writer (p. 21). His solution to this conflict is to separate these two aspects of writing: "Composition and transcription must be separated, and transcription must come last" (p. 24).

Composition of narrative is an important feature of the Focus Unit model. Students are encouraged to draw from their literary background to generate, organize, and translate ideas into the language and structure of narrative; the teacher responds first to their ideas, to each story as a whole. Only after "what is said" has been given adequate consideration is attention turned to "spelling, punctuation, grammar, and neatness." In this way, the teacher reinforces the message that composition is given priority status in the Focus Unit writing projects. The conventions of transcription are emphasized when students are ready to polish their composition for public sharing.

The teacher's feedback is also intended to help beginning writers discover the nature of writing as communication with a potential audience. Young writers, making the transition from speech to written language, must learn to provide relevant meanings and logical connections for this potential audience. To develop this "sense of audience," students are encouraged to read and reread what they write and to ask themselves: "Does this make sense? Does it say what I wanted to say? Will other readers understand it?" Gradually, beginning writers learn to assume the role of critical reader of their own work, to detect problem areas where meaning is unclear, and to make the revisions necessary to produce a cohesive text which conveys the intended meaning.

Thus, reading plays a significant role in the process of story production—prior to as well as during composition. Numerous studies of children's narrative productions have yielded evidence that exposure to and familiarity with stories contribute to the story-making capabilities of young writers (Rentel and King 1983; Applebee 1978; Mandler and Johnson 1977; Stein and Glenn 1979; Botvin and Sutton-Smith 1977; Winograd 1979; Leondar 1977). The literary experiences introduced prior to creative writing in the Focus Unit sequence are intended to help young writers learn about narrative structures, patterns, and language and to build a framework for composition.

In a longitudinal study of beginning writers, Victor Rentel and Martha King (1983) explored the nature of the transition from speech to written language. In particular, they focused on children's acquisition of cohesion, "language's major resource for linking elements of a discourse" (p. 140). The Focus Unit writing activities were designed to help students produce clear, comprehensible narratives and develop cohesion by becoming critical readers of their own compositions.

Exploring literature, the great reservoir of written language, should be an integral part of reading instruction and the language arts curriculum throughout the elementary school years. The transition from oral to written language requires a qualitative leap which carries significant implications for the teacher of reading and writing.

References

Applebee, Arthur N. *The Child's Concept of Story: Ages Two to Seventeen.* Chicago: University of Chicago Press, 1978.

Ausubel, D. P. "The Use of Advance Organizers in the Learning and Retention of Meaningful Verbal Material." *Journal of Educational Psychology* 51 (1960): 267–72.

Botvin, G. J., and B. Sutton-Smith. "The Development of Structural Complexity in Children's Fantasy Narratives." *Developmental Psychology* 13 (1977): 377–88.

Carroll, J., and R. Freedle. *Language Comprehension and the Acquisition of Knowledge.* Washington, D.C.: V. H. Winston and Sons, 1972.

Chomsky, Carol. "Stages in Language Development and Reading Exposure." *Harvard Educational Review* 42 (1972): 1–33.

Clark, Margaret. *Young Fluent Readers: What Can They Teach Us?* London: Heinemann Educational Books, 1976.

Cohen, Dorothy H. "The Effect of Literature on Vocabulary and Reading Achievement." *Elementary English* 45 (1968): 209–17.

Durkin, Dolores. "Children Who Read before Grade One." *The Reading Teacher* 14 (1961): 163–66.

Frase, L. "Learning from Prose Material: Length of Passage, Knowledge of Results, and Position of Questions." *Journal of Educational Psychology* 58 (1967): 266–72.

Goodman, Kenneth. *Miscue Analysis.* Urbana, Illinois: National Council of Teachers of English, 1973.

Leondar, B. "Hatching Plots: Genesis of Storymaking." In *The Arts and Cognition,* edited by D. Perkins and B. Leondar. Baltimore: Johns Hopkins University Press, 1977.

Mandler, J. M., and N. S. Johnson. "Remembrance of Things Parsed: Story Structure and Recall." *Cognitive Psychology* 9 (1977): 111–51.

Pearson, P. D., and D. Johnson. *Teaching Reading Comprehension.* New York: Holt, Rinehart and Winston, 1972.

Rentel, Victor, and Martha King. "Present at the Beginning." In *Research on Writing: Principles and Methods,* edited by Peter Mosenthal et al. New York: Longman, 1983.

Rothkopf, E. Z. "The Concept of Mathemagenic Activities." *Review of Educational Research* 40 (1970): 371–93.

Sanders, Norris. *Classroom Questions. What Kinds?* New York: Harper and Row, 1966.

Smith, Frank. *Comprehension and Learning: A Conceptual Framework for Teachers.* New York: Holt, Rinehart and Winston, 1975.

————. "Making Sense of Reading—And of Reading Instruction." In *Thought and Language/Language and Reading,* edited by Maryanne Wolf, Mark K. McQuillan, and Eugene Radwin, 415–24. Cambridge, Massachusetts: *Harvard Educational Review,* Reprint Series No. 14, 1980.

————. *Writing and the Writer.* New York: Holt, Rinehart and Winston, 1982.

Stein, Nancy. "How Children Understand Stories: A Developmental Analysis." University of Illinois Technical Report, no. 69. Champaign, Illinois: Center for the Study of Reading, March 1978.

Stein, Nancy, and C. G. Glenn. "An Analysis of Story Comprehension in Elementary School Children." In *New Directions in Discourse Processing,* vol. 2, edited by R. O. Freedle. Norwood, New Jersey: Ablex, 1979.

Taba, Hilda. "The Teaching of Thinking." *Elementary English* 42 (May 1965): 534–42.

Winograd, T. A. "A Framework for Understanding Discourse." In *Cognitive Processes in Comprehension,* edited by M. A. Just and P. A. Carpenter. New York: Halsted Press, 1979.

3 Guidelines for Questioning

Questions for the Focus Unit story sessions described in subsequent chapters are drawn primarily from seven general categories. These categories suggest various strategies for interacting with literature and provide guidelines for planning story sessions and formulating questions. The questions associated with each category are used in the Focus Units to guide comprehension as well as composition of narrative and to serve as models for questioning strategies used in critical reading and writing. The ultimate goal is to produce independent readers and writers capable of initiating their own questions as an aid to thoughtful comprehension and production of written language.

Category 1: Setting the Stage for Reading and Writing

The first category includes questions introduced prior to reading or writing. Such questions are designed to focus attention on relevant background information, to invite children to make predictions about story content before reading, and to help children organize relevant information and ideas before writing. In short, category-one questions are associated with preparation, with setting the stage for reading and writing.

At the beginning of a story session, the children were asked to look at the cover, title page, and endpapers of a particular book and to respond to such questions as:

1. What information is provided about this story?
2. Look at the picture on the cover. Can you find clues that tell you about the setting of this story?
3. Are there any words in the title that are unfamiliar to you? Who can explain these words?
4. What does the title tell you about the story? Can you guess from the title what kind of story it will be? Fantasy? True-to-life? Humorous? Can you guess what the story will be about?
5. Can you name any other books by this author or illustrator?
6. What is meant by the words *retold by, translated by, adapted by?*

7. Look at the endpapers. Do you have any questions about them? What additional information about the story is provided in these illustrations?

8. Why is it especially important to look at the copyright date of a science fiction story? What is the meaning of such phrases as "This book is dated" or "That book is out of date"?

9. What do you think the author meant by his or her dedication? (Sometimes the dedication can be best understood after reading or listening to the story.)

The preliminary dialogues generated by questions in category one were used to help children get ready for comprehension. For example, if the children did not have adequate conceptual background to understand a particular story, the initial discussion focused on the unfamiliar concept or concepts. Thus, before reading *Blueberries for Sal* by Robert McCloskey, the teacher asked the children to study the endpapers, which showed Sal and her mother engaged in canning berries. Since most of the children had not been exposed to the process of canning, information was provided to ensure comprehension of the meaning of this story. For another story, the preparatory discussion was used to help the children draw relevant information from their memory. Before listening to *Timothy's Flower* by Jean Van Leeuwen, the children were asked to identify the setting for this story and to discuss its characteristic features. Then, as they listened to the story, they were able to make sense of the events and to understand the significance of a single yellow flower to an urban child.

Discussions about the title or the cover illustration frequently generated predictions about the story which, in turn, set into motion a process of active, purposeful listening or reading. These initial predictions were confirmed, revised, or replaced by new ones as the story unfolded.

Preparation for writing was also guided by questions in this category. Since the focus of each unit provided a central theme or topic for composition, this preparation started with a review of the literature and literary discoveries featured in the story sessions. Then, questions about story structure were introduced to help children organize their thinking prior to and during the creative process. For example:

1. Who is your main character?

2. What other characters will be in your story?

3. Is there a villain in your story?

4. Where will your story take place?

5. Is your story make-believe or true-to-life?

6. What is the problem in your story?

7. How will it be solved?

Category 2: Focusing on the Basic Story

The second category includes questions beginning with *who, what, where,* and *when* and focusing on the characters, plot, and setting. These questions direct attention to the literal level of the story, information given explicitly in the text and/or pictures.

Here are some sample questions which require literal recognition or recall of explicit statements in a story:

1. Who are the main characters?
2. What words are used to describe them?
3. Where does the story take place? Did the clues on the front cover or endpapers help you make an accurate prediction about the setting?
4. When did this story take place? Find the words that tell when it happened. What season of the year was it at the beginning of the story? at the end?
5. What happened before _____? What did _____ do after _____? (These questions ask about the sequence of events.)
6. What did the author tell you about the character's problem? (In some stories, the author provides an explicit statement about the internal problem of the main character; for example, "she is shy," "he was lonely," "she was afraid of monsters," "he had a fear of the sea." In other stories, the central problem is implied and must be inferred by the students.)
7. What happened to this character? What was this character's plan to solve his or her problem? How did he or she manage to escape? (In some stories, the problem is external and obvious, such as the pursuit of the gingerbread boy by a series of hungry characters, the capture of a main character by pirates, or the need to survive on a deserted island.)

Although questions in this second category are generally introduced following the story, at times it is necessary to insert one or more of these questions during the story in order to help children cope with any problems they might have with the basic plot sequence. For example, they may need help to recall a specific character who has reappeared in the story after a series of intervening events. Or they may need to be reminded of information provided early in the story which contributes significantly to the reader's understanding of subsequent events.

Category 3: Preparing for Literary Analysis

Questions in the third category are intended to help children develop an awareness of the structure and language of literature and the skills necessary for literary analysis. These questions draw attention to basic narrative elements (setting, plot, character, style, theme) and the relationships among these elements. In addition, questions in this category are designed to help children use their store of literary skills as a resource for comprehension and composition.

In contrast to the questions in the second category, the questions in this third category require the listener or reader to make inferences about implicit information in the text and to apply his or her literary abilities. Here are some sample third-category questions:

1. What do you know about this character? Look for information in the character's conversations, inner thoughts, and behavior and in the speech, thoughts, and deeds of other characters.

2. Do any of the characters act in ways which are unexpected or surprising? (For example, in the modern fairy tales of Jay Williams, traditional character-types depart from traditional patterns, such as the brave and handsome princess who rescued the vain and passive prince in *Petronella.*)

3. What caused the character's problem?

4. How did the characters change during the story? How would you explain the changes?

5. What information do *you* have about the main character that is not revealed to the other characters? (For example, in William Steig's *The Real Thief,* the author lets the reader know what the main character is thinking. This privileged information is not available to the other characters.)

6. What did the main character learn? What did the other characters learn?

7. Is there a villain in this story? Who do you think is the villain? What role does this villain play in the sequence of events? How would the story be different if this character were not in it?

8. How was the setting important for the development of this story? (For example, the urban setting in *Timothy's Flower* by Jean Van Leeuwen played a key role in this story about a small boy's search for a way to nurture a single yellow flower.)

9. What was the author's message? Why do you think the author wrote this story? What do you think is the most important thing to remember about this story?

10. Think about the title again. What does the title mean to you now?

11. Look at the endpapers again. Can you think of new ways to interpret these pictures now that you know the story? Explain these pictures as symbols for the story's theme.

12. Where do you think the author got his or her ideas for this story?

13. What other stories does this remind you of? Explain how they're connected.

14. Think about the fables we've read. In what way is this story like a fable? How is it different?

15. What special patterns can you find in this story? What other stories have these patterns? (For example, the story might have a parallel plot pattern such as in *Blueberries for Sal* by Robert McCloskey and *Shadow Bear* by Joan Harlow or a story-within-a-story pattern such as in *The Biggest House in the World* by Leo Lionni and *The Chinese Storyteller* by Pearl Buck. Or, the story might include traditional patterns of folklore, such as three sons, three tasks, and three wishes.)

The language of literature is filled with metaphor, simile, idiomatic expression, connotation, allusion, poetry, symbolism, and conventional patterns for introducing and concluding a narrative or describing a traditional character. These sample questions focus attention on the language of literature and clarify figurative language:

1. What is special about the words chosen by the author of this story?

2. What other author writes like this one?

3. Can you identify the writing styles of particular authors?

4. Think about the stories you've read by this author. How would you describe his or her special use of language or style? Are there any stories by this author which seem to depart from this style? (For example, in one discussion of the language patterns used by specific authors, a seven-year-old commented, "I sure was surprised when I found out that Dr. Seuss wrote that story about Bartholomew Cubbins [*The 500 Hats of Bartholomew Cubbins*]. I couldn't believe it at first! It sure is different than those books like *The Cat in the Hat* and *Hop on Pop*.")

5. What words tell you that this is a tall tale? a fairy tale? a legend?

6. Find some words or phrases which are unusual or especially colorful or invented.

7. Find names of characters which have symbolic meaning or special significance or which tell you that the author likes to play with words.

8. Find words which are associated with a specific country or another language.

9. What is another way to say this? Use your own words to explain the meaning of this phrase.

10. What story is the author referring to here? Why mythical hero or heroine does the author want you to associate with the character in this story? What words does the author use to suggest this association?

11. Find words which tell you that this tale is being told by a story-teller. (For example, in *A Story, A Story,* retold by Gail Haley, the opening and closing lines reflect the storyteller's presence: "Once, oh small children round my knee, there were no stories on earth to hear" and "This is my story which I have related. If it be sweet, or if it be not sweet, take some elsewhere, and let some come back to me." This question helped the children become aware of the way the language of written versions of folktales can reflect their origins as oral tales.)

Many of the ideas explored by these and similar questions were used as the starting point for story production. For example, one project involved the creation of a story with a parallel plot; another project focused on the use of interesting words to create vivid images; in another assignment, the children created characters whose behavior revealed thoughts and feelings. Practice in producing a logical plot sequence with basic narrative elements was provided by an assignment in which children wrote the text for a wordless picture book, *The Silver Pony* by Lynd Ward. Fourth-grade and fifth-grade students produced diverse narratives which reflected their individualized interpretations of this remarkable story-in-pictures. In another writing project, the students rewrote in their own words the figurative language used by a particular author. A passage from *Miss Maggie* by Cynthia Rylant provided a good sample for the students to rewrite:

> If his feet had listened to his head, Nat would have bounded out of that house in a flash. But his feet weren't listening. Only his heart.

Category 4: Exploring Implied Meanings and Logical Relationships

The fourth category includes questions about motives, feelings, and thoughts of story characters; reasons behind their behavior; the relationship between events in the narrative sequence; and the underlying theme or message of the story. For the reader, these questions stimulate inferential thinking; for the writer, they set up a framework for evaluating the story-in-progress in terms of coherence and meaning.

The questions associated with this category were often introduced in the course of reading a story aloud to assist comprehension of implied and subtle meanings. Others were asked after the reading was complete. Here are some sample questions:

1. What do you think this character is thinking? What clues help you?

2. How do you think this character feels? What clues help you?

3. Why did _____ finally decide to _____?

4. What was the reason for _____?

5. What goal or purpose was behind this character's behavior? What do you think were his or her intentions?

6. How did the main character feel about the new boy in the first part of this story? How did he seem to feel at the end of the story? What was the reason for this change in attitude?

7. Why do you think the main character behaved the way he or she did? Which character seemed to understand him or her?

8. Why do you think the people feared the stranger who suddenly appeared in their village?

9. Why did this character suddenly run away from the game? How did the other characters interpret this strange behavior?

10. What do you think will happen next? (This question occasionally was inserted at natural transition points in a story so that students could try to predict the outcomes or consequences of the behavior of specific characters or so they could suggest the logical sequence of events.)

As the children wrote their own stories, they were encouraged to ask themselves similar questions about their characters and the sequence of events. For beginning writers, the teacher and peers provided feedback with such questions as "Why did that character do that?" or "How did that character happen to know about the hidden treasure?" Gradually, these young writers began to initiate their own questions to determine the coherence of their narratives and to detect missing links in a particular sequence of events. Building and refining these questioning strategies enabled them to become critical readers of their own writing.

Category 5: Appreciating the Art of Story

Questions in the fifth category help the students to build a foundation for literary appreciation by focusing on literary techniques, forms, and genres and the craft of the author and the illustrator.

Here are some examples of questions designed to call attention to the art of story and the art of illustration:

1. What kind of story is this? (For example, fable, myth, fairy tale, historical fiction, tall tale, etc.)
2. Is it a fantasy or a realistic story?
3. How did this author combine fantasy and realism to create this story? (For example, in such books as *Charlotte's Web* by E. B. White or *The Mermaid's Three Wisdoms* by Jane Yolen.)
4. What techniques did the author use to create such a funny story?
5. Did the characters seem like real people? If so, how did the author create such believable characters? If not, why didn't they seem to be real people?
6. Find examples of the author's use of words to paint vivid pictures.
7. Why do you think this author used a journal to tell this story?
8. Why did this author choose to begin this story with a flashback?
9. How did this author get you to feel anger? sympathy? suspense? frustration? relief? excitement?
10. What clues did the author give you in the beginning of the story to help you guess how it might end?
11. What did this story tell you about the author as a person?
12. What special media or techniques did the artist use to illustrate this story?
13. Why do you think the artist chose this particular style for this tale?
14. How did the artist's media seem to fit the mood of this story?
15. How did the artist show how this character was feeling?
16. Compare two or more artists' interpretations of a traditional fairy tale.
17. What information can you learn from the illustrations in this book which cannot be found by reading the text?
18. Look at various books illustrated by one particular artist. What do you notice?

Children who had begun to feel comfortable as authors were ready to experiment with some of these techniques and styles in creating their own stories and illustrations. To encourage such experimentation, selected questions in this category were revised to serve as suggestions for writing projects:

1. Create word portraits of four different characters in a fairy tale. Then, ask your partner to draw a picture of each of these characters according to your descriptions.

2. Write a story which begins with a flashback.

3. Write a story which makes your audience feel scared, which keeps them in suspense, or which makes them curious about something.

4. Make an illustration for a humorous story about two talking mice. Then, make an illustration for a realistic account of two mice who live in the woods. How will these pictures differ in terms of media and technique?

5. Create a picture of a castle inhabited by an evil sorcerer. Create another picture of a castle in which a lovely princess lives.

6. Describe the place in the forest where a wicked witch lives. Then describe another place in the forest where a kind old woodcutter and his wife live.

7. Write a dialogue between two people having an argument.

8. Write a story in which you give hints or clues in the beginning about how the story will end.

9. Create your own illustrations for the story you heard today. (The teacher had selected a story from a collection without illustrations.) Then, look at the illustrations produced by other students for this project. What differences in interpretation of characters and settings do you find?

Category 6: Recognizing Interconnections in Literature

Questions in the sixth category stimulate students' thinking and awareness beyond a given text, helping them to grasp larger meanings through comparative analysis and synthesis. The young reader/writer who internalizes these larger meanings, literary themes, and narrative structures and patterns can use them to enrich subsequent comprehension and composition experiences.

A central feature of the Focus Unit model is its emphasis on the interconnections and interplay among the diverse narratives which make up the world of literature. The questions in category six are designed to foster the search for and discovery of these connections and relationships. Through comparative studies of a wide variety of literary selections, students develop an awareness of the building/borrowing process through which the oral tradition evolved, the complex links between traditional and modern literature, and the recurring patterns, themes, motifs, and techniques which cross all boundaries of space and time and which reflect the universal qualities of human experience. Young readers gradually learn to approach each new text in light of previous literary experiences and move toward an understanding of the fundamental unity of literature.

Some questions used to generate comparative analyses of narrative elements (character, plot, setting, theme, style), types, subjects, and motifs are included below:

1. What other story character had a problem similar to the one which troubled the character in this story?

2. What patterns do you find in this group of folktales?

3. Which of these stories are about greed? loyalty? friendship? courage? cooperation? pride? justice?

4. What do these five stories say about the nature of courage?

5. What do these modern fairy tales have in common? What did the authors borrow from traditional fairy tales? What technique did these authors use to create humor?

6. Consider these three stories written by the same author. What do you think is this author's attitude toward _____ ?

7. Compare Leo Lionni's modern fables with the traditional fables of Aesop. What similarities and differences do you find? What can you say about the philosophies expressed in these two groups of fables?

8. What do these folktales from _____ tell you about this country and its people? What have you learned about their religions? customs and traditions? occupations? art and architecture? the natural features of this land?

9. The main characters in these three stories have similar problems. How does each character attempt to solve his or her problems? What are the important differences in their responses?

10. How was the youngest child portrayed in each of these modern and traditional stories? How would you explain the similarities?

11. Each of these three stories takes place in a small fishing village. In what other ways are these stories similar? What is the role of setting in these stories?

12. Find clues which suggest that this author is using the form of a traditional legend to tell the story.

13. Look at this list of the stories we have been reading. Which ones would you identify as "quest tales"? Why?

14. We have been reading fables from different countries. What are the special characteristics of these tales? How would you define the fable as a literary form? (After formulating a definition of this genre, the children were asked to test the validity of their definition. New fables were read aloud and analyzed in terms of the specific elements included in their definition. After appropriate revisions were made, the definition was used as the starting point for a writing project in which the children created their own fables.)

15. Look at the list of fables we have read so far. Which ones do you think illustrate the proverb "Pride goeth before destruction, and a haughty spirit before a fall"?

16. Compare the fables of Aesop, the Greek slave, with the fables of La Fontaine, the seventeenth-century French poet.

17. We have been reading legends from different countries. What kinds of questions were addressed in these tales? How did storytellers in different cultures attempt to explain the mysteries of nature? (The children were asked to produce their own explanatory tales. Each child formulated a question, which became the story title, and created a story to answer this question.)

18. Compare the creation myths we have been reading. What are the similarities and differences?

19. One of the characters in each of these stories did not understand the concept of reflection. What problems did this cause for each character? (See, for example, *The Rain Puddle* by Adelaide Holl, *Squawk to the Moon, Little Goose* by Edna Preston, *Flim and Flam and the Big Cheese* by Christian Garrison.)

20. The main characters in these stories learn something about justice, but each one learns something different about this idea. What are some of the different meanings, interpretations, and viewpoints associated with the concept of justice?

The larger ideas and concepts explored in these discussions served as the starting point for composition, which, in turn, served to reinforce and enhance comprehension. For example, for one writing project the children were asked to create a story using some of the recurring motifs and character types found in the folktales of a particular country. Another project focused on a central theme found in a group of international tales. Although at times a whole class was given a single assignment for the writing project, at other times the children were given a list of suggested topics from which to choose according to individual interests. Thus, some children chose to write contemporary versions of traditional tales; others tried to replicate the style of a favorite author or artist; and others decided to rewrite a known story from a different viewpoint or with an alternative ending.

Category 7: Building Bridges between the Story World and the Child's World

The seventh category of questions builds bridges between the story world and the child's own world of reality, imagination, and dreams. Some of the questions in this category encourage children to relate stories to their own experience, to identify with a character's feelings and concerns, and to gain insights about their own lives and their relationships to others. Other questions are designed to expand thoughts beyond "what is" to "what could be." Finally, this category includes questions which prompt children to stand back from the story and to respond to it objectively. They are asked to evaluate the story in terms of their own experience, knowledge, and values as well as information gathered from written sources.

The first type of question in this category is designed to elicit subjective responses to stories. At times, these questions generated comments reflecting intense emotion as children drew from their personal experiences and inner lives. Indeed, the children often needed no prompting to respond spontaneously to a story with personal meanings linking their inner world to the world outside. Below are some sample questions used to help clarify and refine subjective responses to a story.

1. Could this story really happen?
2. How did you feel about this character?
3. Did you ever know someone like this character?
4. Has this ever happened to you? Did you ever feel this way?
5. Did you like the way this character solved his or her problem? What is another way he or she could have solved it?
6. What do you think this character learned about other people and their feelings?
7. What do you think this character will do the next time something like this happens?

The storyteller invites his or her audience to imagine, to dream, and to hope. Children who respond to this invitation, who venture into the story world and discover its hidden treasures, take the first critical step in the process of becoming readers who turn to books for personal enjoyment and growth and of becoming writers who stretch their minds and imaginations to make their own contributions to the world of story. Sample questions that help to stimulate imaginative thinking and dreaming are listed below:

1. What would you have done with those three wishes? (Responses to this question could also be incorporated into writing, painting, or drama.)

2. The character in this story really wanted to become an artist. What do you really want to become?

3. What would you do if Crow Boy (*Crow Boy* by Taro Yashima) became a member of this class?

4. What if you found a monster like Moogi (*Good Night, Orange Monster* by Betty Jean Lifton) in your closet?

5. What if the author asked you to write another ending or a new chapter or a sequel to this story? What do you think you'd write? (These "what if" questions are excellent starting points for imaginative writing and dramatic expression as well as for discussion.)

The third type of question in this category is designed to foster objective evaluations of the author and the story:

1. Do you agree with the author's solution to the problem?

2. Do you think the conclusion was a realistic one?

3. Why do you think this author wrote this book? What was his or her purpose? How was this purpose revealed in the story?

4. What do you think about the way the author describes and treats this character? (It might be especially appropriate to examine the author's portrayal of minority or handicapped characters.)

5. Does the author seem to favor or support any one character? Which one?

6. Could these characters really exist? Could these events really occur?

7. Does the author seem to have strong feelings about a particular issue?

8. Does the author use a particular character to express his or her own message?

9. Is the author trying to convince you to think or feel a certain way? If so, how does he or she do this?

10. Does the author reveal his or her personal attitudes? biases? opinions? Did you approve of or agree with the author's view?

11. Do you think the author tried to show both sides of an issue?

12. How can you determine if the author has treated a historical person or period accurately?

13. Is the central theme of this story presented directly or indirectly?

14. Which character in this story provided wisdom and perspective?

15. Can you identify any characters who protested against the injustice and inequities in this story? Who are they? How did they protest? What does it mean if no one objected to the injustice?

16. Would you recommend this book to a friend? Why?

Concluding Comments

These seven categories were developed to serve as guides for formulating questions that foster critical responses to literature. However, a note of caution about the use of the sample questions may be in order at this point. These questions are offered as suggestions and should be used sparingly. Too many questions and overanalysis can turn the enjoyment of literary exploration and discovery into the drudgery of meaningless drill. Furthermore, each category includes a representative sampling of the range of questions appropriate for the different developmental levels from grades one to six. Thus, before using any of these sample questions, the teacher is urged to consider the age, experience, and learning needs of the children in question as well as their level of involvement and interest at a given time.

The art of teaching is, in large part, the art of asking significant, well-timed questions which stretch students' minds and imaginations, suggest ways to interact with literature, and help them move toward growth and understanding as independent learners.

II Focus Units

4 Toy Animals: A Focus Unit for Grades One and Two

Toy animals play an important role in the lives of most six- and seven-year-olds. Because young children enjoy talking about their animals and frequently bring their favorites to school, stories about stuffed toys were selected for this Focus Unit. The theme was chosen specifically for its relevance and intrinsic emotional appeal for this age group.

Objectives

1. To provide enjoyable and meaningful experiences with literature.
2. To provide a context for independent exploration of books.
3. To provide practice in attending to and comprehending written language.
4. To analyze and compare stories in terms of setting, character, viewpoint, plot, and theme.
5. To provide opportunities for creative expression through the production of original stories.

Bibliography for the Toy Animal Focus Unit

I. Group Story Sessions

Craft, Ruth. **The Winter Bear.** New York: Atheneum, 1975.

This is a gentle story-poem about a child who discovers a toy bear hidden in a tree one cold, wintry day.

Flora, James. **Sherwood Walks Home.** New York: Harcourt, Brace and World, 1966.

Sherwood is a windup bear who is determined to walk home to Robert, his owner, before his motor runs down.

Note: This Focus Unit was originally described by the author in *Language Arts* 54 (May 1977): 537–42, under the title, "Learning to Write by Listening to Literature." Excerpts from the article have been incorporated into this chapter.

Freeman, Don. **Corduroy.** New York: Viking Press, 1968.
> Corduroy, a stuffed bear who lives in a toy department, has several adventures while waiting for someone to buy him and give him a home.

Hughes, Shirley. **David and Dog.** Englewood Cliffs, New Jersey: Prentice-Hall, 1977.
> When David loses his beloved, soft brown toy named Dog, his whole family joins in the search. This is a sensitive story with a satisfying conclusion.

Larranaga, Robert. **Sniffles.** Minneapolis: Carolrhoda Books, 1973.
> Due to an error in a toy factory, a toy dog is made of green tweed instead of fur and has a zipper where there should have been a mouth. He had to wait a long time in a department store before a little boy, allergic to fur, finally chose the little tweed dog as the perfect toy.

Lionni, Leo. **Alexander and the Wind-up Mouse.** New York: Pantheon Books, 1969.
> Alexander, a real mouse, envies his friend Willy, who is the favorite toy of a little girl, and he decides to ask a magic lizard to change him into a toy. However, a subsequent discovery causes him to revise his wish.

Ormondroy, Edward. **Theodore.** Berkeley: Parnassus Press, 1971.
> Lucy's special toy bear, Theodore, has a rather frightening adventure due to Lucy's carelessness. But Theodore is a clever bear and manages to return to Lucy for a joyful reunion.

Waber, Bernard. **Ira Sleeps Over.** Boston: Houghton Mifflin, 1972.
> Ira, excited about sleeping overnight at a friend's house, is troubled with a dilemma: should he bring his teddy bear or leave it at home? His problem is solved when he discovers that his friend, too, sleeps with a teddy bear.

II. Independent Reading

Binzen, William. **Alfred Goes Flying.** New York: Doubleday, 1976.

——. **Alfred the Little Bear.** New York: Doubleday, 1970.

Bornstein, Ruth. **Annabelle.** New York: Thomas Y. Crowell, 1978.

Bull, Peter. **The Teddy Bear Book.** New York: Random House, 1969.

Freeman, Don. **Beady Bear.** New York: Viking Press, 1954.

——. **A Pocket for Corduroy.** New York: Viking Press, 1978.

Hillert, Margaret. "My Teddy Bear." In **Go to Bed! A Book of Bedtime Poems,** selected by Lee Bennett Hopkins. New York: Alfred A. Knopf, 1979.

Hoban, Lillian. **Arthur's Honey Bear.** New York: Harper and Row, 1974.

Howe, Deborah. **Teddy Bear's Scrapbook.** New York: Atheneum, 1980.

Jaques, Faith. **Tilly's House.** New York: Atheneum, 1979.

————. **Tilly's Rescue.** New York: Atheneum, 1981.

Joerns, Consuelo. **The Forgotten Bear.** New York: Four Winds Press, 1978.

Jones, Harold. **There and Back Again.** New York: Atheneum, 1977.

Marcin, Marietta. **A Zoo in Her Bed.** New York: Coward-McCann, 1963.

Memling, Carl. **Little Bear's Mother.** Berkeley: Ariel Books, 1959.

Milne, A. A. **The House at Pooh Corner.** New York: E. P. Dutton, 1928.

————. **Winnie-the-Pooh.** New York: E. P. Dutton, 1926.

Ormondroyd, Edward. **Theodore's Rival.** Berkeley: Parnassus Press, 1971.

Pearson, Susan. **Izzie.** New York: Dial Press, 1975.

Williams, Margery. **The Velveteen Rabbit.** New York: Doubleday, 1926.

Wright, Dare. **Edith and Midnight.** Garden City, New York: Doubleday, 1978.

————.**The Little One.** New York: Doubleday, 1959.

————.**The Lonely Doll.** New York: Doubleday, 1957.

————.**The Lonely Doll Learns a Lesson.** New York: Random House, 1961.

Group Story Sessions

First Session

The Toy Animal Focus Unit was introduced to the children by the teacher reading aloud *Sherwood Walks Home* by James Flora. This humorous story about a windup bear uses repetitive language patterns suggestive of traditional cumulative folktales. The children were encouraged to respond spontaneously to the story before the introduction of specific questions designed to generate discussion and assist comprehension of narrative. The question "What was the problem Sherwood tried to solve?" was intended to focus attention on the plot. "Why questions" were asked to focus on the logical relationships inherent in the narrative—how one event leads to another. For example, the question "Why did Sherwood walk into the bear's cage and then into the lake, instead of going around them?" points to the relationship between Sherwood's limitations as a windup bear and the sequence of events in the story. Other questions were introduced to draw attention to elements of narrative such as form, viewpoint, and setting, as well as position on a reality/fantasy continuum. For example, the question "Does this story remind you of any other stories you've heard?" prompted recall of such familiar folktales as *The Golden Goose, The Gingerbread Boy,* and *Henny Penny.* The children recognized the repetitive pattern characteristic of popular cumulative stories from the oral tradition. In response to the question "Do you think this story could have happened in real life?" the children decided that *Sherwood Walks Home* is a make-believe story. When asked to provide evidence to support this decision, they commented:

> "A windup bear couldn't *really* go that far."

> "A real fish couldn't just walk out of water like that."

> "A policeman wouldn't act like that in real life."

> "Those pictures *look* like make-believe. They're sort of like cartoons."

> "They're just supposed to be funny, not true, not like things really *are.*"

Second Session

Next *The Winter Bear* by Ruth Craft was read aloud, and the children were asked to focus on narrative elements through a comparison of these two storybooks. The children noticed that the rhythm and rhymed lines of *The Winter Bear* differed from the language in Sherwood's story. They observed that one story was set in winter, the other in summer. They noted that the main character in *Sherwood Walks Home* was a toy bear whose thoughts and feelings were revealed by the author, while the main character in *The Winter Bear* was a boy, and the reader was not told how the toy bear felt or what he was thinking. Thus, they discovered that stories are told from different viewpoints and that the author provides information accordingly.

When asked, "Could this story have actually happened?" the children concluded that in contrast to *Sherwood Walks Home, The Winter Bear* was more realistic and that the story could occur in real life. During their discussion the children listed the specific clues they used to arrive at this conclusion:

> "The people talk, but the toy doesn't, so it's more real."

> "Toys can't talk. When they do, you know it's pretend."

"The pictures are pretty and look real."

"It looks like the artist went outside and copied real trees and things."

"The artist didn't try to make the pictures look funny."

"It really *looks* cold and shivery!"

"I think the author [Ruth Craft] really wanted you to think she was telling a true story, but Mr. Flora was just having fun."

The children gradually became literary critics as they discussed the two authors' purposes, characterization, and language techniques, as well as the interaction between the narrative and the illustrations. They were gradually building up a store of knowledge about the basic elements of narrative. Later, they would be able to tap this store as they became involved in the process of producing their own narratives.

Third Session

In this story session, two stories were read aloud and discussed: *Sniffles* by Robert Larranaga and *Corduroy* by Don Freeman. When asked to compare these stories, the children began to make use of the framework which had been developed in the previous discussions. They looked at settings, characters, viewpoint, and the "problems." Then they were asked to think about all four of the stories heard so far. Through synthesis, they discovered common threads: that each toy animal had needed someone, and that two had been left outside while the other two waited in toy departments for a customer to choose them. The discussion soon centered on the children's own experiences with their toy animals. Several children reflected that they liked to pretend that their toys came alive after dark just like Corduroy; others attributed feelings and thoughts to their own beloved animals. This led to an interesting insight: "Maybe Mr. Flora had a toy bear that he loved so much he decided to make up a book about him!" The other children concurred with this child's idea and concluded that "you'd have to own a teddy to really know about the way he feels!"

Fourth Session

After listening to *Alexander and the Wind-up Mouse* by Leo Lionni, the children were asked, "Why did Alexander, the real mouse, envy Willie, the windup mouse?" This question generated responses which indicated their understanding of the basic problem or conflict in the story as well as a spontaneous discussion of the sequence of events. The question "Why did Alexander change his mind about his wish when he finally found the purple pebble?" was intended to help clarify what Alexander learned when he discovered his friend, Willie, in the box of discarded toys.

The next question, "How is this story similar to a fairy tale?" elicited the following responses:

"It has magic."

"Alexander got his wish granted."

"A toy gets changed into a real animal like when a frog gets changed into a prince in a fairy tale."

"The first part didn't seem like a fairy tale, but then when Alexander met the lizard it did. I mean that lizard was sort of like a fairy godmother."

Finally, the children were requested to compare this story with the others introduced in this unit so far. Again, they found a common thread involving themes of neglect and the search for love. There were also several comments about the narrative style. As one child put it, "It was kind of a quiet story."

Fifth, Sixth, and Seventh Sessions

The last three stories read aloud during subsequent story sessions were *Theodore* by Edward Ormondroy, *Ira Sleeps Over* by Bernard Waber, and *David and Dog* by Shirley Hughes. By this time the children were familiar with the process of story analysis and comparative study which had characterized previous discussions. Most of them were ready to initiate their own questions and observations about setting, characters, viewpoint, and plot. For example, they saw that both *Ira Sleeps Over* and *David and Dog* are told from the viewpoint of a human character, while *Theodore* is told from the viewpoint of the toy animal. Thus, of the toy animals found in these three stories, only Theodore assumes the status of a main character whom the reader comes to know as an individual in the course of reading the story. The children noted that both *Theodore* and *David and Dog* incorporated the theme of the "lost and found" toy but that all three of these stories were about a special relationship between a child and his or her toy animal. At this point the children were asked to look at a large wall chart listing the titles of all the stories read aloud in this unit. After a brief review of these stories, they were asked, "In what way are *all* these stories alike?" This question was introduced to guide their discovery of the underlying theme which bound these separate stories into a cohesive structure. As they attempted to formulate a theme statement about this group of stories, one child suggested, "All these stories are about toy animals and children who are special to each other." After deciding that this statement appropriately and concisely identified the theme which unified these stories, the children began to turn their attention to the *distinguishing* features of each story. For example, they noted that Annie, in *Alexander and the Wind-up Mouse,* was the only character who had allowed her favorite toy to be thrown away. While such other characters as David (in *David and Dog*) and Lucy (in *Theodore*) had been somewhat careless and had lost their toys, their final reunions were warm and happy events. Many of the children condemned Annie for her thoughtlessness, but one child countered, "But Mr. Lionni doesn't really say that Annie threw out Willie. I mean, you don't even see Annie and maybe someone else threw Willie into that box and Annie didn't even know about it!" This contribution introduced an alternative perspective into the dialogue and led to further observations about the kinds of information other authors had provided regarding the personal qualities of the diverse characters in this group of stories. At one point in this discussion, several questions were interjected to stretch the children's thinking and to challenge them to apply their knowledge of specific story characters: "How do you think Ira's sister, in *Ira Sleeps Over,* would have responded if Ira had lost his favorite animal like David in *David and Dog?* How do you think David's sister would have responded to Ira's problem? Do you think she would say the same kinds of things that Ira's sister said?"

The children's responses to these questions reflected their grasp of the nature of each of these characters as portrayed in the story. Some impromptu role-playing assisted this process of putting a known character into a new situation (in this case, a scene in another story) and predicting his or her behavior. This experience opened up new possibilities for thinking about story characters and for creating original stories with characters borrowed from familiar stories.

Follow-up Activities for the Whole Class

The first four objectives of this unit were met during the story sessions. The follow-up activities were designed to meet the fifth objective: to provide opportunities for creative expression through the production of original stories. As in other Focus Units, the story sessions helped to set the stage for creative writing: the children gradually accumulated a store of ideas and tools for producing their own narratives.

Following the series of story sessions described above, the children were invited to bring their favorite toy animals to school. A snapshot was taken of each child holding his or her animal, then each child wrote a descriptive paragraph or "sketch" to accompany the photograph. The children were asked to decide on a *viewpoint*: "Who will do the talking, you or your animal?" Many of the children chose to write their paragraph from the viewpoint of their animals and enjoyed the challenge of creating this perspective of the world as seen through the eyes of another.

After writing briefly about their own animals, the children were asked to create stories about imaginary toy animal characters. A few questions, similar to those introduced during the story sessions, were used to remind the children of the narrative elements they had identified during these sessions:

> Who are the characters in your story?
>
> Where will your story take place?
>
> What problems need to be solved?
>
> Is your story real or make-believe?
>
> Who tells the story? Is the most important story character a toy or a child?

Although independence was encouraged, appropriate consideration was given to those children with very limited writing skills. They had the opportunity to dictate their story to a teacher or older student and thus were not excluded from a creative writing experience on the basis of inadequate skills.

As each story was completed, its author illustrated it with one or more pictures. The children decided to compile their stories into an anthology for the school library. The finished product was an attractive book with decorative cardboard covers and a library pocket and card for borrowing. The children were proud to share what they had worked hard to create.

Independent Activities

All the books selected for this unit were placed on a display table in the classroom. The children were encouraged to choose one or more of these stories to read independently. (Several of the children read through the entire collection.) In addition to reading experiences, the children were given other options for independent work. For example, some children painted pictures of their favorite story characters, some wrote poems about their own toy animals, while others decided to work together on a mural depicting scenes from *Winnie-the-Pooh*.

Through such optional activities, the children were given opportunities to pursue new areas of interest, to practice reading and writing skills, and to express themselves in ways that were meaningful and enjoyable for them.

5 Pig Tales: A Focus Unit for Grades One and Two

Animal stories play a major role in the literary experience of young children. Some of these stories include realistic portrayals of animals in their natural environments; in others, the animal characters are disguised people with human traits and behaviors, coping with human conflicts and experiences. Young children's tendency to attribute human thoughts, feelings, and intentions to animals allows children to project their own hopes and fears onto the animal characters in these fantasies. Children's responses to an animal story are bound up with their recognition of the familiar, their own world of experience.

The Focus Unit described in this chapter features animal stories in which pigs play major roles. Pigs have been popular as story characters for generations, and in recent years a variety of delightful and humorous new tales about these appealing creatures has appeared in bookshops and libraries. In this unit, these charming stories served as the context for expanding the children's concept of story and, in particular, for examining a traditional literary element, characterization.

Objectives

1. To enjoy the humor of pig tales.
2. To compare and contrast diverse tales about pigs and to discover connections among stories in a wider context.
3. To explore characterization as a basic narrative element.
4. To provide a context for independent reading.
5. To provide a context for creative writing.

Bibliography for the Pig Tale Focus Unit

I. Group Story Sessions

Augarde, Steve. **Pig.** Scarsdale, New York: Bradbury Press, 1975.
    The other animals are disturbed by Pig's apparent lack of a specific job on their farm. However, their view of him changes when he

41

puts out a fire on the barn roof. Only the reader knows how Pig manages to become a hero by mistake.

Bishop, Claire. **The Truffle Pig.** New York: Coward, McCann and Geoghegan, 1971. (For beginning readers)

Pierre lives with his father and mother in France. They are poor and often hungry, but they finally save enough money to buy a piglet. It is Pierre's job to care for Marcel, the piglet, until he is ready to be made into sausage. When that day arrives, Pierre cannot bear to part with Marcel, who has become a friend. The story has a delightful conclusion, and the reader discovers why Marcel is called "The Truffle Pig."

Galdone, Paul. **The Amazing Pig: An Old Hungarian Tale.** Boston: Houghton Mifflin, 1981.

In this folktale, a peasant boy competes with "Princes and Knights and Noblemen" for the hand of the king's lovely daughter. With the help of his imagination and the family pig, the boy manages to win the princess and eventually to inherit the kingdom.

Jeschke, Susan. **Perfect the Pig.** New York: Holt, Rinehart and Winston, 1980.

Perfect, a pig born the runt of the litter and neglected by his mother and siblings, wishes for wings to escape his unhappy situation. His wish is granted because of an act of kindness, and he flies toward the city and meets Olive, a young artist who befriends him. When Perfect is kidnapped by a greedy and cruel street entertainer, Olive rescues her friend. Their reunion leads to a very satisfying conclusion for a delightful fantasy.

Oxenbury, Helen. **Pig Tale.** New York: William Morrow, 1973.

Told in verse, this is the story of two bored pigs, Bertha and Briggs, who long for riches and adventure. Finding a treasure chest is the first step toward a new life of luxury in the world beyond their sty. However, it doesn't take long for them to discover that happiness can be found in the carefree life they left behind.

Peck, Robert Newton. **Hamilton.** Boston: Little, Brown, 1976.

Hamilton is a pig who loves to eat; he thinks only of food. The other animals tease him when he grows too fat to run and play tag with them. But when Hamilton scares away a hungry wolf who enters the barnyard one night, he gains the respect and gratitude of his animal neighbors. Only the reader is aware that Hamilton became a hero by mistake.

Steig, William. **The Amazing Bone.** New York: Farrar, Straus and Giroux, 1976.

On her way home from school one lovely spring day, a pig named Pearl discovers a small talking bone. They are soon friends, and Pearl decides to take the bone home with her. On the way, a fox captures them, but the bone manages to save the day.

————. **Farmer Palmer's Wagon Ride.** New York: Farrar, Straus and Giroux, 1974.

Farmer Palmer (a pig) and his hired hand, Ebenezer (a donkey), are a delightful pair who experience a series of mishaps on their way home from the market. Their safe return is made possible by their cooperative efforts and the presents Farmer Palmer had selected for his children at the general store.

————. **Roland the Minstrel Pig.** New York: Windmill Books, 1968.

Roland, a talented pig who plays the lute, leaves his friends and sets out in search of fame and wealth. While traveling as a wandering minstrel, he meets Sebastian, a fox who almost succeeds in turning Roland into a "succulent dish." Fortunately, Roland is rescued, and the villain appropriately punished: he is put into the dungeon and given "nothing but stale bread with sour grapes and water."

Tripp, Wallace, adapter. **The Tale of a Pig: A Caucasian Folktale.** New York: McGraw-Hill, 1968.

Living with an old woodsman and his wife is an unusual and clever pig whose secret is discovered one day by a prince riding through the forest. He comes upon the pig as she changes into a lovely maiden who sings of the spell she is under. Her song reveals that the spell can be broken only after she marries. The prince falls in love and marries the pig, in spite of his father's protests. When she is transformed into a beautiful woman following the marriage vows, the Captain of the Guard decides to find another pig who would change into a maiden if he marries her. How he learns a painful lesson about the consequences of envy makes a delightful conclusion.

Walker, Barbara, reteller. **Pigs and Pirates: A Greek Tale.** New York: David White, 1969.

Three Greek swineherds lead a peaceful life on an island tending the pigs of a wealthy prince from the mainland. Because the pigs are clever, the boys teach them many tricks. When pirates appear and attempt to steal the pigs, the three boys use these tricks to outwit the pirates and rescue the pigs.

II. Independent Reading

Berson, Harold. **Truffles for Lunch.** New York: Macmillan, 1980.

Boynton, Sandra. **Hester in the Wild.** New York: Harper and Row, 1979.

Calhoun, Mary, adapter. **The Witch's Pig: A Cornish Folktale.** New York: William Morrow, 1977.

Cole, Brock. **Nothing but a Pig.** Garden City, New York: Doubleday, 1981.

Gackenbach, Dick. **The Pig Who Saw Everything.** New York: Seabury Press, 1978.

Galdone, Paul. **The Three Little Pigs.** New York: Seabury Press, 1970.

Getz, Arthur. **Humphrey, the Dancing Pig.** New York: Dial Press, 1980.

Goodall, John S. **Paddy Pork's Evening Out.** New York: Atheneum, 1973. (Wordless picture book)

————. **Paddy Pork's Holiday.** New York: Atheneum, 1976. (Wordless picture book)

Hoban, Lillian. **Mr. Pig and Family.** New York: Harper and Row, 1980. (For beginning readers)

————. **Mr. Pig and Sonny Too.** New York: Harper and Row, 1977. (For beginning readers)

King-Smith, Dick. **Pigs Might Fly.** New York: Viking Press, 1982. (For advanced readers)

Lobel, Arnold. **A Book of Pigericks.** New York: Harper and Row, 1983.

————. **Small Pig.** New York: Harper and Row, 1969. (For beginning readers)

McPhail, David. **Pig Pig Grows Up.** New York: E. P. Dutton, 1980.

Marshall, James. **Portly McSwine.** Boston: Houghton Mifflin, 1979.

————. **What's the Matter with Carruthers?** Boston: Houghton Mifflin, 1972.

————. **Yummers.** Boston: Houghton Mifflin, 1972.

Miles, Miska. **This Little Pig.** New York: E. P. Dutton, 1980.

Peet, Bill. **Chester the Wordly Pig.** Boston: Houghton Mifflin, 1965.

Rayner, Mary. **Garth Pig and the Ice Cream Lady.** New York: Atheneum, 1977.

————. **Mr. and Mrs. Pig's Evening Out.** New York: Atheneum, 1976.

Stevens, Carla. **Hooray for Pig!** New York: Seabury Press, 1974. (For beginning readers)

————. **Pig and the Blue Flag.** New York: Seabury Press, 1977. (For beginning readers)

Van Leeuwen, Jean. **Tales of Oliver Pig.** New York: Dial Press, 1979. (For beginning readers)

Watson, Pauline. **Wriggles, the Little Wishing Pig.** New York: Seabury Press, 1978.

White, E. B. **Charlotte's Web.** New York: Harper and Row, 1952. (For advanced readers)

Group Story Sessions

First Session

Perfect the Pig by Susan Jeschke was the first book introduced in this Focus Unit. The children were asked to make predictions about the story content based on the title and the picture of the winged pigs on the book cover. In response to the next question, "Can you think of any other stories about pigs?" several titles were recorded on a chart with "Pig Tales" written at the top. As the children caught on to this word play, they enjoyed explaining to others who had not yet seen the humor of the homonym.

After the story was read aloud, the children compared their predictions with the actual story plot. Then three questions were asked to focus attention on the characters in this story:

What was special about the tiny piglet?

What was special about the old sow the little pig helped?

Who was Olive? What was special about her?

The children's responses reflected their grasp of the traits of each character as well as the relationships among them. They recognized that it was the piglet's kindness which led the old sow to grant the wish for wings, that the wings allowed the piglet to escape his unhappy life with an unloving family, and that his escape made it possible for him to meet Olive, who offered him love and security:

"That old sow was just like a fairy godmother!"

"She sure was a funny-looking fairy godmother!"

"Well, lots of times the people with magic powers are *disguised*."

"But a pig's fairy godmother could be a pig!"

"It's like *Cinderella,* sort of. The piglet wasn't treated very nice, but he was good and kind and got his wish granted—just like Cinderella."

The question "How did Perfect's life change after the day of the fog?" was intended to call attention to the movement of the plot as Perfect headed toward danger and into the hands of the villain, a street entertainer who sees Perfect's value as a money-maker. When asked to describe the villain, the children noted the specific clues in the pictures and text which identified the man as a villain. One child commented, "He was just the opposite of Olive. I sure was glad when she found Perfect!" At this point the teacher remarked, "But both Olive and the man earned extra money because of Perfect. Didn't they have the same reason for wanting to keep the pig?" (Olive, an artist, earned money from her paintings of Perfect, while the man collected money from audiences delighted with Perfect's performances.) Several children immediately countered with:

> "But she loved Perfect, and she used the money to buy a house in the country so Perfect would be happy. That man only wanted the money for himself."

> "He didn't really care about Perfect at all. But Olive took such good care of him."

> "And that's the difference!"

Finally, the children were asked, "How is this story like a fairy tale?" They responded:

> "Well, the little piglet left home because he wasn't treated right. It's like those stories with the mean stepmothers. Like *Snow White* and *Cinderella*."

> "And *Hansel and Gretel*."

> "And usually there's a wicked witch or a sorcerer. Like the man who stole Perfect."

> "And fairy tales end happily ever after. Perfect sure was happy to live in the country with someone who loved him. I guess for a pig, the place would seem like a palace!"

As the session drew to a close, the children's attention was directed to the display table with the collection of Pig Tales, and they were invited to select one or more books for independent reading.

Second Session

The book *Pigs and Pirates: A Greek Tale* by Barbara Walker was introduced with an initial discussion of the words *pirate, swineherd, mainland,* and *island*. After the story was read aloud, the children were asked to compare it with *Perfect the Pig*:

"Both stories have people and pigs."

"But the pigs in *Pigs and Pirates* look more *real.*"

"So do the people."

"Both stories had villains who tried to steal the pigs."

"Both stories had pigs who do special things."

"I think *Pigs and Pirates* is more like a real story and *Perfect* is more like a fairy tale."

"There's no magic in *Pigs and Pirates,* and the artist [Harold Berson] tried to make things look real. The pictures in the other story don't look real."

"Maybe that [the incident described in *Pigs and Pirates*] really did happen a long time ago in Greece. At least it's possible. It's impossible for a pig to grow wings."

"But it is possible for someone to find a cute little pig and make it a pet like Olive did!"

Third Session

Farmer Palmer's Wagon Ride by William Steig was read aloud. Many of the children were already familiar with author Steig's wonderful animal characters with human qualities. They recognized that the animals in this story were disguised humans:

"The animals dress like humans and have jobs and houses, and they talk."

"There aren't any people in this story like in the other two."

"If you didn't see the pictures, you could almost forget they were animals."

"But little words tell you. Like when Ebenezer [the donkey] sprained his *hock* and then he *brayed* because it hurt."

"Maybe if Mr. Steig had people instead of animals, it wouldn't be so funny."

Fourth Session

When *The Truffle Pig* by Claire Bishop was read aloud, the children agreed that the pig in this story was realistically portrayed and that the story itself could actually have occurred in real life:

"The people act real and it's really Pierre's story."

"That must happen a lot of times on a farm. Baby animals are so cute, and it gets to be like a pet. But it's really for *food*."

"That's like in *Charlotte's Web*. They wanted to make sausage out of Wilbur, too!"

"Remember that story about that huge bear [Lynd Ward, *The Biggest Bear*]? The boy found it when it was a cute little cub, and then it got too big to keep, and he was so sad."

The children enjoyed the way the dilemma in *The Truffle Pig* was resolved, and they enjoyed learning some new facts—about truffles.

Fifth Session

In this story session, *Pig* by Steve Augarde and *Hamilton* by Robert Newton Peck were read aloud and the pig characters compared. The children recognized that each pig's obsession with food was true to the nature of pigs, that they each had become heroes by mistake, and that in each story the other animals changed their attitude toward the "hero pigs." Several children noted that the animals in both stories lived in natural environments and that most wore no clothes. However, they were intrigued to discover that Hamilton and his mother did wear clothes, which distinguished them from the other animals and set them apart as the main characters.

Sixth Session

The Tale of a Pig: A Caucasian Folktale adapted by Wallace Tripp was read aloud next. The children recognized this as a different type of pig tale in which a human character is transformed into a pig through a magic spell. The following questions were used to guide the discussion:

What kind of story is this? How do you know?

Can you think of any other stories about humans who are changed into animals?

What is unusual about this pig?

How does the storyteller let you know that this unusual pig is actually under a spell?

Which character discovers the secret?

How did the king's Captain of the Guards show his envy? How did he learn a lesson?

Compare this story with other pig tales we've read so far.

Seventh Session

Another folktale, *The Amazing Pig: An Old Hungarian Tale* retold and illustrated by Paul Galdone, was read aloud, and the children compared it with *The Tale of a Pig:*

> "Both stories have kings and castles and royal weddings."

> "But in *The Amazing Pig,* the pig doesn't seem like a character. I mean, that peasant boy really has a pig, but the story is about a pig he makes up with his imagination."

> "But his pig gives him the idea for a way to trick the king and get the princess. So the pig is important even though you only see him in real life on one page."

> "I think the title should have been *The Amazing Boy*—because *he's* the important character. He outwitted the king."

Eighth Session

A very different type of tale was introduced next: *Pig Tale* by Helen Oxenbury. The children thoroughly enjoyed the humorous adventures of Bertha and Briggs, two pigs who are bored with life in the country and long for "money and riches" to enjoy the world beyond their sty. Oxenbury's pictures were also a source of great delight.

By this time in the Focus Unit, the children were ready to explore characterization and plot sequence without the help of the teacher's questions. The children noted that in the beginning of the story the pigs are found in a natural setting, but their desire for something more and their discovery of a treasure chest take them into the complex world of humans, banks, cars, uncomfortable clothing, and electric appliances. The children saw that at the end of the story the pigs had learned their lesson:

> "They learned that you shouldn't try to be something you're not."

> "They learned that 'there's no place like home.' Like in *The Wizard of Oz!*"

After its introduction in this group session, this particular book was chosen again and again for individual enjoyment.

Ninth and Tenth Sessions

The next two sessions were devoted to two more pig tales by William Steig: *Roland the Minstrel Pig*. Steig's first book for children, and *The Amazing Bone*. These books were discussed in the tenth session:

"In both stories the animals are like regular people. They talk and wear clothes. And Roland plays a lute, and Pearl goes to school."

"Roland and Pearl are both sort of special people . . . I mean pigs. They're both kind of gentle and friendly."

"Both stories have a villain. A fox, of course!"

"I know why it's a fox! Because the fox is always the enemy of pigs."

"I watched a TV show that explained about that. The fox is the *predator* and the pig would be the *prey*."

"But also in stories, the fox is always sly and tricky, like Sebastian."

"And cunning."

"But in both stories the fox has some feelings. Like when he felt sorry for Pearl when she started to cry, and in the other one the fox really seemed to appreciate Roland's songs. Remember, he said, 'It's a *shame* to eat him, but I must!' "

"*The Amazing Bone* is like a fairy tale because of the magic bone."

"But the other story has a king and a palace and everything. The king is a lion. That's perfect!"

"In both stories the fox got punished. That was so funny when the Bone made him shrink."

"I liked it when the fox was put in jail and got sour grapes. It's like that story in our big Aesop book."

"And Roland got what he wanted—to be a famous musician."

Eleventh Session

The final story session was reserved for the children to talk about the stories they had read independently. For example, several children had read *Hooray for Pig!* and *Pig and the Blue Flag,* both by Carla Stevens. They discovered that Pig is the main character in each story and that his problem is similar in each tale. They were able to relate this problem to situations in their own lives:

"In *Hooray for Pig!* the problem is he can't swim, but his friend Otter teaches him how. He's a good teacher."

"In the other book, Pig is too fat to run fast and stuff in gym so he hates gym."

"And Otter is the gym *teacher.* And Raccoon is Pig's friend again, but he's not always such a nice friend."

"I know. Like when he says things that hurt Pig's feelings. But at the end, he really tries to help Pig *try,* and Pig wins the game for the team."

"So then he started to like gym."

"The animals are like real kids in those books. Like if you can't do something so great, then you don't like to have to do it."

"I remember when I couldn't ride my two-wheeler, and I said, 'Dad, my foot hurts. I can't go out.' But now, I ride it all day!"

"It was the same for me—when I was just learning how to swim. Now it's easy as pie. But I know just how he [Pig] felt when he didn't want to go near the water!"

As this sharing time continued, the children discussed other books they had read and frequently related the stories to their own experiences. At the conclusion of this session, there were a number of requests for the teacher to read aloud specific books. As a result, special story sessions were arranged to share with the whole group such favorites from the independent reading list as *Yummers* by James Marshall, *Chester the Wordly Pig* by Bill Peet, *Pigs Might Fly* by Dick King-Smith, *Mr. and Mrs. Pig's Evening Out* by Mary Rayner, *The Pig Who Saw Everything* by Dick Gackenbach, and, of course, *Charlotte's Web* by E. B. White.

Creative Writing

In preparation for writing original pig tales, a list of the stories read aloud and those read independently was recorded on the Pig Tale chart in the story corner. The children were asked to consider the characters in these stories in terms of the following questions:

Which pig characters were like humans? Look for clues such as clothing, speech, habits, setting, etc.

Which ones were like pigs, true to their nature?

In which stories were there human as well as animal characters?

In which stories were all the characters animals?

What was special about each pig?

In this group of stories, what were some of the problems facing the pig characters? the human characters?

In which stories did the main character(s) leave home?

In which stories was there a villain? Which villains were the natural enemies of pigs?

Which stories had magic?

After reviewing the stories recorded on the chart, the children, using these questions as guidelines, were ready to create their own pig tales. The first step was to decide what kind of story each wanted. Would their characters be realistic or fanciful? Would there be human characters as well as animals? Would they use magic? What special qualities would their main character have? What problem would the character have to solve? Once they had made some decisions about the nature of the story they wanted to write, the children were anxious to get started, to put their ideas on paper. Some of the children found it helpful to draw one or more pictures about their story idea prior to writing the text. Others preferred to illustrate the story after it was written.

In his book *Writing and the Writer* (1982), Frank Smith distinguishes between two aspects of writing: composition and transcription. The former involves "getting ideas, selecting words, and grammar," while the latter involves "the physical effort of writing, spelling, capitalization, punctuation, paragraphs, and legibility" (p. 20). Smith points out that "composition and transcription can interfere with each other" (p. 21). While every child needs practice to improve transcription skills, it is important to clarify the specific instructional goals of writing assignments. The creative writing projects associated with the Focus Unit are intended to provide opportunities to generate and translate ideas into the language and structure of narrative. Composition is primary; transcription is secondary. That is, the child is encouraged to focus on the story first and to attend to letter reversals, misspelled words, punctuation errors, and so forth after the story has been recorded. For this reason, children who were just beginning to develop encoding skills were given the option of dictating their story ideas to the teacher. Most of these beginning writers were enthusiastic about using their newly acquired transcription skills to produce their own pig tales, but a few were not yet ready to combine the two aspects of writing, transcription and composition. They elected to dictate their stories in order to give full attention to the composition process, but in subsequent writing projects these children had sufficient confidence to write out their stories.

The end products of this creative writing project—narratives which had been proofread, corrected, and, in some cases, revised—proved to be a source of great amusement when read aloud. Each child had managed to create a unique pig character, and most of the children produced coherent plot sequences injected with humor and imagination. The nature of their compositions seemed to indicate that the literary experiences in the story sessions had contributed significantly to the quality of their written work. Children learn to read by reading; they learn to write by writing. Their reading experiences provide the foundation for writing, and writing experiences provide the foundation for reading. In short, this describes the essence of the Focus Unit model.

References

Smith, Frank. *Writing and the Writer*. New York: Holt, Rinehart and Winston, 1982.

Ward, Lynd. *The Biggest Bear*. Boston: Houghton Mifflin, 1952.

6 Roger Duvoisin: A Focus Unit for Grades One and Two

Yetta M. Goodman has defined reading as a "private, ongoing, long-distance discussion between the reader and the author" (Goodman and Burke 1980, p. 18). In this Focus Unit, young readers were introduced to the work of popular children's author-illustrator Roger Duvoisin (1904–1980). A primary purpose of the unit was to help children understand the nature of the interaction between producers (speakers and writers) and comprehenders (listeners and readers) of language in communication. One way for children to learn about the interactive nature of language is to become aware of the producers of texts they read. Another way is for children to become producers and, as authors, to develop an awareness of their potential audience, the comprehenders.

The reading process is an interaction between an author and a reader; each participant in this dialogue brings a knowledge of language and the world to the text. The reader, using this prior knowledge, generates meaning from the text by reconstructing the author's meaning and then responds intellectually, emotionally, and/or aesthetically to this meaning.

In this unit about Roger Duvoisin, the children gained experience as comprehenders interacting with a producer as they discovered the style and technique of this author-illustrator. The children also gained experience as producers, by becoming author-illustrators and by developing an awareness of potential comprehenders.

Objectives

1. To introduce young readers to Roger Duvoisin, author of more than 40 books for children and illustrator of 140 books.
2. To encourage children to discover and appreciate the style, techniques, and themes of a particular author.

Note: This Focus Unit was first implemented with second-grade children in 1977 and was originally described by the author in *Language Arts* 55 (October 1978): 832–36, under the title "Literary Awareness: A Basis for Composition." The unit was repeated in 1981 with children in grades one and two. Portions of the article in *Language Arts* have been included in this chapter.

3. To help young readers begin to understand the nature of the interaction between authors and readers by becoming acquainted with an author and by becoming authors, thus expanding their experience and skills as comprehenders and producers of written language.

4. To provide a context for independent reading.

Bibliography for the Roger Duvoisin Focus Unit

I. Group Story Sessions: Books Written by Roger Duvoisin

The Crocodile in the Tree. New York: Alfred A. Knopf, 1973.

At first, the animals on Sweetpea farm are suspicious of Crocus the crocodile. But once convinced of his gentle nature, they help hide him from Mr. and Mrs. Sweetpea. Eventually, Crocus even convinces Mrs. Sweetpea that his intentions are friendly.

Crocus. New York: Alfred A. Knopf, 1977.

The animals of Sweetpea farm respect Crocus and admire his four long rows of sharp teeth. Crocus is devastated when a severe toothache leads to the removal of all of his beautiful teeth. Fortunately, his problems are solved and his self-esteem restored at the end of this charming tale.

The Importance of Crocus. New York: Alfred A. Knopf, 1980.

Crocus is convinced that in comparison to the other farm animals, he has no special talents and serves no special functions. However, his feelings of worthlessness disappear when a pond is added to Sweetpea farm. This crocodile becomes the champion swimmer and diver and protects the farm animals from their enemies. By the end of this tale, all the animals discover the importance of Crocus.

Lonely Veronica. New York: Alfred A. Knopf, 1963.

When men come with cranes and bulldozers and destroy the peace of their river, the hippopotamuses leave—except Veronica, who decides to stay behind and watch. Later, Veronica finds herself alone in a city and dreams of being back in the jungle and the hippopotamus river. The foreman of the crew rescues Veronica from city life and takes her to his father's farm.

Our Veronica Goes to Petunia's Farm. New York: Alfred A. Knopf, 1962.

Initially, the animals on the farm of Petunia the goose are suspicious of Veronica the hippopotamus and refuse to speak to this strange newcomer. Hurt by their rejection, Veronica stays in her house, too melancholic to eat. But with the help and concern of each of the animals, Veronica recovers, and friendly relations are established.

Veronica. New York: Alfred A. Knopf, 1961.

Veronica, a hippopotamus who longs to be different, famous, and conspicuous, leaves her mud bank, her river, and the other hippopotamuses. However, when she eventually finds herself in the midst of a busy city, she discovers that "one can be too conspicuous" and longs to return to her riverbank. Veronica learns the importance of being true to one's nature.

Veronica's Smile. New York: Alfred A. Knopf, 1964.

Veronica, like Crocus the crocodile, feels she serves no useful purpose on Mr. Pumpkin's farm. A series of events convinces her that her big mouth allows her to help others, and she is happy to discover that she is, indeed, a very useful member of the farm community.

II. Independent Reading

A. Other Books Written by Roger Duvoisin

A for the Ark. New York: Lothrop, Lee and Shepard Books, 1952.

All Aboard! New York: Grosset and Dunlap, 1935.

Angelique. New York: McGraw-Hill, 1960.

Chanticleer. New York: Grosset and Dunlap, 1947.

The Christmas Cake in Search of Its Owner. American Artists' Group, 1941.

The Christmas Whale. New York: Alfred A. Knopf, 1945.

Day and Night. New York: Alfred A. Knopf, 1960.

Donkey-Donkey: The Troubles of a Silly Little Donkey. Chicago: Albert Whitman, 1933.

Easter Treat. New York: Alfred A. Knopf, 1954.

The Happy Hunter. New York: Lothrop, Lee and Shepard Books, 1961.

The House of Four Seasons. New York: Alfred A. Knopf, 1956.

Jasmine. New York: Alfred A. Knopf, 1973.

A Little Boy Was Drawing. New York: Charles Scribner's Sons, 1932.

The Missing Milkman. New York: Alfred A. Knopf, 1967.

Periwinkle. New York: Alfred A. Knopf, 1976.

Petunia. New York: Alfred A. Knopf, 1950.

Petunia and the Song. New York: Alfred A. Knopf, 1951.

Petunia, Beware! New York: Alfred A. Knopf, 1958.

Petunia, I Love You. New York: Alfred A. Knopf, 1965.

Petunia's Christmas. New York: Alfred A. Knopf, 1952.

Petunia's Treasure. New York: Alfred A. Knopf, 1975.

Petunia Takes a Trip. New York: Alfred A. Knopf, 1953.

Snowy and Woody. New York: Alfred A. Knopf, 1979.

Spring Snow. New York: Alfred A. Knopf, 1963.

Two Lonely Ducks: A Country Book. New York: Alfred A. Knopf, 1955.

Veronica and the Birthday Present. New York: Alfred A. Knopf, 1971.

What Is Right for Tulip. New York: Alfred A. Knopf, 1969.

B. Selected Books Illustrated by Roger Duvoisin

Fatio, Louise. **The Happy Lion.** New York: McGraw-Hill, 1954. (First in a series)

Freschet, Berniece. **The Old Bullfrog.** New York: Charles Scribner's Sons, 1968.

————. **The Web in the Grass.** New York: Charles Scribner's Sons, 1972.

Haviland, Virginia. **Favorite Fairy Tales Told in France.** New York: Little, Brown, 1959.

Holl, Adelaide. **The Rain Puddle.** New York: Lothrop, Lee and Shepard Books, 1965.

Menotti, Gian-Carlo. **Amahl and the Night Visitors.** New York: McGraw-Hill, 1952.

Miles, Patricia. **The Pointed Brush.** New York: Lothrop, Lee and Shepard Books, 1959.

Schlein, Miriam. **Little Red Nose.** New York: Abelard-Schuman, 1965.

Tresselt, Alvin. **The Beaver Pond.** New York: Lothrop, Lee and Shepard Books, 1970.

————. **Follow the Wind.** New York: Lothrop, Lee and Shepard Books, 1950.

————. **Hide and Seek Fog.** New York: Lothrop, Lee and Shepard Books, 1965.

————. **It's Time Now.** New York: Harper and Row, 1969.

————. **Sun Up.** New York: Lothrop, Lee and Shepard Books, 1949.

————. **Wake Up, City!** New York: Lothrop, Lee and Shepard Books, 1957.

————. **Wake Up, Farm!** New York: Lothrop, Lee and Shepard Books, 1955.

————. **What Did You Leave Behind?** New York: Lothrop, Lee and Shepard Books, 1978.

————. **White Snow, Bright Snow.** New York: Lothrop, Lee and
   Shepard Books, 1947.
————. **The World of the Candy Egg.** New York: Lothrop, Lee and
   Shepard Books, 1967.
Tworkov, Jack. **The Camel Who Took a Walk.** New York: E. P. Dutton,
   1951.

C. Reference Material about Roger Duvoisin

Commire, Anne, editor. **Something about the Author: Facts and Pictures
   about Contemporary Authors and Illustrators of Books for Young
   People,** vol. 2. Detroit: Gale Research, 1972.
Freeman, Muriel. "The Duvoisins." *Publishers Weekly* (February 28,
   1977).
Hopkins, Lee Bennett. **Books Are by People: Interviews with 104 Au-
   thors and Illustrators of Books for Young Children.** New York:
   Citation Press, 1969.
Kirkpatrick, D. L., editor. **Twentieth-Century Children's Writers.** New
   York: St. Martin's Press, 1978.
Locher, Frances C., editor. **Contemporary Authors: A Bio-Bibliograph-
   ical Guide to Current Writers in Fiction, General Nonfiction,
   Poetry, Journalism, Drama, Motion Pictures, Television, and Other
   Fields.** Detroit: Gale Research, 1964 to present.

Story Sessions

First Session

Veronica was the first of the books by Roger Duvoisin selected for reading
aloud during the group sessions. Many of the children were already
acquainted with his book *Petunia,* and some recognized the name of the
author-illustrator. *Petunia* and the other stories about this silly goose who
learned some important lessons from her various adventures had been
placed on the display table in the classroom with other books written and
illustrated by Duvoisin, and the children were encouraged to select books
from this collection for independent reading. *Veronica* introduced a new
story character, a hippopotamus who yearned to become conspicuous.
After listening to this first story about Veronica, the children familiar
with Petunia compared these two story characters:

"Both wanted to be special and different."

"They wanted something *more.* Petunia wanted to be wise and
Veronica wanted to be conspicuous and famous."

"Both learned a lesson at the end of the story."

The following questions were introduced to generate further discussion:

What does *conspicuous* mean? What is the opposite of *conspicuous*?

Where was Veronica most conspicuous? Why?

Where was she inconspicuous? Why?

Why do you think Veronica wanted to be conspicuous?

What makes this story so funny?

This series of questions was designed to focus on the meaning of *setting* in narrative structure and the importance of setting in the unfolding of a story. The children began to grasp the idea that humor can be created by locating a character in an unusual setting. Veronica was conspicuous on a busy city street; her size and inexperience with city life occasioned a series of comical misadventures. Several children who had read *Petunia Takes a Trip* observed the similarities between these two stories:

"Petunia and Veronica both looked so funny in the middle of a city."

"But they both learned to appreciate their own home."

Second Session

Our Veronica Goes to Petunia's Farm was read aloud in the second story session. The children were delighted with the idea that Veronica had joined Petunia the goose and the other familiar animals on the farm Mr. Duvoisin had created. Their spontaneous comments about this story reflected their recognition of the literary technique in which a story character is placed in an unusual or unexpected setting. One child commented, "In this story Mr. Duvoisin put Veronica on a farm. That's another place where hippopotamuses don't belong."

The question "How did the farm animals respond to Veronica's arrival?" was introduced to stimulate an exploration of the story theme:

"The other animals refused to be friends at first because they didn't think Veronica belonged."

"She seemed strange and different so they wouldn't even talk to her."

"But then Veronica got so sad because no one was friendly. So she didn't feel like eating or doing anything."

"When the other animals realized Veronica was sick, they all tried to get her better."

"That's when they found out that Veronica is really friendly and kind."

"So they learned a lesson!"

"They learned that even if someone is different or *foreign,* you can be friends."

When asked to compare this story with *Veronica* in terms of the lessons learned, one child observed:

"In the first story, Veronica learned that she was *too* conspicuous in the city and that it was better to go back where she belonged. In the second story, she wanted to belong on that farm but the other animals had to get used to her first. They learned a lesson in that story."

At this point, the children discussed the story in terms of personal experiences and feelings. Many had identified with Veronica as the outsider. They too had once been new to a neighborhood or school and recognized the experience of rejection and isolation.

At the conclusion of the session, the teacher printed on 4 x 6-inch cards some of the new words encountered in Duvoisin's books: *conspicuous, inconspicuous, paradise, foreigner, appetite, vendor, demolish,* and *thistle.* After each of these words was discussed, the children were invited to add to this collection as they came across new or interesting words during subsequent group or independent reading experiences. These words were stored in a box labeled "Mr Duvoisin's Words" and decorated with drawings of Petunia, Veronica, and Crocus. Later in the unit, a group of advanced readers used these words in a special project described in the Seventh Session.

Third Session

Lonely Veronica was read aloud next. The initial responses were:

"Look! Mr. Duvoisin put Veronica back at her river again with all the other hippopotamuses—like in the first story."

"It's also like the first story because Veronica wanted to be different and ended up in the city again."

"But she didn't like it and wanted to go home."

"The ending was different though. The foreman, Joe, decided to take her to his father's farm—for a *pet!*"

"I think we should have read this story before the one about Veronica going to the farm."

This last comment generated interest in the copyright dates of these three stories about Veronica. When they discovered that *Lonely Veronica* (1963) was published after *Our Veronica Goes to Petunia's Farm* (1962), the children wondered if the farm in *Lonely Veronica* could be Petunia's farm. Their questions about the sequence of these stories—such as "Why didn't Mr. Duvoisin write *Lonely Veronica* second, before she went to Petunia's farm?"—remained unanswered. The children were unable to write to the author because Duvoisin died before they became involved in this particular Focus Unit. However, it was apparent from their questions and comments that they considered the Veronica stories as connected episodes in a total sequence.

Fourth Session

When *Veronica's Smile* (1964) was read aloud, the children noted that this book was published the year after *Lonely Veronica* and that Veronica was back with Petunia again on Mr. Pumpkin's farm. After a discussion of the setting, plot, and theme of this story, the children were asked to compare the Veronica stories. Most recognized that each story ended with a lesson or moral similar to those found in fables. To clarify this point, the last few pages of each story were reread in order to discover the lesson learned. In *Veronica's Smile,* the children identified Petunia's final words as the key lines: "You see, Veronica, when we do what we can with what we have, everyone is happy." They decided that the key line in *Veronica* was, "One can be *too* conspicuous." In *Lonely Veronica,* the lesson was summed up in Veronica's comment to her friend Alexander: "I think there are no good *old* days; there are no good *new* days. There are only bad and good days." *Our Veronica Goes to Petunia's Farm* provided more of a challenge, but the children finally agreed that the rooster's comment, "She is *our* hippopotamus," was the key line. One child commented: "I think he meant that Veronica was the same as them even though she looks so different. That was the lesson the other animals learned."

Fifth Session

A new character, Crocus the crocodile, was introduced in the fifth session in which both *The Crocodile in the Tree* and *Crocus* were read aloud. By this time, very few teacher-initiated questions were needed to generate discussion. The children recognized that Crocus, like Veronica, lived on a farm, an unusual setting for a crocodile, and that he too encountered mistrust, fear, and suspicion before the other animals learned to appreciate him as an individual. They noted that Duvoisin had created a new farm belonging to Mr. and Mrs. Sweetpea and housing a new group of animal characters. Several commented on the cooperative nature of these animals:

> "Bertha the duck and Coco the dog had all the good ideas, but *all* the animals helped hide Crocus."

> "They worked together and cooperated so Crocus wouldn't get caught."

Others pointed out the humorous elements of Crocus, the crocodile who "only uses his teeth for smiling" and who brings bouquets to Mrs. Sweetpea when he discovers their mutual love of flowers. Finally, they identified the moral at the end of each story: " 'Life is so beautiful when we have so much in common with a friend,' mused the crocodile" in *The Crocodile in the Tree,* and " 'Don't we all need something that makes us feel important?' wondered Bertha the toothless duck. 'For Crocus it's his teeth' " in *Crocus.*

Sixth Session

Prior to this session, the teacher and several children gathered biographical information about Roger Duvoisin from various sources in the library (see the reference section of the bibliography). At the beginning of this session, the children were asked what they had learned about Duvoisin from the stories he had written. Their comments were recorded on a chart:

> "Mr. Duvoisin likes animals."

> "He has a good sense of humor."

> "He lets you get to know certain characters by writing different books about the same ones."

> "His stories are sort of like fables. They have a lesson at the end."

> "His animal characters talk and act like people."

> "He likes to put his characters in unusual settings to make us laugh."

> "His pictures are like cartoons."

> "His animals have special personalities."

Then the biographical information, collected by the "library committee," was shared with the group. The children were delighted to learn that Duvoisin had illustrated many books written by such familiar authors as Alvin Tresselt and Louise Fatio and to discover that the latter was Duvoisin's wife. They decided to include her *Happy Lion* books on the display table with her husband's books.

Seventh Session

Finally, *The Importance of Crocus* was read aloud, including the brief biographical sketch on the last page, which concludes with the words, "Mr. Duvoisin's warm and gentle humor lives on in the last book he wrote and illustrated, *The Importance of Crocus,* which was completed just prior to his death in 1980."

The children were obviously moved by these words, and one comment seemed to express their feelings at that moment: "Even though we never really *met* Mr. Duvoisin, it feels like we've lost a good friend." The title of his last book gave them the idea for a special project, a book called "The Importance of Mr. Duvoisin," which they dedicated to him. The book included biographical data and their own impressions of him as an artist and individual, comments about favorite stories, drawings of his special animal characters, and riddles about the books read during the group sessions. The last section of the book, prepared by a group of advanced readers, defined some of the words used by Duvoisin, used them in humorous sentences, and illustrated them.

Eighth Session

The children were invited to share their independent reading experiences in the final story session. Those not yet ready to read the books in this collection were paired with children who could read to them, so all the children were prepared to contribute to the discussion. Several children had read *The Happy Hunter* and identified Duvoisin's familiar technique for creating humor. In this story, it is a hunter who loves animals and who would not think of harming a single one. Others read *Snowy and Woody*, the story of three friends — Snowy, a polar bear; Woody, a woodland bear; and Kitty, a gull—who help each other when threatened by hunters. The children compared *Snowy and Woody* to *The Happy Hunter:*

> "In some ways it's similar because Snowy leaves the arctic, his home, and goes to a warmer place. But it's not really a funny story like the others."

> "It's a story about friendship—how they help each other even though they're all different."

> "Snowy's white coat protected him in the snow and Woody's brown coat protected him in the grassy meadow. That's called *camouflage.* Let's put that in our word box!"

Many of the children enjoyed reading *The Happy Lion* by Louise Fatio, Duvoisin's wife, and discovering that this author had used the technique which they had found in Duvoisin's stories:

"This is another story about a character who ends up in a setting he doesn't really belong in."

"As soon as the Happy Lion left the zoo, the people stopped being so friendly. They thought he was dangerous."

"The funniest part was when the Happy Lion walked down the street, and he just couldn't figure out why everyone suddenly screamed and ran away!"

"It ends up like these other stories when Petunia and Veronica decided they'd rather be in their own place after their adventures in the *people* world!"

Creative Writing

The writing project for this Focus Unit involved the creation of stories with new characters in unusual settings. Before working independently, the children met in a group for a preparatory activity. A sheet of paper on a large easel was divided into two columns: one column was headed Characters, the other, Settings. First, Duvoisin's characters and settings were listed. Then the children thought of new animal characters and settings that would provide an unusual or unexpected context. This activity reinforced the literary technique they were to use and provided various ideas to help the children get started.

By this time, the children were ready to begin their own compositions. Most worked independently; those with limited writing skills dictated their ideas to the teacher. Again, all the children, regardless of individual differences in skill level, participated in the creative process and composed original stories. Each completed story was illustrated, bound into a separate book, and shared with the group during the final session. For many of the children, the knowledge that their stories would eventually be heard or read by others seemed to play an important role in the writing process. At various intervals they asked a neighbor to listen to what they had written so far in an attempt to get feedback from a "comprehender." That is, these young writers had apparently begun to internalize the idea of "audience awareness" as a significant dimension of communication.

The children's books were added to the Focus Unit collection on display in the classroom. A few of the titles selected for these original stories were:

"The Whale in the Swimming Pool"

"The Flea Who Wanted to be Famous"

"The Mouse on the Ski Slope"

"The Rabbit on the Moon"

"The Elephant in the Dancing Class"

"The Hippopotamus Who Came to School"

"The Day Veronica Stepped out of Her Book and into the Classroom"

"The Polar Bear Who Took a Vacation in Hawaii"

The children's grasp of the recurring story ideas, themes, and literary techniques in Duvoisin's books was reflected in their own compositions. They had discovered some of the basic tools used by authors to create prose and poetry. The children's growing knowledge of these literary tools and of the interactive nature of language enriched the quality of their comprehension and production of written narrative.

Reference

Goodman, Yetta M., and Carolyn Burke. *Reading Strategies: Focus on Comprehension.* New York: Holt, Rinehart and Winston, 1980.

7 Jay Williams: A Focus Unit for Grades Four and Five

An important objective of each Focus Unit is to open doors into the world of literature for young people. It is the responsibility of parents and teachers to serve as guides in the exploration of this world. In this Focus Unit, students were introduced to the genre of modern fairy tales by examining some of the books written by Jay Williams (1914–1978). His fairy tales were used to demonstrate some of the basic characteristics of this genre, and students discovered some of Williams's special qualities as well: his style and literary techniques, his wonderful sense of humor, and his diverse interests. This Focus Unit was designed to expand the students' capacity for literary appreciation and to introduce them to new sources of reading enjoyment.

Objectives

1. To introduce the students to author Jay Williams.
2. To provide a context for discovering literary techniques used in modern fairy tales.
3. To provide a context for creating original fairy tales.
4. To provide a context for discovering new possibilities for personal reading enjoyment.

Bibliography for the Jay Williams Focus Unit

I. Group Story Sessions: Stories Written by Jay Williams

"Petronella." In **The Practical Princess and Other Liberating Fairy Tales.** New York: Parents' Magazine Press, 1978.

Petronella, youngest child of King Peter XXVI and Queen Blossom, decides to seek her fortune. With the help of a little old man

Note: Brief portions of this chapter originally appeared in "Reading and Discussing Fairy Tales—Old and New" in *The Reading Teacher* 35 (March 1982): 656–59. Reprinted with permission.

who rewards her for her kindness, Petronella manages to rescue a prince. However, he has none of the usual qualities associated with fairy-tale princes, and she chooses the enchanter instead.

"The Silver Whistle." In **The Practical Princess and Other Liberating Fairy Tales.** New York: Parents' Magazine Press, 1978.

Just before she dies, the Wise Old Woman of the West gives her daughter, Prudence, a magical silver whistle. Prudence goes out to make her way in the world, becomes a witch's servant, and is commanded to get the magical mirror of Morna from the Wazar. Successful in this quest, Prudence hands the mirror over to the witch, only to discover that the witch plans to use it to win Prince Pertinel. Prudence foils the witch's evil scheme and ends up marrying the prince herself.

II. Independent Reading

A. "Liberated Heroines" in Fiction and Folklore

Corbett, Scott. **The Hockey Girls.** New York: E. P. Dutton, 1976.

Crayder, Dorothy. **She, the Adventuress.** New York: Atheneum, 1973.

Dalgliesh, Alice. **Courage of Sarah Noble.** New York: Charles Scribner's Sons, 1954.

de la Mare, Walter. **Mollie Whuppie.** New York: Farrar, Straus and Giroux, 1983.

de Paolo, Tomie. **Helga's Dowry: A Troll Love Story.** New York: Harcourt Brace Jovanovich, 1977.

George, Jean. **Julie of the Wolves.** New York: Harper and Row, 1972.

Katz, Bobbi. **The Manifesto and Me—Meg.** New York: Franklin Watts, 1974.

———. **Rod-and-Reel Trouble.** Chicago: Albert Whitman, 1974.

Knudson, R. R. **Zanbanger.** New York: Harper and Row, 1977.

L'Engle, Madeleine. **A Wrinkle in Time.** New York: Farrar, Straus and Giroux, 1962.

Lindgren, Astrid. **Pippi Longstocking.** New York: Viking Press, 1950.

———. **Ronia, the Robber's Daughter.** New York: Viking Press, 1983.

Lofts, Norah. **The Maude Reed Tale.** Nashville: Thomas Nelson, 1972. (Historical fiction)

Lurie, Alison. **Clever Gretchen and Other Forgotten Folktales.** New York: Thomas Y. Crowell, 1980.

Miles, Betty. **The Real Me.** New York: Alfred A. Knopf, 1974.

Minard, Rosemary. **Long Meg.** New York: Pantheon Books, 1982.

————, editor. **Womenfolk and Fairy Tales.** Boston: Houghton Mifflin, 1975.

O'Dell, Scott. **Carlotta.** Boston: Houghton Mifflin, 1977.

————. **Island of the Blue Dolphins.** Boston: Houghton Mifflin, 1960.

————. **Sarah Bishop.** Boston: Houghton Mifflin, 1980.

Phelps, Ethel, editor. **The Maid of the North and Other Folktale Heroines.** New York: Holt, Rinehart and Winston, 1981.

————. **Tatterhood and Other Tales.** Old Westbury, New York: Feminist Press, 1978.

Pogrebin, Letty Cottin, editor. **Stories for Free Children.** New York: McGraw-Hill, 1982.

Stamm, Claus. **Three Strong Women: A Tall Tale from Japan.** New York: Viking Press, 1962.

Taves, Isabella. **Not Bad for a Girl.** New York: M. Evans, 1972.

Tolan, Stephanie. **The Liberation of Tansy Warner.** New York: Charles Scribner's Sons, 1980.

Winthrop, Elizabeth. **Marathon Miranda.** New York: Holiday House, 1979.

Yolen, Jane. **The Emperor and the Kite.** Cleveland: World, 1967.

B. Biographies of Women

Bowman, Kathleen. **New Women in Medicine.** Chicago: Children's Press, 1976.

Brownmiller, Susan. **Shirey Chisholm: A Biography.** New York: Doubleday, 1970.

Buckmaster, Henrietta. **Women Who Shaped History.** New York: Macmillan, 1966.

Clapp, Patricia. **Dr. Elizabeth: The Story of the First Woman Doctor.** New York: Lothrop, Lee and Shepard Books, 1974.

Davidson, Margaret. **The Story of Eleanor Roosevelt.** New York: Four Winds Press, 1969.

DeLeeuw, Adele. **Maria Tallchief: American Ballerina.** Champaign, Illinois: Garrard, 1971.

De Pauw, Linda. **Seafaring Women.** Boston: Houghton Mifflin, 1982.

Dobrin, Arnold. **A Life for Israel: The Story of Golda Meir.** New York: Dial Press, 1974.

Epstein, Sam, and Beryl Epstein. **She Never Looked Back: Margaret Mead in Samoa.** New York: Coward, McCann and Geoghegan, 1980.

Felton, Harold. **Deborah Sampson: Soldier of the Revolution.** New York: Dodd, Mead, 1976.

——. **Mumbet: The Story of Elizabeth Freeman.** New York: Dodd, Mead, 1970.

Fox, Mary. **Lady for the Defense: A Biography of Belva Lockwood.** Harcourt Brace Jovanovich, 1975.

Gleasner, Diana. **Breakthrough: Women in Writing.** New York: Walker, 1980.

Greenfield, Eloise. **Mary McLeod Bethune.** New York: Thomas Y. Crowell, 1977.

——. **Rosa Parks.** New York: Thomas Y. Crowell, 1973.

Haskins, James. **Barbara Jordan.** New York: Dial Press, 1977.

Leone, Bruno. **Marie Montessori: Knight of the Child.** St. Paul: Greenhaven Press, 1978.

McGovern, Ann. **The Secret Soldier: The Story of Deborah Sampson.** New York: Four Winds Press, 1975.

——. **Shark Lady: True Adventures of Eugenie Clark.** New York: Four Winds Press, 1978.

Meigs, Cornelia. **Jane Addams: Pioneer for Social Justice.** New York: Little Brown, 1970.

Morrison, Dorothy. **Chief Sarah: Sarah Winnemucca's Fight for Indian Rights.** New York: Atheneum, 1980.

——. **Ladies Were Not Expected: Abigail Scott Dunniway and Women's Rights.** New York: Atheneum, 1977.

Noble, Iris. **Susan B. Anthony.** New York: Julian Messner, 1975.

Olney, Ross R. **Janet Guthrie: First Woman at Indy.** New York: Harvey House, 1978.

Peare, Catherine. **The Story of Helen Keller.** New York: Thomas Y. Crowell, 1959.

Scheader, Catherine. **They Found a Way: Mary Cassatt.** Chicago: Children's Press, 1977.

Sterling, Dorothy. **Freedom Train: The Story of Harriet Tubman.** New York: Doubleday, 1954.

Stoddard, Hope. **Famous American Women.** New York: Thomas Y. Crowell, 1970.

Veglahn, Nancy. **The Mysterious Rays: Marie Curie's World.** New York: Coward, McCann and Geoghegan, 1977.

Walker, Greta. **Women Today: Ten Profiles.** New York: Hawthorn Books, 1975.

C. Humorous Modern Fairy Tales and Fables

Aiken, Joan. **A Necklace of Raindrops.** New York: Doubleday, 1968.

Alexander, Lloyd. **The Four Donkeys.** New York: Holt, Rinehart and Winston, 1972.

Broun, Heywood. **The Fifty-first Dragon.** New York: Prentice-Hall, 1968.

Bulla, Clyde. **My Friend the Monster.** New York: Thomas Y. Crowell, 1980.

Cunliffe, John. **The Great Dragon Competition and Other Stories.** New York: André Deutsch, 1980.

Dahl, Roald. **The BFG.** New York: Farrar, Straus and Giroux, 1982.

de Paolo, Tomie. **The Knight and the Dragon.** New York: G. P. Putnam's Sons, 1980.

Gardner, John. **Dragon, Dragon and Other Tales.** New York: Alfred A. Knopf, 1975.

————. **Gudgekin the Thistle Girl and Other Tales.** New York: Alfred A. Knopf, 1976.

————. **The King of the Hummingbirds and Other Tales.** New York: Alfred A. Knopf, 1977.

Grahame, Kenneth. **The Reluctant Dragon.** New York: Holiday House, 1938.

Heide, Florence, and Sylvia van Clief. **Fables You Shouldn't Pay Any Attention To.** Philadelphia: J. B. Lippincott, 1978.

Krensky, Stephen. **Castles in the Air and Other Tales.** New York: Atheneum, 1979.

Lee, Tanith. **Princess Hunchatti and Some Other Surprises.** New York: Farrar, Straus and Giroux, 1972.

McGowen, Tom. **Dragon Stew.** Chicago: Follett, 1969.

MacLachlan, Patricia. **Moon, Stars, Frogs and Friends.** New York: Pantheon Books, 1980.

Nesbit, E. **The Last of the Dragons.** New York: McGraw-Hill, 1980.

Sage, Alison. **The Ogre's Banquet.** Garden City, New York: Doubleday, 1978.

Thurber, James. **The 13 Clocks.** New York: Simon and Schuster, 1950.

————. **The Wonderful O.** New York: Simon and Schuster, 1957.

Williams, Jay. **Everyone Knows What a Dragon Looks Like.** New York: Four Winds Press, 1976.

————. **The King with Six Friends.** New York: Parents' Magazine Press, 1968.

————. **One Big Wish.** New York: Macmillan, 1980.

———. **Philbert the Fearful.** New York: W. W. Norton, 1966.

———. **Seven at One Blow.** New York: Parents' Magazine Press, 1972.

———. **Stupid Marco.** New York: Parents' Magazine Press, 1970.

Wise, Williams. **Sir Howard the Coward.** New York: G. P. Putnam's Sons, 1967.

Yolen, Jane. **The Acorn Quest.** New York: Thomas Y. Crowell, 1981.

———. **Sleeping Ugly.** New York: Coward, McCann and Geoghegan, 1981.

Zaring, Jane. **The Return of the Dragon.** Boston: Houghton Mifflin, 1981.

D. Other Books Written by Jay Williams

Augustus Caesar. New York: Row, Peterson, 1951.

A Bag Full of Nothing. New York: Parents' Magazine Press, 1974.

The Battle for the Atlantic. New York: Random House, 1959.

A Box Full of Infinity. New York: W. W. Norton, 1970.

The Burglar Next Door. New York: Scholastic Book Services, 1976.

The Cookie Tree. New York: Parents' Magazine Press, 1967.

The Counterfeit African. New York: Oxford University Press, 1944.

Danny Dunn and the Homework Machine (with Raymond Abrashkin). New York: McGraw-Hill, 1958. (Science fiction series)

Eagle Jake and Indian Pete. New York: Rinehart, 1947.

Forgetful Fred. New York: Parents' Magazine Press, 1974.

The Good-For-Nothing Prince. New York: W. W. Norton, 1969.

The Hawks Tone. New York: Henry Z. Walck, 1971. (ESP fantasy)

The Hero from Otherwhere. New York: Henry Z. Walck, 1972.

The Horn of Roland. New York: Thomas Y. Crowell, 1968. (The adventures of Roland, Charlemagne's daring and loyal knight)

I Wish I Had Another Name (with Winifred Lubell). New York: Atheneum, 1962. (Verse)

Joan of Arc (with Charles W. Lightbody). New York: American Heritage, 1963. (Includes paintings, illuminations, drawings, and maps of the Middle Ages)

Knights of the Crusades (with Margaret B. Freeman). New York: American Heritage, 1962. (Illustrated with the arts and armaments of the Crusade era)

Leonardo da Vinci (with B. Lowry). New York: Harper and Row, 1965.

Life in the Middle Ages. New York: Random House, 1966.

The Magic Gate. New York: Oxford University Press, 1949.

The Magic Grandfather. New York: Four Winds Press, 1979.

Magical Storybook. New York: American Heritage, 1972.

The Spanish Armada (with Lacey B. Smith). New York: American Heritage, 1966.

The Stolen Oracle. New York: Oxford University Press, 1943.

The Surprising Things Maui Did. New York: Four Winds Press, 1979. (Legend of Maui, a Polynesian deity)

The Sword and the Scythe. New York: Oxford University Press, 1946.

The Sword of King Arthur. New York: Thomas Y. Crowell, 1968. (Based on Sir Thomas Malory's *Le Morte d'Arthur*)

The Time of the Kraken. New York: Scholastic Book Services, 1977.

To Catch a Bird. New York: Crowell Collier and Macmillan, 1968.

The Tournament of the Lions. New York: Henry Z. Walck, 1960.

The Water of Life. New York: Four Winds Press, 1980.

What Can You Do with a Word? New York: Macmillan, 1966.

The Wicked Tricks of Tyl Uilenspiegel. New York: Four Winds Press, 1975. (Four tales of a Dutch folk hero)

The Youngest Captain. New York: Parents' Magazine Press, 1972.

Medusa's Head. New York: Random House, 1960.

Moon Journey. New York: Crown, 1977. (Based on the work of Jules Verne)

The People of the Ax. New York: Henry Z. Walck, 1974. (Science fiction)

Petronella. New York: Parents' Magazine Press, 1973.

Pettifur. New York: Scholastic Book Services, 1977.

The Practical Princess. New York: Parents' Magazine Press, 1969.

The Practical Princess and Other Liberating Fairy Tales. New York: Parents' Magazine Press, 1978.

A Present from a Bird. New York: Parents' Magazine Press, 1971.

Puppy Pie. New York: Crowell Collier and Macmillan, 1962.

The Question Box. New York: W. W. Norton, 1965.

The Reward Worth Having. New York: Scholastic Book Services, 1977.

The Roman Moon Mystery. New York: Oxford University Press, 1948.

School for Sillies. New York: Parents' Magazine Press, 1969.

The Siege. New York: Little, Brown, 1954. (Nonfiction book on the Crusades)

The Silver Whistle. New York: Parents' Magazine Press, 1971.

E. Reference Material about Jay Williams

Commire, Anne, editor. **Something about the Author: Facts and Pictures about Contemporary Authors and Illustrators of Books for Young People.** Detroit: Gale Research, 1971 to present.

Kirkpatrick, D. L., editor. **Twentieth-Century Children's Writers.** New York: St. Martin's Press, 1978.

Group Story Sessions

First Session

To provide a common literary background for exploring the modern fairy tales of Jay Williams, the students were asked to read several traditional folktales and fairy tales prior to the first story session. At this session they identified some distinctive features of these tales from the oral tradition, referring to the symbolic and one-dimensional nature of the characters, the common motifs, and the recurring patterns and themes. Then "Petronella" by Jay Williams was read aloud and discussed. In response to the first question, "How is this story similar to traditional fairy tales?" the students identified characteristic patterns:

"It's about a king and queen and three children."

"The three children go out to seek their fortunes."

"The youngest one is kind to an old man, but the two older ones don't care about him."

"The youngest one is rewarded for kindness."

"This is the first step in the quest. The reward is very helpful advice for reaching the goal."

"It has a 'happily ever after' type of ending."

Then the students were asked, "How is this story *unlike* the traditional fairy tale?" They noted that Williams made his princess "a tall, handsome girl with flaming red hair" instead of the more typical dainty and delicate type; that it was the princess who did the brave deeds, who had the exciting adventures, and who eventually rescued the prince; that the prince in the story was lazy and selfish and showed none of the usual attributes of a fairy-tale prince; that the enchanter lived in "a comfortable-looking house, surrounded by gardens and stables and trees heavy with fruit" instead of in a stark and barren setting; and that the story ended with the princess deciding to marry the enchanter instead of the prince.

Responses to the third question, "What techniques did Mr. Williams use to create humor?" reflected the students' awareness that certain expected patterns associated with the fairy tale as a traditional literary genre had been violated. They recognized that the humor was created through a series of twists and reversals and contemporary touches. They also noted that an appreciation of this humor depended on one's knowledge of the traditional fairy-tale pattern. In his book *From Two to Five* (1963), Kornei Chukovsky explores this aspect of humor and children's delight in the incongruous, the absurd, and incorrect juxtapositions found in prose and poetry. Chukovsky suggests that the pleasure children derive from listening to or creating nonsense verse is related to their eagerness to *play* with the ideas they have mastered: "When we notice that a child has started to play with some newly acquired component of understanding, we may definitely conclude that he has become full master of this item of understanding; only those ideas can become toys for him whose proper relation to reality is firmly known to him" (p. 103).

The authors of humorous modern fairy tales play with what is known about traditional fairy tales and assume that their readers have already acquired this knowledge. The ability of a reader to comprehend and appreciate the humor of tales such as "Petronella" depends on recognition of the twists, reversals, and incorrect juxtapositions as they relate directly to the *expected* in traditional fairy tales.

The final question raised in the discussion of "Petronella" was "What issue do you think Mr. Williams was addressing in this story?" Most of the students agreed that Williams seemed to be expressing his concern about the sexist role-playing associated with fairy tales in particular and found in too many children's books in general. Several suggested that the story of "Petronella," with its strong heroine and weak hero, served to offset the rather one-sided view of women presented in traditional tales. One fifth-grade girl commented: "Mr. Williams probably wanted to call attention to the way these old tales are so prejudiced against women. There are some other good stories like this one in *Stories for Free Children* [edited by Letty Cottin Pogrebin]. They're from *Ms Magazine*."

Second Session

In the second session, Jay Williams's "The Silver Whistle" was read aloud, and the discussion was similar to that of "Petronella." The story was compared to traditional fairy tales, especially those with the "quest" pattern and with such common motifs as wicked witches, magic objects, three tasks, and a prince in search of a bride. Several students recognized story elements drawn from two Russian tales, *Baba Yaga* by Ernest Small and *Vasilisa the Beautiful* by Thomas Whitney. The heroine in "The Silver

Whistle" was compared to Petronella and identified as another example of the strong, intelligent, independent female character, a striking contrast to the traditional passive princesses sitting quietly and protected in castle gardens. One student pointed out the copyright date for the first edition of "The Silver Whistle" was 1971 and commented: "Mr. Williams entered the women's liberation movement at a very early stage!" In response to this observation, another student exclaimed, "Oh, so that's what it means— 'and other *liberating* fairy tales'! That whole collection must have the same kinds of stories about liberated women."

Third Session

The next session introduced other examples of books featuring liberated heroines. The students selected at least two stories to read independently and to discuss in class. By the end of the session, there were requests for more stories about liberated heroines. A list of titles was recorded in a folder and hung in the book corner of the classroom. The preliminary list was expanded as additional titles were recommended by teachers, librarians, and students. One student who had just studied the art of calligraphy volunteered to decorate the folder and to record the titles in calligraphy. A few weeks later, those students who had developed a special interest in the books in this category decided to establish a book club to share and discuss the books. The teacher helped with arrangements for a meeting space and with scheduling problems, and this special interest group met regularly, twice a month, for the remainder of the school year. The complete list of titles eventually recorded in the Liberated Heroines folder and used as a basic reference by the book club is included in the bibliography of books for this Focus Unit.

Fourth Session

This session was scheduled after most of the students had read at least two selections from the group of humorous modern fairy tales. They discussed the tales in terms of the techniques and patterns explored during the first two sessions in which Jay Williams's "Petronella" and "The Silver Whistle" were introduced. For example, those who had read John Gardner's "Dragon, Dragon" identified the underlying structure of the classic fairy-tale sequence and the twists and contemporary touches woven into this structure to produce humor. One student had recognized Gardner's allusion to the Aesop fable "Mice in Council" ["But the wise cobbler said gloomily, 'It's all very well to talk about it—but how are you going to do it?' " (p. 4)]. Another student commented, "This story seemed closer to a regular fairy tale than 'Petronella.' It didn't have a message about women's rights, and it ended up with the youngest son killing the dragon, saving the two older brothers, and getting the princess and half the kingdom!"

Jane Yolen's *The Acorn Quest* was recognized by several students as a spoof on the legend of King Arthur. They especially appreciated Yolen's wonderful games with words and names such as King Earthor, an owl; Sir Runsalot, a mouse; Sir Gimmemore, a rabbit; Sir Tarryhere, a turtle; and the Wizard Squirrelin. One student commented, "I liked the way Ms. Yolen mixed the funny and the serious in that little story. I mean, even though you're sort of chuckling all through it, there are messages about hope and friendship and courage, too."

The Last of the Dragons by E. Nesbit was compared to "Petronella" and "The Silver Whistle." One student observed: "In this story there are *three* characters who are changed from their traditional roles—the princess was pretty and nice but also a great fencer and brave, and *she* wanted to fight the dragon; the prince didn't like fighting, he was more interested in *studying;* and the dragon didn't really like to eat princesses, he just wanted friends and to drink *petrol!*"

A student who had read *Seven at One Blow* by Jay Williams suggested that a different technique was used for this story: "It starts out almost exactly like 'The Brave Little Tailor,' but then Mr. Williams made up a whole new ending." As each student added observations, discoveries, and insights about the specific stories they had selected to read independently, the discussion gradually moved toward some general conclusions about humorous modern fairy tales and the way different writers play with classic fairy-tale form and content and impose humorous twists and reversals and contemporary revisions on traditional characters, settings, themes, and language.

Creative Writing

The broad overview of characteristic features of the modern fairy tales included in this Focus Unit provided the context for the creative writing project planned for the first segment of this unit. The students created their own modern fairy tales, responding enthusiastically to the challenge of blending the contemporary with the traditional without altering the classic form to the point that the new story would be beyond recognition as a modern fairy tale. For example, they learned to use contemporary language somewhat sparingly when they discovered the humorous effect of a few slang expressions from the 1980s sprinkled into the more formal speech of kings and queens in the fairy-tale world. One student observed, "The humor seems to be related to the surprise of an unexpected word or action or thing. Like here, in my story, I have this regular prince going off to battle this regular dragon—but he climbs on his white Honda motorcycle instead of a white horse!"

The sharing of these original stories demonstrated a high quality of interaction as students responded with genuine delight and appreciation to their classmate's creative efforts and sense of humor. The tales produced by these young authors reflected their understanding of the traditional fairy tale as a literary genre and as the basis for modern fairy tales. The students had obviously drawn from their diverse experiences with classic tales as well as from their exposure to the modern tales of Jay Williams, John Gardner, and others to produce their own unique blends of humor and fantasy.

More about Jay Williams

The next segment of this Focus Unit involved a closer look at Jay Williams and the broad spectrum of books produced by this gifted writer. The first step entailed some library research. Assigned the task of bringing to class some biographical information about Williams, the students gained firsthand experience with library skills in their search through relevant reference materials. Their quest led them to such basic references as *Something about the Author* and *Twentieth-Century Children's Writers,* which, in turn, directed them to more specific references. The results of the students' research, recorded in their notebooks, was shared in class. A biographical sketch of Williams was compiled from the information and recorded by a volunteer scribe. The next step was to generate a complete list of Williams's publications for young people. The students discovered that he had also written for adults but decided to confine their list to "books intended for kids." As this list grew, the students became increasingly impressed with the diversity it reflected. When the list seemed to be complete, the books were categorized in terms of genre: historical fiction, modern fairy tale, science fiction, folklore, legend, and nonfiction.

The students selected at least one book from this list for independent reading and shared their reading experiences in a way that might stimulate others to choose that book. Most of the students responded positively to these peer recommendations. The end result was that more books by Williams were read and enjoyed by more students. In the process, students discovered new interest areas for further personal reading. For example, one student developed a taste for science fiction while another student became interested in the Middle Ages. One student who had enjoyed reading about King Arthur was delighted to discover *The Magic Grand-*

father, a story about an eleven-year-old boy whose grandfather has the same powers as King Arthur's Merlin. Students who especially appreciated the humor of *The Wicked Tricks of Tyl Uilenspiegel* went to the library in search of additional tales about this folk hero. And so it went: as interests spread, so did reading involvement.

The final assignment of the Focus Unit was to write about Jay Williams—to try to capture the essence of the man and the artist, using explicit and implicit information gathered from biographical data and from the products of his pen. The form used for this assignment was an obituary or eulogy for this author, who died July 12, 1978. The students were very serious and thoughtful as they attempted to portray the significance of the life of a man whom they had never met but who had become a friend through the literature he had written.

References

Chukovsky, Kornei. *From Two to Five.* Berkeley: University of California Press, 1963.

Small, Ernest. *Baba Yaga.* Boston: Houghton Mifflin, 1966.

Whitney, Thomas. *Vasilisa the Beautiful.* New York: Macmillan, 1970.

8 The Night: A Focus Unit for Grades One and Two

Bed in Summer

In winter I get up at night
And dress by yellow candle-light.
In summer, quite the other way,
I leave to go to bed by day.

Robert Louis Stevenson

The Night Focus Unit is most appropriately introduced into the classroom at that time of the year when days are suddenly shorter and the night grows longer, when children wake up in morning darkness and night falls long before bedtime. The idea for this Focus Unit evolved in response to children's questions about the change from daylight saving time to standard time, which had brought more darkness into their waking hours, their fears and concerns associated with this darkness, and their interest in the night world itself.

The story sessions of the Night Focus Unit were planned to coincide with a science unit about night and day, about the sun, moon, and stars, and about the nocturnal creatures who are awake in the night world. Thus, literature and science were integrated into a cohesive framework for the study of night. The fact and fantasy, the natural and supernatural, the known and unknown, the science and the mystery associated with the night world—all became topics for exploration.

Objectives

1. To introduce stories which address children's questions and concerns about the night world.
2. To provide children with opportunities to express, explore, and share personal questions, concerns, and fears associated with the night in a supportive environment.
3. To provide opportunities to apply factual information in responding to fiction.
4. To improve story comprehension skills with special emphasis on:
   a. identifying basic narrative components—setting, plot, character, theme.

79

    b. identifying and comparing problem-solving strategies of diverse story characters.

    c. identifying logical relationships among story events.

5. To promote independent reading.

6. To provide the context and stimulus for creative writing and other forms of creative expression.

Bibliography for the Night Focus Unit

I. Group Story Sessions

Alexander, Anne. **Noise in the Night.** New York: Rand McNally, 1960.

Sherri hears a strange noise in the night and engages her family in various attempts to identify it. However, it is Sherri who eventually solves the mystery of the noise in the night and surprises everyone with her discovery.

Babbitt, Natalie. **The Something.** New York: Farrar, Straus and Giroux, 1970.

Mylo is a small monster who overcomes his fear of the dark and "the Something" which he meets in a dream one night.

Conford, Ellen. **Eugene the Brave.** Boston: Little, Brown, 1978.

Eugene is a timid little possum who is afraid of the dark and refuses to join his family when they go out at night to search for food. His sister, Geraldine, decides to cure him of his fear.

Crowe, Robert. **Clyde Monster.** New York: E. P. Dutton, 1976.

Clyde is a little monster who is afraid to go to bed in his cave at night because he believes there are people hiding in the dark ready to get him.

Duvoisin, Roger. **Day and Night.** New York: Alfred A. Knopf, 1960.

This is the story of two friends, an owl called Night and a poodle called Day. Their evening conversations disturb the sleep of the Pennyfeather family until Bob Pennyfeather thinks of a solution which pleases all concerned.

Fenner, Carol. **Tigers in the Cellar.** New York: Harcourt, Brace and World, 1963.

At night, when it is dark, a little girl hears tigers prowling and growling in the cellar. One night she creeps quietly out of her room into the dark hall. "There they were. At the foot of the stairs were two tigers." Her nighttime adventures with these two tigers are woven into a fabric of reality and fantasy, wishes and dreams.

Lifton, Betty Jean. **Good Night, Orange Monster.** New York: Atheneum, 1972.

Ken is afraid of the monster in his closet. Moogi, the monster who lives in Ken's closet, is afraid of boys. Ken and Moogi meet, become friends, and help each other overcome their fears.

Mayer, Mercer. **There's a Nightmare in My Closet.** New York: Dial Press, 1968.

A little boy, concerned about a "nightmare" in his closet, decides to confront the unknown monster who has caused him such anxiety at bedtime.

Schubert, Ingrid, and Dieter Schubert. **There's a Crocodile under My Bed!** New York: McGraw-Hill, 1981.

Peggy is startled by a crocodile under her bed, but her parents do not take her discovery seriously. Peggy's fears turn to delight when she actually meets James, the crocodile under her bed.

Wildsmith, Brian. **The Owl and the Woodpecker.** New York: Franklin Watts, 1971.

The Woodpecker's tapping disturbs the Owl's sleep and sets into motion a heated argument in which the other forest animals become active participants. They manage to resolve their differences, and peace returns to the forest.

II. Independent Reading

A. Fiction

Aardema, Verna. **Why Mosquitoes Buzz in People's Ears.** New York: Dial Press, 1975.

Bannon, Laura. **Little People of the Night.** Boston: Houghton Mifflin, 1963.

Bendick, Jeanne. **A Fresh Look at Night.** New York: Franklin Watts, 1963.

Bonsall, Crosby. **Who's Afraid of the Dark?** New York: Harper and Row, 1980.

Bradbury, Ray. **Switch on the Night.** New York: Pantheon Books, 1955.

Brown, Margaret Wise. **Wait Till the Moon Is Full.** New York: Harper and Row, 1948.

Crews, Donald. **Light.** New York: Greenwillow Books, 1981.

Dragonwagon, Crescent. **When Light Turns into Night.** New York: Harper and Row, 1975.

———. **Your Owl Friend.** New York: Harper and Row, 1977.

Elkin, Benjamin. **Why the Sun Was Late.** New York: Parents' Magazine Press, 1966.

Fisher, Aileen. **In the Middle of the Night.** New York: Thomas Y. Crowell, 1965.

Fox, Siv Cedering. **The Blue Horse and Other Night Poems.** New York: Seabury Press, 1979.

Gackenback, Dick. **Harry and the Terrible Whatzit.** New York: Seabury Press, 1977.

Hoban, Russell. **Bedtime for Frances.** New York: Harper and Row, 1960.

Hopkins, Lee Bennett. **Go to Bed! A Book of Bedtime Poems.** New York: Alfred A. Knopf, 1979.

Hutchins, Pat. **Good Night, Owl!** New York: Macmillan, 1972.

Jarrell, Randall. **The Bat-Poet.** New York: Macmillan, 1964.

Keats, Ezra Jack. **Dreams.** New York: Macmillan, 1974.

Memling, Carl. **What's in the Dark?** New York: Parents' Magazine Press, 1971.

Moss, Elaine, compiler. **From Morn to Midnight.** New York: Thomas Y. Crowell, 1977.

Rockwell, Anne. **The Dancing Stars: An Iroquois Legend.** New York: Thomas Y. Crowell, 1972.

Russo, Susan. **The Moon's the North Wind's Cooky: Night Poems.** New York: Lothrop, Lee and Shepard Books, 1979.

Ryan, Cheli Duran. **Hildilid's Night.** New York: Macmillan, 1971.

Sendak, Maurice. **In the Night Kitchen.** New York: Harper and Row, 1970.

Shulivitz, Uri. **Dawn.** New York: Farrar, Straus and Giroux, 1974.

Skofield, James. **Night Dances.** New York: Harper and Row, 1981.

Udry, Janice. **The Moon Jumpers.** New York: Harper and Row, 1959

Waber, Bernard. **Ira Sleeps Over.** Boston: Houghton Mifflin, 1972.

Ward, Lynd. **The Silver Pony.** Boston: Houghton Mifflin, 1973.

B. Nonfiction

Asimov, Isaac. **The Moon.** Chicago: Follett, 1966.

———. **Stars.** Chicago: Follett, 1968.

Branley, Franklyn. **A Book of Stars for You.** New York: Thomas Y. Crowell, 1967.

———. **The Moon Seems to Change.** New York: Thomas Y. Crowell, 1960.

Engelbrektson, Sune. **The Sun Is a Star.** New York: Holt, Rinehart and
Winston, 1963.

Gans, Roma. **Birds at Night.** New York: Thomas Y. Crowell, 1968.

Goudy, Alice. **The Day We Saw the Sun Come Up.** New York: Charles
Scribner's Sons, 1961.

Hurd, Edith T. **The Mother Owl.** Boston: Little, Brown, 1974.

Jobb, Jamie. **The Night Sky Book: An Everyday Guide to Every Night.**
Boston: Little, Brown, 1977.

Kuskin, Karla. **A Space Story.** New York: Harper and Row, 1979.

Rey, H. A. **Find the Constellations.** Boston: Houghton Mifflin, 1962.

Rinard, Judith. **Creatures at Night.** Washington: National Geographic
Society, 1977.

Selsam, Millicent. **Night Animals.** New York: Four Winds Press, 1979.

Shapp, Martha, and Charles Shapp. **Let's Find Out What's in the Sky.**
New York: Franklin Watts, 1961.

Group Story Sessions

First Session

Good Night, Orange Monster by Betty Jean Lifton was read aloud first
to introduce one of the major themes found in stories about night: nighttime fears. The children easily identified with Ken, the character who was
afraid of monsters in his closet, and they were delighted to meet the other
main character, Moogi, a small furry monster who lived in Ken's closet.
This story served as a stimulus for the spontaneous sharing of personal
apprehensions, anxieties, and scary experiences associated with the night.
As each child contributed to this interaction, others nodded with understanding and seemed reassured to discover common bonds of feelings and
fears. Surely it is helpful for children to know that they are not alone.

After exploring the theme of this story in terms of their own personal
experiences, the children were asked to turn their attention to the story
itself and to think about the characters, plot, and setting: "Who are the
two main characters? What are their problems? Where does the story
take place?" These questions were intended to lead the children toward a
discovery of the parallel plots woven together in this story. After identifying the two main characters, the children saw that each had a problem
(Ken was afraid of monsters, while Moogi was afraid of boys) and each
character had his own setting. Eventually, one girl reached the conclusion,
"It's like having two stories in one! The first story starts out in the
bedroom about Ken and his family and his fear of monsters, and the

second story is in the closet about Moogi and *his* family and his fear of boys." Responses to the next question, "How did Ken and Moogi change by the end of the story?" reflected the children's grasp of the way the problems were solved as well as the evidence of character development in this story:

> "Ken wasn't afraid of monsters anymore because he met Moogi and they got to be friends."

> "The same thing with Moogi. He wasn't afraid anymore either. And they both made little monsters and boys with that monster-making machine. I've got one like that."

> "They both sort of helped each other with their problem."

> "Ken didn't need his light on when he went to bed so that means he's not afraid anymore."

> "And he wasn't afraid to have the closet door open at night either."

> "Ken's mom knew he was growing up but she didn't know *how* he solved his problem. Moogi's mom and dad could see that Moogi was growing up, too."

Second Session

The Something by Natalie Babbitt, another story about nighttime fears, was read aloud next. When asked, "Who is the main character and what is his problem?" the children responded by comparing this story with *Good Night, Orange Monster:*

> "Mylo is a little monster just like Moogi and he's afraid of the dark because he thinks a Something will get him and it's a human."

> "But it's different because Moogi is a *nocturnal* creature. He's awake at night and sleeps in the day, but Mylo sleeps at night."

> "But Mylo meets the Something just like Moogi meets Ken. And he makes a clay statue of it just like Moogi made that boy out of plastic stuff."

> "And that's how they solved their problem. They all stopped being afraid after they got to *know* the thing they were afraid of."

> "And they all kept their little statues even after they stopped being afraid. Mylo put it next to his bed, but he wasn't afraid of the dark anymore."

> "Last night I saw a big thing in my room, and I woke up my dad and he came in and turned on the light, and it was the clown lamp on my dresser!"

In these excerpts, one sees evidence of critical thinking which takes the children beyond literal comprehension of a story. They were able to make valid comparisons with the story read in the first session; they applied their new knowledge of nocturnal animals to this comparative analysis; and they related the story themes to their own experiences with nighttime fears.

The final question in this session, "Why did Mylo's mother buy him the clay?" brought diverse interpretations:

> "She felt bad that Mylo was unhappy, so she brought him a present to cheer him up."

> "I think she got him clay because she thought he would get so busy making stuff that he'd forget all about being afraid of the dark."

> "Maybe she knew if he *made* the thing he was afraid of he wouldn't be afraid of it. So that's why she chose clay."

> "Maybe she read *Good Night, Orange Monster* and that's how she knew!"

> "She couldn't. She's just a character in a story! She brought him the clay because she felt bad that she couldn't really help him with his problem and she felt better because she could show that she loved him even though she couldn't help him."

Third Session

Clyde Monster by Robert Crowe was read and compared with the first two stories. The children immediately recognized the similarities between Clyde, Mylo, and Moogi: all three were small monsters who feared the dark and people. However, many of the children said they didn't like the way this story ended. The teacher's attempt to help the children understand and explain their negative reactions is illustrated in the following dialogue from the session:

Teacher: Why didn't you like the ending?

Child 1: Well, Clyde was still afraid at the end of the story. He didn't really solve his problem.

Teacher: How did you decide that he was still afraid?

Child 1: Because he still wanted the light on. When Ken stopped being afraid, he didn't need the light on.

Child 2: But Clyde didn't say that. He didn't even have a light. He lived in a cave!

Child 1: He did so. He was still afraid of the dark!

Teacher: Let's go back and look at the book. Here it is. Clyde said to his parents, "Could you leave the rock open just a little?" What did he mean? Maybe the picture on the last page will help.

Child 3: Oh, I get it! The rock was like the *door* to the cave and the *moonlight* came in.

Child 1: See! I was right. He still wanted it to be light because he was still afraid.

Child 4: That's why those other two stories were better because everyone got rid of their problems at the end and so it was a happy ending, but Clyde looked sort of sad because he was pretty much the same at the end.

Child 5: He should have changed at the end. Nothing really happened.

Teacher: How did Clyde's parents try to help him?

Child 1: They told him a kind of story to make him not be afraid anymore.

Child 2: But it was sort of a fake story, and I don't think Clyde really believed it. And his dad was mad because he wasn't acting brave.

Child 6: Clyde didn't *do* anything like Ken and Moogi and Mylo did.

Child 7: I think Clyde's parents probably wanted to be helpful just like Ken's mom and Moogi's and Mylo's. But it's better if he did something himself to solve his own problem.

Child 8: I liked the other stories better because I liked the characters. Clyde was sort of boring, and he looked so sad all the time. I would much rather have Moogi come to my house than Clyde!

The children's comments seemed to reflect their expectations about narrative sequence and their disappointment regarding the apparent lack of a satisfactory resolution of the monster's problem in *Clyde Monster*. In addition, the children's observations indicated that they grasped the connection between the success of Ken, Moogi, and Mylo in overcoming their nighttime fears and these characters' active involvement in the process of solving their problem by identifying and confronting the source of their fear.

Fourth Session

By the fourth story session, the children were ready to make accurate predictions as they listened to *There's a Crocodile under My Bed!* by

Ingrid and Dieter Schubert. For example, they anticipated the parents'
rational response to Peggy's exclamation on the second page, "There's a
crocodile under my bed!" and they were not at all surprised to find out
on the fourth page that there really was a crocodile under her bed. The
children found several parallels with *Good Night, Orange Monster* and
presented their observations spontaneously:

> "James [the crocodile] had a special reason for being under Peggy's
> bed just like Moogi had a special reason for being in Ken's closet."
>
> "And in both stories the children played with them when their
> parents weren't around."
>
> "And they made models together. Like Ken and Moogi made those
> plastic monsters, and James and Peggy made that egg carton croc-
> odile."
>
> "And in both stories the parents tried to make the kids think it was
> just their imagination."
>
> "In the end, Peggy wasn't scared anymore."
>
> "I thought it was like *Good Night, Orange Monster* because it sort
> of has two stories too. One story's about Peggy and her parents in
> her house and then there's the other story about what happened to
> James in the Land of Crocodiles."

Fifth Session

Eugene the Brave by Ellen Conford was read aloud next. The children
were asked to list the important things they had learned about each of the
main characters, a family of possums. This question generated a discussion
about the specific and distinguishing characteristics of these story characters as well as their general characteristics as nocturnal creatures. In the
process, they identified Eugene's problem (his fear of the dark), the diverse
responses of the family members, and the various strategies used in the
attempt to solve this problem.

Several questions were introduced to help the children think about the
episode in which Geraldine implements her plan to cure Eugene and to
help them understand the rather subtle meanings behind her actions:

> What was Geraldine's plan for curing Eugene of his fear of the dark?
>
> How did she get him to do a brave deed?
>
> Do you think she really had hurt her leg when she called Eugene to
> help her?

Additional questions were used to focus attention on attitudinal changes
in the central story character as well as in the readers/listeners:

How did Eugene feel about himself at the end of the story?

How did his experience with his sister, Geraldine, help him solve his problem?

What did you think of Geraldine in the beginning of the story?

How did you feel about her by the end of the story?

Were you surprised by what she did? Why?

The last group of questions about Geraldine was intended to highlight an attitudinal change in readers/listeners as they gain new information about a particular story character and revise their initial impression or opinion about that character. This story provides an excellent opportunity for such reader involvement and the discovery that overt behaviors of characters cannot always be used as accurate indications of internal motives and feelings.

This group session was concluded with a consideration of the various strategies used by family members to help Eugene with his problem. For example, the children were asked to contrast the strategy used by Randolph (Eugene's brother) with Geraldine's strategy and to speculate on the reason for Geraldine's eventual success. The children observed that everyone, especially Randolph, seemed to be sympathetic about Eugene's problem but that it was Geraldine who really helped Eugene to help himself. One child compared this story to *Good Night, Orange Monster:* "Ken's mom just told him not to be scared because there's no such thing as monsters. But Ken had to see for himself! And he found out that it doesn't really help to hide! It was the same for Eugene." At this point, other children brought into the discussion their own experiences with fears and the various responses of siblings and parents.

Sixth Session

There's a Nightmare in My Closet by Mercer Mayer and *Tigers in the Cellar* by Carol Fenner were selected next. Before the two stories were read aloud, the children's attention was drawn to key words in the titles: *nightmare* and *cellar*. These words were discussed in terms of denotations, connotations, and personal associations. This exploration of two emotionally charged words set the stage for listening to and discussing the stories. After identifying the basic elements and plot sequence of each narrative, the children compared the two stories with each other and with the five stories read in previous sessions:

> "In the story about the nightmare, the boy finds out that the creature in his closet is a crybaby, and when the girl in the other story meets the tigers, one is crying!"

"It's the same in *Good Night, Orange Monster*. When they meet the things they're afraid of, they're not scary or terrible at all!"

"And they all stopped being afraid as soon as they met the thing."

"The mother in *Tigers in the Cellar* sure sounded familiar! When the girl tried to tell her about the tigers, her mom just said, 'Nonsense!' like the other parents said in those other stories."

"I think that midnight ride with the tigers really was a dream."

"Maybe she just *imagined* the tigers—like sometimes you have a pretend friend."

"I think they really were there—just like Moogi was really there. Those tigers would be nice pets."

"In *The Something* it seemed like a regular dream. Remember how the pages were all dark when he met that girl and she said, 'You're in my dream' and Mylo said, 'No it's my dream'?"

"I don't think it matters if it was a dream or not. At least they stopped being afraid."

Seventh Session

When the children heard *Noise in the Night* by Anne Alexander, they immediately recognized the basic story pattern identified in the previous stories and gradually identified common themes:

"She found out what the noise was so she wasn't scared anymore."

"She tried to draw a picture of it—just like Ken and Mylo tried to make the things they were scared of."

"And her parents tried to help but she solved her own problem."

"In all the stories something is scary if you can't see it. But when you know what it is, it's not as scary anymore."

"It's like that Spook House on Halloween. *Everything* was scary until they turned the light on!"

"That's why the nighttime is so creepy—because of the dark."

"That's why the scary things live in closets and cellars. It's always dark and creepy in those places."

Eighth Session

Since the children had been studying the habits and characteristics of nocturnal creatures as part of a science unit, two stories about nocturnal creatures were selected: *The Owl and the Woodpecker* by Brian Wildsmith and *Day and Night* by Roger Duvoisin. The children enjoyed demonstrating their new knowledge about nocturnal animals as they discussed these stories, and they recognized that the problem in each story was a consequence of the particular sleep patterns of these animals. The children also noted that in each story the friendship was initiated by an incident in which one character rescues the other.

Independent Reading and Extension Activities

The collection of books selected for the Night Focus Unit included both iction and nonfiction titles as well as various elementary science texts ind reference books which the children could choose to read independently during the regularly scheduled quiet reading time. To extend their independent reading experiences, several advanced readers were selected to work as a group with the teacher on a project involving the production of "information books." Each child selected a topic of particular interest (such as stars, the moon, nocturnal animals), collected information about this topic, and then wrote and illustrated a booklet on the topic. When each booklet was completed, it was placed on the display table with the other books about night.

Another group of children created a picture book of their favorite characters from the night stories they had heard in the story sessions or read during the quiet reading time. Each child drew a picture of his or her favorite character and wrote a caption on the bottom of the page to explain who it was. These pages were bound together into a large book which also became part of the Focus Unit collection.

A third group created riddles about the stories read independently and copied them onto 5 x 8-inch cards with the answers written on the back. These cards were held together with a steel notebook ring. On the top card was printed: "Can you guess this story?" This book was added to the Night book display, as were extra blank cards to encourage other children to add their own riddles.

A fourth group of children worked on a "Word Book," which consisted of new or interesting words found in the books read aloud or independently. Each child selected one or more words to contribute to the book. They printed one word in the top right-hand corner of the page, illustrated the word in the center of the page, and used the word in a sentence at the bottom of the page. When all the pages were completed, the children arranged the words alphabetically and bound the pages together into a book, using notebook rings so new pages could be added later.

Many of the children enjoyed sharing the Night books with their parents. Some borrowed books from the classroom collection, and others found the same or similar stories at their local libraries. One child brought home *The Bat-Poet* by Randall Jarrell for his parents to read to him at bedtime. He and his parents were delighted with this beautiful story, and the child told his classmates about the book during one of the story sessions. As a result, this particular book was selected by a number of other children to be read at bedtime. This is a nice example of the way reading experiences in the classroom can be extended into the home. In fact, a number of parents reported that this initial experience turned out to be the catalyst for the establishment of a more regular read-aloud time as part of the bedtime routine.

Creative Writing

In preparation for creating night poems, the children were asked, "What do you think of when you think of night?" in order to generate a list of words and phrases about night. This list was recorded on a large chart; it included such topics as sounds of night, dreams, nightmares, shadows, monsters, ghosts, the moon and stars, wind, nocturnal animals, going to bed, thoughts in bed, and so on. After the chart was filled with the children's own thoughts about night, the teacher shared with them a few of the thoughts expressed by several poets using different poetic forms:

> Everyone is asleep
> There is only the moon
> And me.
>
> Seifu-jo

> The harvest moon is so bright!
> My shadow walks home with me.
>
> Sodō

> The Night
>
> The night
> creeps in
> around my head
> and snuggles down
> upon the bed,
> and makes lace pictures
> on the wall
> but doesn't say a word at all.
>
> Myra Cohn Livingston

In Bed

When I am in bed
I hear
footsteps of the night
sharp
like the crackling of a dead leaf
in the stillness.

Then my mother laughs
downstairs.

                                   Charlotte Zolotow

Charlie's Bedtime

Can you bring me a glass of water?
Can I have a little juice?
Can I say goodnight to Daddy again?
Will you read me Dr. Seuss?

Will I see you in the morning, Mommy?
Can I keep on the light?

Oh—
If only I'd find a real way
To chase away the night.

                                   Lee Bennett Hopkins

Night Comes . . .

Night Comes
leaking
out of the sky.
Stars come
peeking.
Moon comes
sneaking,
silvery-sly.
Who is
shaking,
shivery—
quaking?
Who is afraid
of the night?

Not I.

                                   Beatrice de Regniers

Thus, the stage was set for the creative writing process through a
brainstorming session in which the children examined their own thoughts
about night and through exposure to poets who have translated similar
thoughts into the art form of poetry. When the children began to write

their own night poems, they were ready to draw from their literary and experiential background to produce diverse expressions of individual thoughts, feelings, and perceptions reflecting a blend of reality and imagination, wishes and dreams.

The completed poems were illustrated with the help of the art teacher, who suggested a wax resist technique in which black tempera paint was washed over a crayon drawing of the night scene conveyed by the poem. These illustrated night poems were exhibited on a bulletin board adjacent to the Night Focus Unit collection of fiction and nonfiction books, textbooks, reference materials, and books created by the children. The total display reflected the diverse but related experiences generated by this Focus Unit.

Following this classroom writing activity, a number of children expressed an interest in doing further work with poetry. In response, the teacher organized these children into a small group and had them read *The Blue Horse and Other Night Poems* by Siv Cedering Fox as a stimulus for creating their own book of poems with a common theme. Their assignment was to create poems in answer to the question posed on the first page of this book, " . . . and what do you think of before you fall asleep?" The children responded enthusiastically to this challenge to their minds and imaginations. Inspired by the poetry in this book, they let their thoughts take flight as they engaged in creative language play.

Design of the Focus Units

An underlying objective of this and every Focus Unit is to provide appropriate challenges and rich language and thinking experiences for *all* children in heterogeneous classrooms. During the story sessions, each child is encouraged to contribute to the group discussions according to his or her own unique background, interests, and cognitive ability. These discussions involve a sharing of ideas and experiences in which each child can learn from the contributions of peers. The collection of books for independent reading is sufficiently diverse to provide for the various reading skills and interests in any one classroom. The activities promoting this independent reading and the classroom projects involving various forms of creative expression are also tailored to a wide range of interests and talents. Learning experiences are created or modified to provide for special gifts or learning difficulties or in response to immediate interests expressed by individual children. The Focus Unit model functions as an open invitation to all children to become actively involved with literature. The form and extent of that involvement will vary from one child to the next.

The recognition of individual differences is evident in the implementation of the Night Focus Unit. At the same time, the Focus Unit, as an instructional design, is essentially a group experience in which common questions, concerns, and interests are shared and explored. The Night Focus Unit is structured to generate an awareness of these shared concerns and experiences, which eclipse individual differences. That is, common questions and interests associated with the nighttime serve to bind diverse individuals into a cohesive group. Furthermore, it is important for children to be given reassurance, on the one hand, that they are special and unique as individuals and, on the other hand, that they have much in common with those around them.

9 The Sea: A Focus Unit for Grades Four and Five

The relationship of people to the sea is the theme which connects the stories selected for this Focus Unit. Most of the children for whom this unit was designed had at some time in their lives discovered the power of the sea through firsthand experience. Several had expressed their fascination with the sea; they had felt its mystery and beauty. People's response to the sea can be found in ancient legends and myths, traditional folktales and fairy tales, poetry, and ballads as well as in contemporary fiction. Feelings about the sea have always been ambivalent. Its power and mystery inspire feelings of awe and wonder as well as terror and hatred. The sea is a source of life and death, providing sustenance and mobility as well as engendering terrifying destruction. Storytellers and writers the world over have been moved to interpret the dual nature of the sea through themes of good and evil, fascination and dread, love and hate, life and death. The tales included in the Sea Focus Unit were selected to illustrate the different kinds of legends and folklore of the sea that are part of our literary heritage and to provide a sampling of diverse literary genres, motifs, themes, and styles.

Objectives

1. To provide exposure to diverse tales of the sea found in traditional and modern literature.
2. To promote growth in the ability to analyze literary selections in terms of genre, characters, motifs, themes, and symbolism.
3. To expand reading interests and to promote independent reading.
4. To provide a context and assistance for creative writing.

Bibliography for the Sea Focus Unit

I. Group Story Sessions

Hearn, Lafcadio. "Urashima." In **The Boy Who Drew Cats.** New York: Macmillan, 1963.

Urashima Taro frees a tortoise from his fishing line and returns it to the sea. As a reward for this kind deed, the Dragon King of the Sea invites Urashima to marry his daughter and to live with her on an enchanted island.

Hodges, Margaret. **The Wave.** Boston: Houghton Mifflin, 1964.

In this ancient Japanese tale, a wise old man sets fire to his own rice fields in order to draw the villagers away from a tidal wave which threatens to engulf the village.

Uchida, Yoshiko. "The Magic Mortar." In **The Magic Listening Cap: More Folk Tales from Japan.** New York: Harcourt, Brace and World, 1955.

This is a folktale about a poor man whose wealthy brother refuses to lend him even a small amount of rice. A magic mortar brings good fortune to the poor man and his wife but causes the greedy brother to be punished for his wickedness.

————. "The Sea of Gold." In **The Sea of Gold and Other Tales from Japan.** Boston: Gregg Press, 1980.

Hikoichi, a cook on a fishing boat, befriends the fish of the sea and feeds them every evening for many long years. Although mocked by the fishermen, Hikoichi is rewarded for his generosity by the King of the Sea.

Watson, William. "The Ballad of Semmerwater." In **A Storyteller's Choice,** edited by Eileen H. Colwell. New York: Henry Z. Walck, 1963.

This poem is based on a legend about Semmerwater, a deep and mysterious lake in which lies buried a lost city, punished for its pride, ". . . deep asleep till Doom."

Wetterer, Margaret K. **The Mermaid's Cape.** New York: Atheneum, 1982.

A young Irish fisherman falls in love with a beautiful mermaid. When she drifts too close to shore, he steals her "shimmering sea-green cape," preventing her return to the sea and giving him power over her.

Yolen, Jane. **Greyling: A Picture Story from the Island of Shetland.** Cleveland: World, 1968.

A fisherman and his wife long for a child of their own. One day the fisherman finds a small grey seal stranded on a sand bar. When he brings it home, it becomes a human child. The couple love him as a son, but because they know he is a Selchie, they never allow him in the sea. According to legend, the Selchies are "men upon the land and seals in the sea."

————. "The Wind Cap." In **The Hundredth Dove.** New York: Thomas Y. Crowell, 1977.

"There was once a lad who would be a sailor but his mother would not let him go to the sea." Thus begins the tale of Jon, who saves the life of a tiny green turtle and is rewarded with a magic cap full of wind—"the kind that sailors most desire." Jon runs off to sea where he discovers that his magic wind cap carries with it the potential for both good and evil.

II. Independent Reading

Aiken, Joan. **The Kingdom under the Sea and Other Stories.** London: Jonathan Cape, 1971.

Andersen, Hans Christian. "The Little Mermaid." In **The Complete Fairy Tales and Stories,** translated by Erik Christian Haugaard. New York: Doubleday, 1974.

Anderson, Lonzo. **Arion and the Dolphins.** New York: Charles Scribner's Sons, 1978.

Asbjörnsen, Peter C., and Jörgen Moe. "Why the Sea Is Salt." In **A Cavalcade of Sea Legends,** edited by Michael Brown. New York: Henry Z. Walck, 1971.

Babbitt, Natalie. **The Eyes of the Amaryllis.** New York: Farrar, Straus and Giroux, 1977.

Bowden, Joan. **Why the Tides Ebb and Flow.** Boston: Houghton Mifflin, 1979.

Brown, Michael, editor. **A Cavalcade of Sea Legends.** New York: Henry Z. Walck, 1981.

Bulla, Clyde. **Jonah and the Great Fish.** New York: Thomas Y. Crowell, 1970.

Cumberlege, Vera. **Shipwreck.** Chicago: Follett, 1972.

d'Aulaire, Ingri, and Edgar d'Aulaire. "Danaüs, Perseus and the Gorgon." In **Book of Greek Myths.** New York: Doubleday, 1962.

————. "Thor and the Jotun Aegir." In **Norse Gods and Giants.** New York: Doubleday, 1967.

Dobrin, Arnold. **Taro and the Sea Turtles: A Tale of Japan.** New York: Coward-McCann, 1966.

Dolch, Edward. **Stories from Japan.** Champaign, Illinois: Garrard, 1960.

Felton, Harold. **True Tales of Stormalong: Sailor of the Seven Seas.** New York: Prentice-Hall, 1968.

Grimm Brothers. **The Fisherman and His Wife,** retold by Randall Jarrell. New York: Farrar, Straus and Giroux, 1980.

Hearn, Lafcadio. "The Gratitude of the Samebito" and "The Story of Kogi the Priest." In **The Boy Who Drew Cats.** New York: Macmillan, 1963.

Houston, James. **Tikta' Liktak: An Eskimo Legend.** New York: Harcourt, Brace and World, 1965.

Hunter, Mollie. **The Kelpie's Pearls.** New York: Funk and Wagnalls, 1966.

————. **A Stranger Came Ashore.** New York: Harper and Row, 1975.

Kingsley, Charles. "Andromeda." In **A Cavalcade of Sea Legends,** edited by Michael Brown. New York: Henry Z. Walck, 1971.

Lawrence, John. **The Giant of Grabbist.** New York: David White, 1968.

Littledale, Freya. **The Magic Fish.** New York: Scholastic Book Services, 1967.

McHargue, Georgess. **The Mermaid and the Whale.** New York: Holt, Rinehart and Winston, 1973.

Manning-Sanders, Ruth. **A Book of Mermaids.** New York: E. P. Dutton, 1967.

Matsutani, Miyoko. **The Fisherman under the Sea.** New York: Parents' Magazine Press, 1969.

Mohan, Beverly. **Punia and the King of the Sharks.** Chicago: Follett, 1964.

Nic Leodhas, Sorche. "The Drowned Bells of the Abbey." In **A Cavalcade of Sea Legends,** edited by Michael Brown. New York: Henry Z. Walck, 1971.

O'Dell, Scott. **The Black Pearl.** Boston: Houghton Mifflin, 1967.

————. **Island of the Blue Dolphins.** Boston: Houghton Mifflin, 1960.

Phumla. **Nomi and the Magic Fish: A Story from Africa.** New York: Doubleday, 1972.

Price, Margaret, adapter. "Perseus and Andromeda." In **Myths and Enchantment Tales.** New York: Rand McNally, 1960.

Sakade, Florence, editor. **Urashima Taro and Other Japanese Children's Stories.** Rutland, Vermont: Charles E. Tuttle, 1959.

————. "Why the Jellyfish Has No Bones." In **Little One-Inch and Other Japanese Children's Favorite Stories.** Rutland, Vermont: Charles E. Tuttle, 1958.

Sperry, Armstrong. **Call It Courage.** New York: Macmillan, 1940.

Steinbeck, John. **The Pearl.** New York: Viking Press, 1947.

Stoutenburg, Adrien. "Five Fathoms Tall: Stormalong." In **American Tall Tales.** New York: Viking Press, 1966.

Taylor, Mark. **The Fisherman and the Goblet.** Los Angeles: Golden Gate Junior Books, 1971.

Tennyson, Alfred Lord. "The Kraken." In **A Cavalcade of Sea Legends,** edited by Michael Brown. New York: Henry Z. Walck, 1971.

Thiele, Colin. **Storm Boy.** New York: Harper and Row, 1963.

Turska, Krystyna. **Tamara and the Sea Witch.** New York: Parents' Magazine Press, 1971.

Yolen, Jane. **The Mermaid's Three Wisdoms.** Cleveland: World, 1978.

———. **The Wizard Islands.** New York: Thomas Y. Crowell, 1973.

Group Story Sessions

First Session

"The Sea of Gold" from Yoshiko Uchida's *The Sea of Gold and Other Tales from Japan* was the first story read aloud in this Focus Unit. To focus attention on literary genre, the children were asked, "What clues could you use to identify this as a traditional folktale?" In response, several children pointed to the full title of the book. One child explained, "The title is like the titles of other collections of old folktales, so I figure this must be a collection of Japanese folktales." Another child added, "The words *adapted by* on the book cover would be another clue that these tales are *retellings* of old, old stories from the past." A third child noted, "The book has *398* on it, so that means it's from the fairy-tale shelves in the library." When one child exclaimed, "But it just *sounds* like a folktale," a second question was introduced: "In what ways is this tale, "The Sea of Gold," similar to other folktales you've read or heard?" Their responses reflected an awareness of characteristic patterns found in folktales:

> "The cook was rewarded for being kind to the fish like in that old story about the fisherman and his greedy wife [Brothers Grimm]."
>
> "It has magic in it. The reward was gold from the King of the Sea."
>
> "And the ending is pretty typical. Hikoichi [the cook] lived happily ever after!"

Finally, they were asked to think of a word or label which would best describe each of the characters in this tale. They decided that the words *good* and *kind* would be appropriate words for Hikoichi, that the fishermen who had mocked him were *greedy* and *selfish,* and that the old fisherman who understood that the gold was Hikoichi's reward for his years of kindness to the fish was described as *wise.* The purpose of this question was to draw their attention to the symbolic nature of folktale characters by classifying these characters in terms of the broad spectrum of human virtue and folly.

This first story session was concluded with an assignment: the students were instructed to select and read independently one or more of the traditional folktales found in the Sea Focus Unit collection. In addition, they were asked to record (in a notebook designated for written responses to reading experiences) the title of each story chosen for independent reading, what clues they had used to identify this story as a folktale, what story patterns they had found, and what words they would use to describe the main characters. The written analysis of stories read independently served to reinforce the oral analysis which had been generated by teacher questions during the group story sessions. The group sessions in each Focus Unit provide a model for literary analysis and experience with questions designed to guide comprehension and appreciation and to stimulate higher-level thinking. The oral discussions in these group sessions are intended to serve as preparation for independent written responses to literature.

Second Session

When "Urashima" by Lafcadio Hearn was read aloud, several children said they had read other versions of this Japanese folktale in other collections (Edward Dolch, *Stories from Japan,* and Florence Sakade, *Urashima Taro and Other Japanese Children's Stories*) and in a single edition (Miyoko Matsutani, *The Fisherman under the Sea*). When asked to compare "Urashima" to "The Sea of Gold" and to the stories they had selected for their independent reading, the children responded with various references to recurring patterns and motifs:

> "Hikoichi and Urashima were both rewarded for being kind to sea creatures."

> "And both were rewarded by a supernatural character—the King of the Sea."

> " 'Urashima' is like another story I read in that same book about a priest who's kind to fish and gets to go into the kingdom under the sea as a reward" ["The Story of Kogi the Priest"].

> "*The Fisherman and His Wife* [Grimm] is the same way. He lets the fish go free and gets rewarded with wishes."

"I read *Taro and the Sea Turtles* [Arnold Dobrin]. It's about a boy who saves these big turtles, and then when he gets into trouble with some pirates who want his gold, those turtles come along and save him and take him home."

"That sounds exactly like my story! I read *Arion and the Dolphins* [Lonzo Anderson]. The dolphins really like Arion and his lute music, and when the sailors try to steal Arion's gold and to kill him, he jumps in the sea, and the dolphins save him and carry him home. That was a good story!"

Third Session

"The Magic Mortar" by Yoshiko Uchida and "The Ballad of Semmerwater" by William Watson were read aloud to introduce another pattern found in folklore: rewards for kindness and goodness balanced by punishments for greediness and cruelty. The children focused on this pattern as they compared this folktale and poem.

"The greedy brother [in 'The Magic Mortar'] is sort of like that city by the lake of Semmerwater because they [the people in the city] were punished for being so selfish and cruel to that beggar and they all ended up at the bottom of the lake!"

"But the herdsman was nice to the beggar so I'm sure *his* cottage didn't go under!"

"The beggar who came to Semmerwater is like that old man in 'The Magic Mortar' because both were sort of in charge of the rewards and punishments and had magical powers."

"It's like *The Fisherman and His Wife.* The fisherman got rewarded because he was kind to the fish, but his wife was so greedy and selfish and mean that she got punished. The fish had magical powers like the old man and the beggar in those other stories."

"I read a really good pirate story called 'The Drowned Bells of the Abbey' [Sorche Nic Leodhas]. The pirates tried to steal the bells, but they were magical bells and pulled the pirates into the water, so the pirates ended up on the bottom of the sea, too!"

"In my story [*Arion and the Dolphins*] the sailors who try to steal Arion's gold get a very surprising punishment! But I'm not going to tell the ending!"

One child summed up this exploration of the reward/punishment pattern:

"It seems that a lot of the stories are about *justice.* So if a character is good, he gets rewarded, and if he's bad, he gets punished. It seems to me that practically all those fairy tales from the older days were about justice."

Fourth Session

After *The Wave* by Margaret Hodges was read aloud, the children were asked to think about its theme. They decided that this story showed the destructive power of the sea and the human struggle to survive its raging fury. They saw that it was the selfless action of a wise old man that enabled the villagers to escape from the tidal wave which destroyed their village. One girl commented, "It was sort of like escaping from an angry sea monster." The children were asked, "How is the sea viewed in some of the other stories we've discussed?" and their responses reflected growing recognition of the dual nature of the sea and the conflicting interpretations found in this Focus Unit. They commented on the difference between the storytellers who seemed to be most impressed with the beauty and mystery of the underwater world and who imagined wonderful kingdoms under the sea, and those storytellers who saw the sea in a more practical sense, as a powerful element bearing both the promise of survival and the threat of death. One child observed: "In some of the stories, going down into the sea is a reward like in 'Urashima,' but in other stories it's a punishment like in 'The Magic Mortar' and 'The Ballad of Semmerwater.' " Another child commented, "A lot of the stories are about fishermen, and the sea is really important for them because that's how they earn a living. But it's also dangerous like when a storm comes. That's what happened in my story, *The Giant of Grabbist*" (John Lawrence). A girl who had read the Russian fairy tale *Tamara and the Sea Witch* (Krystyna Turska) added, "In my story, there's a wicked sea witch. A lot of times stories have scary creatures coming out of the sea like monsters and serpents. That's the *evil* part of the sea." The other side was presented by a child who had read *Nomi and the Magic Fish* (Phumla): "In my story there's a magic fish who's like the fairy godmother in *Cinderella*. So that's the *good* part of the sea." Thus, the children moved toward synthesis as they discussed what these diverse stories, unified by a common focus, had to say about humankind's relationship to the sea.

Fifth Session

Greyling by Jane Yolen and *The Mermaid's Cape* by Margaret K. Wetterer were read aloud to introduce two families of sea creatures: the Selchies and the mermaids. These two modern fairy tales are each based on ancient legends: *Greyling* grew out of the legends of the Selchies told on the Scottish island of Shetland, and *The Mermaid's Cape* was created from ancient Celtic legends of the merfolk.

Independent Reading

The children were asked to select and read another sea tale which represented a different genre, such as a tall tale, a myth or legend, a survival
tale, a ghost story, modern fantasy, or realism. In preparation for this
selective process, various literary genres were discussed and examples were
pulled from the Sea Focus Unit collection to help the children become
familiar with various types of literature.

To generate interest in longer stories or novels, the teacher presented
brief "book talks" about such books as *Island of the Blue Dolphins* by
Scott O'Dell, *Storm Boy* by Colin Thiele, *Shipwreck* by Vera Cumberlege,
The Black Pearl by Scott O'Dell, *Tikta' Liktak* by James Houston, *The
Eyes of the Amaryllis* by Natalie Babbitt, and *The Kelpie's Pearls* by
Mollie Hunter. Again, this independent reading assignment included a
request to record the title of each book, its genre, and comments about
characters, story patterns, and themes. A follow-up group session was
planned to allow the children to share and discuss what they had read
and the ideas and observations they had recorded for this assignment.

The follow-up discussion was initiated by inviting the children to compare the stories they had read independently and those heard in the group
sessions. Several children who had become particularly intrigued by the
mermaid stories volunteered to open the discussion with a few comments
about some of the differences they had found:

> "*The Mermaid and the Whale* [Georgess McHargue] was a funny
> story, but 'The Little Mermaid' [Hans Christian Andersen] and *The
> Mermaid's Three Wisdoms* [Jane Yolen] were serious."

> " 'The Little Mermaid' was written like a fairy tale, but it was
> awfully sad. So was that story about the mermaid who married the
> fisherman [*The Mermaid's Cape*], but the ending was happier."

> "*The Mermaid's Three Wisdoms* was written like it was a true story
> but with fantasy mixed in. I thought it was sort of like *Charlotte's
> Web* [E. B. White]; when you *read* the book, you just *believe* what's
> happening, like you get used to the idea of a twelve-year-old girl
> having a mermaid for a friend just like you really care about that
> spider as if she were human!"

Mollie Hunter's *A Stranger Came Ashore* had been recommended for
independent reading to those children who had expressed an interest in
the Selchie folk. One child commented: "I read *A Stranger Came Ashore*
after we heard about Selchies in that story, *Greyling*. I guessed pretty
early on in the book that the stranger was really a Selchie, but I was
surprised when it turned out that he was an evil character. He was like a
sorcerer with magic powers. He was so different from Greyling, who was

so nice to the fisherman and his wife." Another child added: "I read that, too. It takes place in the Shetland Islands just like *Greyling,* and Finn Learson [the Selchie] saved the boy from drowning just like Greyling saved the fisherman from drowning. But Finn only did it because it was part of his evil plan!"

This sharing session continued with further contributions involving analysis of the characters, themes, and patterns in the books read independently. At the conclusion of this session, the children were asked to think about the underlying theme which they had discussed earlier and which bound these sea tales together: humans' relationship to the sea. Again, the children focused on the dual nature of the sea, its potential for both good and for evil. They were able to give examples to further substantiate the validity of this concept as it gradually developed in the course of their cumulative experiences with sea literature:

> "I read *Call It Courage* [Armstrong Sperry]. The boy in this story was afraid of the sea; he saw it as his enemy."

> "In my story, it was exactly opposite. I read that tall tale about Stormalong [Adrien Stoutenburg], who just loved the sea! He wanted more than anything to leave home and go to sea!"

> "I read *Shipwreck* [Vera Cumberlege]. It's about a boy and his dad who go out in a lifeboat to try to save these sailors whose ship got wrecked at sea. The sea is terrible in that story."

> "In the story of 'Andromeda,' [Charles Kingsley] there's a really horrible sea monster."

> "The Midgard Serpent [in *Norse Gods and Giants* by Ingri and Edgar d'Aulaire] was evil, too."

> "But those dragon kings in those Japanese stories could be really nice. They were so fancy with their jewels and silk robes and great palaces. Those storytellers probably thought of the sea as a beautiful place."

> "I read *The Black Pearl* [Scott O'Dell]. It seemed to combine all those different feelings about the sea. Like this one character, Salazar, made his living from the sea, but he also died in the sea. And the Manta Diablo [monster devilfish] was an evil creature, but Ramón, the main character, also thought it was beautiful!"

Creative Writing

To prepare for the creative writing assignment, a group session was held to provide a review of the ideas and concepts which had accumulated during the preceding group and independent experiences with the sea tales. After a brief review of the stories, motifs, characters, and themes, the teacher read aloud "The Wind Cap" by Jane Yolen. The children's responses to this tale reflected their readiness to draw from the literary background they had been building in the course of this Focus Unit. Excerpts taken from their discussion of this story demonstrate their capacity for literary analysis and their recognition of story patterns and themes which might have been borrowed from or inspired by traditional legends and folklore:

> "I think we should categorize it as a fairy tale. It starts out like those old stories: 'There was once a lad . . . ,' and it happened long ago and far away, and it has magic and a fairy creature."

> "And the characters don't have regular names. They're just called 'the mother,' 'the sailors,' 'the captain'—except the boy. But he doesn't have a last name or anything."

> "I know why he's called Jon! This story is sort of like 'Jonah and the Whale,' and I bet Ms. Yolen named her character after the Jonah in the Bible!"

> "Maybe she read 'Jonah and the Whale' when she was in the fourth grade!"

> "What about *The Fisherman under the Sea* [Miyoko Matsutani]? Maybe she read that, too! Because in both stories the main character was kind to a turtle, and they got rewarded when the turtle changed into a supernatural creature."

> "It's a lot like that story about the boy who rescued those two big sea turtles and they saved his life [*Taro and the Sea Turtles*]."

> "I think Mrs. Yolen was thinking about King Midas. Remember? He got a wish granted because once he was kind to Bacchus' old teacher, but then when he got his wish it turned out to be both good and bad! The same thing happened to Jon: that magic wind cap turned out to be good and bad!"

> "This story reminds me of 'Old Stormalong.' They both wanted to go to sea, but their mom said, 'No, you better just stay on land!' "

Finally, the children were instructed to become authors and to make use of their knowledge of literature and the sea to create their own sea tales. Some of the children chose to write stories in the tradition of the classic fairy tale, while others created explanatory tales or stories of adventure and suspense. The stories which evolved reflected the diverse interests and styles of the children as well as their attempts to utilize the rich literary background that had been made available to them. Their

stories included a wide range of interesting characters: mermaids, change-
lings, sea gods, pirates, dragon kings, sea monsters, magical fish, kindly
fishermen, greedy sailors. They wrote about good versus evil, kindness
rewarded, wickedness punished, and the magic of the sea world. Many of
the children managed to capture the characteristic language and melody
of legend and folklore in their own tales.

Before producing the final copy of their stories and appropriate illustrations, each child met with the teacher to discuss necessary corrections
and possible improvements. *How to Make Your Own Books* (1974) by
Harvey Weiss provided the basis of group instruction in the art of book
binding so that the children could bind their stories and illustrations into
a book. The stories were shared with other classes and displayed in the
school library. Each book was a source of pride for its author, and the
children were able to experience one of the special joys of authorship as
they watched others enjoy what they had written.

Reference

Weiss, Harvey. *How to Make Your Own Books.* New York: Thomas Y. Crowell,
    1974.

10 Folktale Patterns: A Focus Unit for Grades Three and Four

The focus of this unit is on the recurring patterns which connect folktales from different countries. Three groups of books were selected to represent three different folktale patterns: the theft of magical objects, the use of superpowers by others to assist the hero, and "circle stories," or stories where the main characters greedily ask their benefactors for more and more, until they ask too much and end up back where they started.

As these tales were read aloud and discussed during the group sessions, the children were encouraged to discover the common pattern or "second-level story" which characterized the stories in each group. In the process, the children made other discoveries about the nature of folktales in particular and the oral tradition in general. They became aware of the building/borrowing process underlying the creation and recreation of traditional tales around the world and through the ages. In addition, the children discovered a new source for reading enjoyment—the folktale and fairy-tale section of the library.

Objectives

1. To introduce folktales from different countries.
2. To discover patterns which connect tales from different countries.
3. To learn about the nature of the oral tradition in general and the folktale in particular.
4. To provide opportunities for creative writing and other forms of creative expression.
5. To expand independent reading interests.

Bibliography for the Folktale Patterns Focus Unit

I. Pattern 1: The Theft of Magical Objects

A. Group Story Sessions

Chase, Richard, reteller. "Jack and the North West Wind." In **The Jack Tales.** Boston: Houghton Mifflin, 1943.

The "Jack Tales" have been told for generations in the mountain country of North Carolina and have their roots across the ocean. In this particular tale, Jack sets out to stop the North West Wind from blowing into their little house. But an old man intervenes and gives Jack a magic tablecloth, a magic rooster, and a magic club. When the tablecloth and rooster are stolen by "some rowdy boys," the last gift is used to retrieve these gifts. At the end of the tale, we are told that Jack and his mother "were both doin' pretty well. . . . They had that old rickety house fixed up tight against the wind, too."

Domanska, Janina. *Palmiero and the Ogre.* New York: Macmillan, 1967.

When Palmiero runs away from home to escape his mother's scolding, a lonely and gentle ogre gives him a job. One day the ogre suggests that it is time for Palmiero to go home for a visit and lends him a magic donkey who coughs up jewels when he hears the words "giddy-up, Neddy!" The donkey is stolen by a greedy innkeeper, but because the ogre also gives Palmiero a magic stick, Palmiero is able to retrieve the donkey and to return to his home in triumph.

Faulkner, Georgene, reteller. "The Lad and the North Wind." In **The Flying Ship.** New York: Grosset and Dunlap, 1931.

This is a traditional Norwegian tale about a poor boy who is given three magic gifts by the North Wind. Two of the gifts are stolen by a greedy innkeeper before the boy reaches home. The third gift, a stick, is used to convince the innkeeper to return the stolen treasures to the rightful owner, and the boy and his mother "lived in peace and plenty on the gifts of the North Wind."

Jameson, Cynthia. **The Flying Shoes.** New York: Parents' Magazine Press, 1973.

In this Russian folktale, an old man has a pair of magic shoes which he wove himself as a lad. When the shoes are stolen first by a youth, then by a merchant, and finally by the tax collector, each thief discovers that the shoes have a will of their own. Indeed, the villains are punished appropriately for their greed, and the shoes return to the old man.

Riordan, James. **The Three Magic Gifts.** New York: Oxford University Press, 1980.

Ivan the Rich and Ivan the Poor are two brothers who live in a Russian village. When Ivan the Poor manages to get a magic cloth from the Wind, it is stolen by his envious brother. When Ivan the

Poor gets a magic goat from the Sun, it is stolen by his greedy brother. When Ivan the Poor gets a magic sack from the Frost, two strong men leap out and beat Ivan the Rich until he returns the cloth and goat to his brother. "Never did he cheat his brother again."

Towle, Faith M., reteller. **The Magic Cooking Pot.** Boston: Houghton Mifflin, 1975.

A poor man in ancient India prays to the Goddess Durga to help him feed his hungry family. Because he is a good man, the goddess answers his prayers with a magic cooking pot which is always filled with rice. When the magic pot is stolen by a wicked innkeeper, the Goddess Durga gives the poor man a pot full of demons to help him retrieve his first magic pot from the villain. The author uses batik, a traditional Indian art form, to illustrate this Indian folktale.

Werth, Kurt, adapter. **The Cobbler's Dilemma: An Italian Folktale.** New York: McGraw-Hill, 1967.

Simon the cobbler is so friendly and talkative and such a gossip that he never seems to get any work done. His wife and nine children go without food because of his foolishness. When he goes to the Wise Man for help, Simon receives a magic basket and a magic rooster. Because of Simon's loose tongue, the wonderful gifts are stolen by an innkeeper. But the Wise Man also gives Simon a magic broomstick which he uses to persuade the innkeeper to return the gifts. Although Simon is not allowed to keep the gifts, he learns to tend to his own business—cobbling.

Zemach, Harve, adapter. **Too Much Nose: An Italian Tale.** New York: Holt, Rinehart and Winston, 1967.

An old man gives each of his three sons a magic gift and sends them out into the world to seek their fortunes. The second son, a rather gullible young man, meets a greedy and cunning queen who manages to trick him and his two brothers out of their treasures. The second son finds two magic fruits: one causes noses to lengthen, the other causes noses to shorten. He uses this discovery to trick the queen into returning the gifts. In the end, the three brothers have their treasures, but the greedy queen has too much nose!

B. Additional References

Asbjörnsen, Peter C., and Jörgen Moe. "The Lad Who Went to the North Wind." In **East of the Sun and West of the Moon and Other Tales.** New York: Macmillan, 1963.

Barbeau, Marius, collector. "The Princess of Tomboso." In **The Golden Phoenix and Other Fairy Tales from Quebec.** Don Mills, Ontario: Oxford University Press, 1980.

Chang, I. C. "The Three Gifts." In **Tales from Old China.** New York: Random House, 1969.

Grimm Brothers. "The Nose." In **Fairy Tales.** Cleveland: World, 1947.

Hampden, John. "The Donkey Which Made Gold." In **The House of Cats and Other Stories.** New York: Farrar, Straus and Giroux, 1967.

Hardendorff, J. B. "Per and the North Wind." In **Tricky Peik and Other Picture Tales.** Philadelphia: J. B. Lippincott, 1967.

Hutton, Warwick, reteller. **The Nose Tree.** New York: Atheneum, 1981.

Littledale, Freya, reteller. **The Magic Tablecloth, the Magic Goat, and the Hitting Stick.** New York: Scholastic Book Services, 1971.

II. Pattern 2: Helpful Characters with Superpowers

A. Group Story Sessions

Grimm Brothers. "The Golden Goose." In **Grimm's Fairy Tales,** retold by Rose Dobbs. New York: Random House, 1955.

Simpleton, the youngest of three brothers, is given a goose with gold feathers in return for his kindness to a little old man. This is the beginning of a series of events leading Simpleton ever closer to marrying a princess and inheriting a kingdom. The little old man returns three more times and uses his special powers to help Simpleton with the tasks imposed by the king.

Ness, Evaline, adapter. **Long, Broad, and Quickeye.** New York: Charles Scribner's Sons, 1969.

Assisted by three companions with supernatural powers, a young prince rescues a beautiful princess imprisoned in a mysterious castle by a wicked sorcerer. When the prince and his three faithful friends manage to break the spell, the evil wizard is transformed into a black bird. This creature vanishes, and suddenly all living things surrounding the castle are once again restored to life . . . including the knights who had been turned to stone after failing to rescue the princess.

Ransome, Arthur, reteller. **The Fool of the World and the Flying Ship: A Russian Tale.** New York: Farrar, Straus and Giroux, 1968.

The Fool of the World is the youngest of three sons of an old peasant and his wife. Although his family thinks very little of him, the Fool sets out to win the hand of the czar's daughter in marriage. Because of his kindness and cheerful manner, he is befriended by an old man and seven others with supernatural powers. With their help, he manages to complete the improbable tasks set by the czar and, in the end, marries the princess.

Williams, Jay. **The King with Six Friends.** New York: Parents' Magazine Press, 1968.

King Zar is a young king in search of a kingdom. Along the way, he meets six unusual individuals who decide to join him on his travels. At last they reach a fine city with a beautiful castle in which lives a princess in search of a husband. Before she marries, her suitor must pass all the tests set by her father, a task King Zar's six friends help him accomplish.

B. Additional References

Artzybasheff, Boris. **The Seven Simeons: A Russian Tale.** New York: Viking Press, 1961.

Association for Childhood Education International. "The Flying Ship." In **Told under the Green Umbrella.** New York: Macmillan, 1962.

Bishop, Claire, reteller. **The Five Chinese Brothers.** New York: Coward-McCann, 1938.

Fillmore, Parker, reteller. "Longshanks, Girth, and Keen." In **The Shepherd's Nosegay: Stories from Finland and Czechoslovakia.** New York: Harcourt, Brace, 1958.

Grimm Brothers. **The Four Clever Brothers.** New York: Harcourt, Brace and World, 1967.

————. "Six Servants." In **Tales from Grimm,** translated by Wanda Gag. New York: Coward-McCann, 1936.

Haviland, Virginia, reteller. "Drakestail." In **Favorite Fairy Tales Told in France.** Boston: Little, Brown, 1959.

Lang, Andrew. "The Seven Simons." In **Crimson Fairy Book.** New York: McGraw-Hill, 1966.

Manning-Sanders, Ruth. "Long, Broad, and Sharpsight." In **A Book of Wizards.** New York: E. P. Dutton, 1966.

III. Pattern 3: Circle Tales

A. Group Story Sessions

Godden, Rumer. **The Old Woman Who Lived in a Vinegar Bottle.** New York: Viking Press, 1972.

An old woman returns a little fish to the sea and is rewarded for her kindness. After she is granted her first modest wish, she becomes increasingly bold, greedy, and selfish. She demands more and more for herself until finally she finds herself back where she started—but much wiser for her experience.

Grimm Brothers. **The Fisherman and His Wife,** translated by Elizabeth Shub. New York: Greenwillow Books, 1978.

A fisherman catches and returns to the sea a large flounder, who offers to grant the wishes of the fisherman's wife, Ilsebill. But her greed angers the flounder, as she asks to move from their night pot to a cottage to a castle to a palace and upward to the position of pope. Finally, the couple find themselves back again at the night pot.

Hurlimann, Ruth. **The Proud White Cat,** translated by Anthea Bell. New York: William Morrow, 1977.

A proud Tom Cat is certain that no other cat is worthy to be his wife. With the wise guidance of Mrs. Vixen, he considers and rejects the finest ladies as potential brides. Tom Cat ends up recognizing his own foolish pride and marries none other than Katy Cat.

McDermott, Gerald, adapter. **The Stonecutter: A Japanese Folktale.** New York: Viking Press, 1975.

Tasaku is a lowly stonecutter who envies a prince. A mountain spirit grants his wishes for wealth and increasing power until Tasaku becomes a mountain. "But Tasaku felt the sharp sting of a chisel. It was a lowly stonecutter, chipping away at his feet."

B. Additional References

Association for Childhood Education International. "The Fisherman and His Wife." In **Told under the Green Umbrella.** New York: Macmillan, 1962.

Grimm Brothers. **The Fisherman and His Wife.** New York: Pantheon Books, 1957.

————. **The Fisherman and His Wife,** retold by Margot Zemach. New York: W. W. Norton, 1966.

Hawthorne, Nathaniel, reteller. **The Golden Touch.** New York: McGraw-Hill, 1959.

Lang, Andrew. "The Fisherman and His Wife." In **The Green Fairy Book.** New York: McGraw-Hill, 1966.

Ransome, Arthur, reteller. "The Golden Fish." In **Old Peter's Russian Tales.** New York: Penguin Books, 1974.

Group Story Sessions for Pattern 1: The Theft of Magical Objects

First Session

The Magic Cooking Pot by Faith M. Towle was selected to introduce the first group of tales in this three-part Focus Unit. The children were asked to look carefully at the cover, title page, and several illustrations to discover what kinds of information could be gathered about this book before it was read aloud. Their comments helped to introduce the folktale. One child noticed that the illustrations reminded him of a book about India he had at home. When asked to identify the particular art form used for these illustrations, several children correctly responded with the term *batik*. A child who had recently learned about this traditional Indian art form at a local art gallery class explained the process of making batiks using textiles, dyes, and wax.

The title was the source of further information. One child commented, "The title has the word *magic* so it must be a make-believe story. It's fantasy." A look at the title page confirmed that this was a tale from India and informed them that the story was "retold and illustrated by Faith M. Towle." One child responded, "That means she's the one who did all those batik pictures. That must have taken ages!" Although most of the children knew the meaning of *illustrated,* they were not familiar with the word *retold.* The teacher then briefly explained the difference between a story written by a particular author and a story which has been retold or adapted from the oral tradition and recorded in written form.

After reading *The Magic Cooking Pot* aloud, the teacher asked, "Why did the goddess give the poor man the magic pot?" This question served to highlight a basic motif in folktales: good deeds and kindness are rewarded. The next question was designed to focus attention on the plot sequence in this story: "What are the four most important parts of this story?" One child came up with this retelling in four parts:

> "First, a poor man got a magic pot from a goddess because he's a good man.
> Second, a greedy innkeeper stole it.
> Third, the poor man got another pot with demons in it to scare the innkeeper.
> Fourth, he got his magic pots back and went home to his family and they all lived happily ever after!"

Following the first story session, the children recreated this basic plot sequence using crayons and paper divided into four equal sections. The art project helped to reinforce their grasp of the underlying plot pattern, which they were soon to discover in all the stories in this first group.

Subsequent Sessions

During subsequent story sessions, books on this same theme, eventually categorized by the children as the "tales of stolen magical objects," were read aloud in the following order: *The Three Magic Gifts* by James Riordan, *Too Much Nose: An Italian Tale* by Harve Zemach, *The Cobbler's Dilemma: An Italian Folktale* by Kurt Werth, "The Lad and the North Wind" by Georgene Faulkner, *The Flying Shoes* by Cynthia Jameson, *Palmiero and the Ogre* by Janina Domanska, and "Jack and the North West Wind" by Richard Chase.

Each of these story sessions opened with a consideration of the book cover, title page, and illustrations to generate a search for clues regarding the origins and content of each tale. The children became familiar with such terms and phrases as *retold by, reteller, a retelling of, adapted by, translated by,* and *from an old Indian tale.* Sometimes they found that the title revealed a great deal about the story, such as the Russian tale *The Three Magic Gifts,* while other titles presented more of a challenge. Thus, before reading *The Cobbler's Dilemma: An Italian Folktale,* the teacher suggested that the dictionary would help clarify the meanings of the two unfamiliar words in this title. As soon as the meaning of *dilemma* was revealed to them, several children asked, "What *was* his dilemma?" After listening to the story, they were able to answer their question.

After each new story was read aloud, the children were asked to compare it to stories read in previous sessions. They found the common plot pattern which connected the stories in this group, but they noted significant differences as well. For example, the comparison of *The Magic Cooking Pot,* set in India, with *Palmiero and the Ogre,* set in Italy, yielded the following dialogue:

> "In *The Magic Cooking Pot* the poor man got rice, but in the other story Palmiero got diamonds and jewels."
>
> "I think Palmiero got better magic. What's so great about rice?"
>
> "Maybe if you're really poor and really hungry, you'd think it'd be better to get something to eat!"
>
> "In India everyone eats a lot of rice, and it's very good for you. But there are lots of people there who don't have anything to eat so they get sick. So they would be so happy to get a magic pot with all that rice!" (This contribution came from a girl born in India, who had recently returned from an extended visit with her family in that country.)
>
> "In that other story [*Palmiero and the Ogre*] the people don't look so poor, so they probably would be happier with the jewels. Anyway, it's from Italy and they eat *pasta* there!"

After all the tales in the first group had been introduced in the story sessions, the children were asked to identify the common features of the tales:

"All the stories had magic things. Sometimes three magic things, sometimes two and even one—like in *The Flying Shoes*."

"The magic things were given to people who were poor but good. It's like a reward, but it's something they need."

"Sometimes the magical things come from a goddess or a little old man or the North Wind or a good ogre. But every story has a special 'giver' character."

"Usually the magic gifts get stolen because the character is too trusting or foolish or talks too much."

"And the magic things are stolen by greedy and rich people—like that queen or those innkeepers . . ."

" . . .or the merchant and the tax collector in *The Flying Shoes!*"

"But the greedy people are always punished—usually by one of the magic things."

"Like that cane or the pot of demons."

"And all the stories end happily and the good people get what they want and the bad people get what they *deserve!*"

"How come so many of the stories have greedy *innkeepers?*"

"It's sort of like owning a big hotel, I think, so you get rich and then when you get too rich, you get greedy."

"I don't think that's always so true. I know some rich people who aren't greedy like that. They even give a lot of money away to poor people."

At this point, the teacher commented on the validity of this last comment and the importance of judging people as individuals, not in categories. Then she asked the children to try to explain why so many of the rich characters in these folktales were described as greedy and selfish. This question, intended to generate divergent thinking, led to a lively discussion in which all the children participated. One child responded with this explanation: "Well, rich people get everything they want, so then they get spoiled. So then they want everything for themselves. So they're greedy." Another child added, "Yes. They just get used to getting their own way so they expect to get whatever they want. Maybe those stories were told in the olden days to teach them *not* to be greedy."

Finally, after locating on a wall map each of the countries from which these stories originated, the children were asked to try to explain how

stories from so many different parts of the world could be so similar. As
the children explored possible explanations for such a phenomenon, they
gradually moved toward an understanding of the dynamic quality of these
oral tales, traveling through time and space from faraway places and
ancient days to their own classroom:

> "Maybe someone in one country went to visit people in another
> country and after dinner they all sat around the fire and he told his
> favorite story. Later, his friends might've told that story to some
> neighbors, but they changed it a little but kept the important parts."

> "And maybe they told *their* favorite story to the visitor and he told
> it to his family when he got home and then when his children grew
> up they told it to *their* children and on and on . . ."

> "And everytime someone told it, the story got changed a little—so it
> was different but really the same story."

> "Sometimes it got told in one language and then *translated* into
> another so some of the words were different!"

> "A lot of times when you tell a story you've heard you forget some
> parts of it and so you make up new things."

> "Like maybe you can't remember the three magic gifts so you could
> just make them up."

> "But people had to keep telling the story or it would get lost."

> "I'm glad these stories got put into books so we can keep them. I
> bet a lot of stories people made up got lost in the olden days. But
> now they get put into books."

> "That's what the Grimm Brothers did, remember? They copied down
> the stories people told out loud so they could save them."

Creative Writing for Pattern 1

By this time the children were familiar with the pattern associated with
this group of folktales, and they were ready to create their own "tale of
stolen magical objects." To guide them in this process, several questions
were recorded on large chart:

> Where and when does your story take place?

> Who is the main character?

> Who is the villain?

> What magical objects are stolen?

> What happened?

After their stories were written and illustrated, the children shared them in the next story session. Giving children opportunities to share what they have created is an important dimension of the writing experiences structured into the Focus Unit. When the teacher sets aside adequate time for their original stories to be presented in the group sessions, the children see that their work is valued, that their efforts are given recognition. The teacher shows that what the children have written is as important as the books read aloud. In addition, the children receive feedback as their listeners respond with comments or questions. For example, a frequent type of response to child-written stories presented in these group sessions reflected confusion generated by gaps in the story sequence. In many instances, these gaps resulted from a lack of "audience awareness." That is, the child-writer had the total story sequence in mind but failed to record sufficient information for the readers/listeners to grasp the intended meaning. Growth in composition skills involves growth in the capacity to consider the perspective of potential readers/listeners of written communication. The peer feedback to these young authors served to highlight the importance of audience awareness in written communication.

The tales of stolen magical objects produced by these children provided the teacher with valuable information about each child's grasp of narrative structure in general and about this folktale pattern in particular. The tales were evaluated in terms of logical sequence, plot coherence, character development, use of dialogue, sense of humor, imaginative elements, sensitivity to language and form of folktale, and general language usage. These evaluations provided a basis for helping the children build on their strengths and improve areas of weakness.

Group Story Sessions for Pattern 2: Helpful Characters with Superpowers

First Session

The Fool of the World and the Flying Ship by Arthur Ransome introduced the group of folktales containing characters with superpowers. The children were interested in the Caldecott Medal sticker on the cover of this attractive picture book, so the significance of this literary honor was discussed. They found additional information on the book's cover, such as the now-familiar words *retold by* and the information that this was "a Russian tale." However, the title raised some questions, setting the stage for purposeful listening when the story was read aloud.

To focus attention on the plot pattern characteristic of this group of folktales, the children were again asked to retell the story in four parts. The following plot sequence was finally generated and recorded on the large chart in the story corner:

1. The youngest son shared his food with the old man who helped him get the flying ship so he could marry the princess.
2. He made friends with seven men with special superpowers.
3. They helped him do each of the hard tasks ordered by the czar. The tasks were to prove he's good enough for the czar's daughter.
4. He did the tasks and married the princess.

Several children volunteered to create a series of pictures to illustrate this plot sequence.

Second Session

After listening to the second story in this group, *Long, Broad, and Quick-eye* by Evaline Ness, the children compared it with *The Fool of the World:*

"The hero in both stories had friends with special powers."

"Their friends helped the heroes get the princess because they [the heroes] were friendly and nice."

"Both stories had a villain who made the hero do hard things. In the first story the czar was mean because he really was trying to get rid of the Fool."

"And in the other one that wizard is the villain."

"And both stories end with a wedding."

"They end 'happily ever after!' "

Third Session

"The Golden Goose" by the Brothers Grimm was the next story selected to illustrate this particular folktale pattern. Most of the children were familiar with these famous collectors and recorders of the oral tradition in Germany.

After reading this story aloud, the teacher asked the children to compare it with the two previous tales and to identify and formulate a label for the pattern connecting the three folktales:

"It's like *The Fool of the World* because it starts out with three sons, and the youngest is called Simpleton, which is kind of like the Fool."

"And there's an old man who helps him because he shares the food. It's the same in both stories."

"And the old man is magical because he changes the food into good stuff."

"This story is sort of like those other stories about stolen magical objects. At least at first it seemed that way when the innkeepers wanted to steal the golden feathers from his magical goose."

"But Simpleton doesn't get fooled. He just goes right on!"

"Then when he makes the princess laugh he's supposed to get to marry her, but the king makes him do more tasks, just like in *The Fool of the World*."

"The last part is the same. I mean, he gets superfriends to help him."

"All three stories have those characters with superpowers."

"And it ended with another wedding!"

"In this story the *last* task was to get a flying ship, and in *The Fool of the World*, the *first* task was to get a flying ship."

"But all three stories have those characters with superpowers."

"And they always help the hero."

"That's the *pattern!*"

"We could call them the stories with helpful supercharacters."

After some additional discussion, consensus was reached, and the story pattern was recorded on the chart.

Fourth Session

The final story in this segment of the Focus Unit was *The King with Six Friends* by Jay Williams. When the book was held up before the group to signal the opening of the session, the first comments were:

"It says 'by Jay Williams.' It doesn't say 'retold by.' "

"He must have made up the story then."

"I know a lot of his books. He writes good stories."

"The title shows that there's a king in the story, so it's going to be like a folktale probably."

"*The King with Six Friends.* I bet the six friends have superpowers!"

"They're probably helpful friends, too. But I wonder what sort of tasks a *king* would have to do?"

At this point, Jay Williams's story was read aloud. The children's predictions were confirmed and their questions answered. Indeed, throughout the presentation of the story, they were actively predicting each new event. The story itself seemed to invite such cognitive participation and to generate the excitement of anticipating the author's plan while the plot unfolded. The teacher had set the stage for such involvement by inviting the children to apply their newly acquired knowledge of folktale patterns as they responded to this modern folktale.

After the story was read aloud, the children were asked to compare it with those read previously and to consider it in terms of the pattern statement recorded on the chart.

> "This story is a lot like the other ones. It has characters with special powers, and they're all helpful. And the hero has tasks to do to get a princess."

> "But it's sort of different, too. Like the hero is a king instead of a peasant, but he's poor like a peasant. And it's the king who figures out what to do—instead of the friends."

> "Mr. Williams made up this story, but he must have gotten his ideas from those old stories."

> "Anyway, all these stories have the pattern. They all have helpful supercharacters!"

Creative Writing for Pattern 2

The second writing project for this unit involved the construction of stories around the pattern of supercharacters. The first step in the creative process was to draw a portrait of one or more original characters with special superpowers and to label each portrait with an appropriate name, descriptive of the particular talent of that character. These original characters became the helpful companions in the stories created by the children. The completed stories and portraits were again shared in a group session. Signs of improvement in literary abilities were duly noted by peers as well as the teacher, thus demonstrating that an appreciative audience can be a significant motivating force for young authors.

Group Story Sessions for Pattern 3: Circle Tales

First Session

The third and final segment of this Focus Unit began with a Grimm tale, *The Fisherman and His Wife*. Several of the children were familiar with this old tale, and, of course, by now all the children were acquainted with the Brothers Grimm. The teacher asked for an explanation of the meaning of "translated by Elizabeth Shub" in case anyone needed further clarification of this concept.

After the story was read aloud, the children were asked to retell the story in three parts—beginning, middle, and ending:

"In the beginning they were poor and lived in an old night pot."

"In the middle, the fisherman got wishes because he was kind to a magic fish. The wife kept asking for castles and palaces and to be a king and emperor and pope. She got too greedy and proud. So the magic fish got mad!"

"In the end, the fish took back all the stuff she wished for, and they ended up back in their old night pot again."

The following questions were introduced to generate further analysis of this picture book:

What words would best describe the fisherman?

What words would best describe his wife?

How does the artist show changes in the sea as the story progresses?

How does she show the changing mood of the flounder as each new request is made by the fisherman?

If this were a fable, what lesson or moral might be included at the end?

Second Session

The Stonecutter: A Japanese Folktale by Gerald McDermott was read aloud next, and the children compared it with *The Fisherman and His Wife:*

"They're different because one's from Japan and one's from Germany."

"The pictures are really different. This one [*The Stonecutter*] looks like *collage.* I've made collage pictures."

"But both stories start and end at the same place." (To confirm her point, this child read aloud the first and last paragraphs of *The Stonecutter*.)

"Both the stonecutter and the fisherman's wife wanted too much power, so they didn't get any more wishes."

"And they both learned not to be so greedy . . ."

". . . and proud!"

"*The Stonecutter* is sort of like a fable, too. Like it teaches a lesson."

Then, the teacher wrote on the chart the words of an ancient proverb, "Pride goes before the fall," and asked the children to explain its meaning and how it might relate to these two stories.

Third Session

The third book read aloud was *The Old Woman Who Lived in a Vinegar Bottle* by Rumer Godden. The teacher also read an interesting note by the author, explaining that this was an old folktale told to her by her mother, who had heard it from her nurse. "As far as I know," writes Godden, "this is the first time this version has been written down." What a nice illustration of the nature of the transmission of the oral tradition from generation to generation and from storyteller to storywriter.

The children required no teacher-initiated questions to begin their comparative analysis of these three tales. They noted obvious similarities: the granting of wishes to reward goodness and kindness; the gradual swelling of greed, selfishness, and pride reflected in each new wish; the growing anger of the supernatural agents of magic in response to unreasonable demands; and the final return to the original setting of the story.

The children pointed out that the old woman in Rumer Godden's tale had much in common with the fisherman's wife in the Grimm story, but they also noted significant differences between the two tales:

> "The fisherman's wife was really mean and bossy in the first place, and she stayed that way all the way through."

> "I bet even when she ended up back in that old hut she's still going to be mean and bossy."

> "I agree! But the old woman started out nice, and then she got kind of carried away with all those things. But in the end, she got back to her old self and you could tell she was wiser at the end. She learned her lesson!"

The teacher interrupted the dialogue briefly at this point to ask the child to find the portion in the text which supported this statement. Once located, the appropriate lines were read aloud and the dialogue continued.

> "But the magic fish forgave her because she apologized and changed back to being nice and kind again." (This child spontaneously located the supporting evidence in the text and read it to the group.)

> "I liked that ending the best. It's the happiest one."

> "I know. Me, too. I liked the part when the fish said he thought it was going to be a sad story but it turned out good."

When the children were asked to identify the pattern that connected these tales, they responded with comments such as, "All the main characters ended up just where they started from!" One child observed that these stories were "sort of a lot like circles," and the others decided that "circle stories" would be a good name for tales with this pattern. To reinforce the circular nature of this plot pattern, the children were supplied with drawing paper, scissors, and compasses and instructions for making a circle divided into equal wedges, like a pie. Then, each child chose one of the three circle stories to illustrate with a drawing in each wedge, the first wedge representing the beginning as well as the ending of the story.

Fourth Session

In the final session, the children were introduced to *The Proud White Cat* by Ruth Hurlimann. According to the jacket flap, the book is "based on a medieval German fable." Information on the copyright page also indicated that this tale is part of German folklore. The children enjoyed this information search, discovering the kinds of information a reader can find in various parts of a book and learning the proper terms for each component of a book. In fact, special interest in the dedication page emerged in the course of the Folktale Patterns Focus Unit; this information served to personalize the author, artist, or reteller and to bring the individual closer to the children. After listening to *The Proud White Cat,* the children agreed that it fit the pattern of the circle stories, although it was the only one in which the characters were talking animals instead of humans. They saw it as most similar in plot development to the tale of *The Stone Cutter,* but they felt that the ending was more like that in *The Old Woman Who Lived in a Vinegar Bottle* because the cat did learn a lesson and "sort of had a second chance." They observed that these two tales were more like "the happily ever after kind of story." Again, the children were encouraged to locate and read aloud the specific lines at the conclusion of each story which would support their comments.

Summarizing Session for the Three Folktale Patterns

Finally, as a move toward synthesis, the children were asked to look at a list of all the story titles in each of the three groups of folktales and to search for patterns which could connect these tales. After much discussion, they decided that in all the stories "someone was rewarded for being kind or good or for sharing and that pride and greed and wickedness were punished." They also identified some recurring patterns found in some, but not all, of the tales:

"The three sons and three tasks."

"The youngest son was simple or foolish at first."

"But he always ended up better than the first two brothers."

"And most stories ended up with a wedding, and the hero marries the princess."

"They all take place long ago and far away."

"There's usually some kind of magic or supernatural things or people with special powers."

"Usually, the poor people get more food and stuff they need."

"Most of the stories end happy."

These recurring patterns were recorded on a wall chart and used as the starting point for a creative writing project which drew this Folktale Focus Unit to a close.

Creative Writing

For the final project, the children created original folktales, drawing from the literary background they had acquired in the course of this three-part Focus Unit. The major purpose of this writing assignment was to reinforce as well as to assess their grasp of the essential characteristics of the folktale as a literary genre and some of the recurring patterns found in these traditional tales. After the stories were completed and then shared in the group session, they were added to the Focus Unit collection. Many became popular choices for independent reading, certainly a form of high praise for any young author.

Independent Reading

A basic objective of each Focus Unit is to provide opportunities to expand independent reading interests. Throughout the Folktale Patterns Focus Unit, the children were encouraged to select books in the collection to read independently. At the end of the unit, several of the children went to the library in search of more "old stories." Others followed their example, and the folktale and fairy-tale section became generally recognized as a good place to find books for independent reading enjoyment. Apparently, a new area of interest had been established among these young readers.

11 Japan: A Focus Unit for Grades Five and Six

In her book *Touch Magic: Fantasy, Faerie and Folklore in the Literature of Childhood* (1981), a collection of essays on fairy tales and folk literature, Jane Yolen stressed that one of the basic functions of folklore "is to provide a way of looking at another culture from the inside out" (p. 16). This Focus Unit on Japan provides an example of a social studies curriculum in which the literature of a particular country serves as the starting point for studying it "from the inside out."

During the initial segment of this unit, selected tales from the folk literature of Japan were read aloud to the whole class. In addition, students chose at least four other traditional tales to read independently from a display of books for this Focus Unit. The students' challenge was to glean from these tales as much as they could about Japan: the traditions and way of life of its people and its history, economy, geography, art, and religions. Although they made a number of interesting discoveries, the students soon found that their exploration of the folk literature was yielding more questions than answers. At this point, various nonfiction accounts of Japan, including social studies textbooks, were used as another source of information about this country, its past and present.

Modern literature served as a third source: literary tales rooted in ancient tradition, poetry, contemporary realistic fiction, and historical fiction. These three sources provided a foundation for building a rich and well-balanced picture of Japan.

Objectives

1. To expose students to the folk literature of Japan.
2. To provide a rich and many-layered picture of Japanese culture through its literature.
3. To give students experience in a multisource approach to the study of a particular culture.
4. To help students expand their horizons and develop a world view—the first steps toward reaching the insights, understandings, and compassion so essential for world peace.

Bibliography for the Japan Focus Unit

I. Group Story Sessions

Brenner, Barbara. **Little One Inch.** New York: Coward, McCann and
Geoghegan, 1977.

A childless couple pray to the gods for a child. A boy is born to
them, but he is "no bigger than a finger." When he is old enough to
go out in the world, he is hired to be a bodyguard for Michiko, a
merchant's daughter. After he saves her from two terrible oni, the
boy and Michiko find the oni's hammer and make a wish. Michiko
becomes the same size as the one-inch lad. They marry and live
happily ever after.

Coerr, Eleanor. **Sadako and the Thousand Paper Cranes.** New York:
Dell, 1977.

Sadako lived in Japan from 1943 to 1955. She was in Hiroshima
the day the atom bomb fell, and she died ten years later of leukemia
caused by radiation from the bomb. Sadako's story is a moving
tale of courage, love, and tragedy. In the hospital a friend reminds
her of an old legend, "If a sick person folds one thousand paper
cranes, the gods will grant her wish and make her well again."
Sadako folded 644 cranes before she died. Her classmates folded
the rest.

Hearn, Lafcadio. "The Boy Who Drew Cats." In **The Boy Who Drew
Cats and Other Tales of Lafcadio Hearn.** New York: Macmillan,
1963.

When a goblin rat terrorizes the priests in a Buddhist temple, the
cats painted by a boy on large white screens jump out and kill the
rat.

———. "The Story of Kogi the Priest." In **The Boy Who Drew Cats and
Other Tales of Lafcadio Hearn.** New York: Macmillan, 1963.

A gentle priest is rewarded for his great kindness to all living
creatures. The Dragon King grants his wish to enjoy the pleasures
and freedom of a fish in the Water World. When he fails to heed
the warning of the Dragon King, the priest-turned-fish is caught by
a fisherman, is sold to a cook, and feels the pain of the knife. This
is a strange and mystical tale told by Kogi the priest about his own
experience.

Ike, Jane Hori, and Baruch Zimmerman. **A Japanese Fairy Tale.** New
York: Frederick Warne, 1982.

This is the story of a remarkable couple—a husband who has accepted a repulsive physical appearance so that his wife can be beautiful, and a wife who learns about inner beauty from her husband.

Laurin, Anne. **Perfect Crane.** New York: Harper and Row, 1981.

Gami, a lonely magician, makes a folded paper crane and then gives life to the perfect white bird. Gami's life is happy until the crane says, "I must join the flock and fly to follow the sun."

Luenn, Nancy. **The Dragon Kite.** New York: Harcourt Brace Jovanovich, 1982.

Ishikawa is a Robin Hood-type thief living during the late 1600s or early 1700s. He builds a remarkable dragon kite to carry him up to the golden dolphins on the roof of the castle belonging to the son of the shogun. He plans to steal the dolphins in order to buy a hundred bags of rice for the hungry villagers. Ishikawa reaches his goal, but he is caught and sentenced to death along with his family and the kite maker. Just prior to the execution, a red and silver dragon appears and rescues the prisoners.

Uchida, Yoshiko, reteller. "The Golden Axe." In **The Magic Listening Cap: More Folk Tales from Japan.** New York: Harcourt, Brace, 1955.

When a poor woodcutter is rewarded for his kindness and honesty by the goddess of the water, his neighbor envies his good fortune. The neighbor seeks riches from the water goddess but is punished for his greed.

———. "The Old Man of the Flowers." In **The Dancing Kettle and Other Japanese Folk Tales.** New York: Harcourt, Brace, 1949.

An old man and woman are rewarded for their kindness to a little dog, Shiro. A cruel and greedy neighbor, envious of the old couple's good fortune, attempts to use Shiro to gain riches for himself. When this fails, he kills Shiro and is justly punished.

———. "The Sea of Gold." In **The Sea of Gold and Other Tales of Japan.** Boston: Gregg Press, 1965.

Gentle Hikoichi works as a cook on a fishing boat. For many years he feeds the fish and talks to them each morning. For his kindness to the fish, Hikoichi is rewarded by the King of the Sea.

———. "Urashima Taro and the Princess of the Sea." In **The Dancing Kettle and Other Japanese Folk Tales.** New York: Harcourt, Brace, 1949.

Urashima Taro, a young fisherman, is rewarded for his kindness to a tortoise. He is invited to live in the Palace of the Sea with the princess. In time, he decides to return home, and the princess gives him a lovely box, which she forbids him to open. When Urashima discovers that he has been away for three hundred years, he forgets the warning of the princess and opens the box. Suddenly, he is an old man, 300 years older than a moment before.

II. Independent Reading

A. Traditional Literature

Bang, Garrett. **Men from the Village Deep in the Mountains and Other Japanese Folktales.** New York: Macmillan, 1973.

Bartoli, Jennifer, reteller. **The Story of the Grateful Crane.** Chicago: Albert Whitman, 1977.

Baruch, Dorothy, reteller. **Kappa's Tug-of-War with Big Brown Horse: The Story of a Japanese Water Imp.** Rutland, Vermont: Charles E. Tuttle, 1962.

Bryant, Sara Cone. **The Burning Rice Fields.** New York: Holt, Rinehart and Winston, 1963.

Dolch, Edward. **Stories from Japan.** Champaign, Illinois: Garrard, 1960.

Dorson, Richard M. **Folk Legends of Japan.** Rutland, Vermont: Charles E. Tuttle, 1962.

Floethe, Louise, reteller. **A Thousand and One Buddhas.** New York: Farrar, Straus and Giroux, 1967.

Francis, Frank, reteller. **Timimoto's Great Adventures.** New York: Holiday House, 1969.

Harris, Rosemary, reteller. **Child in the Bamboo Grove.** New York: S. G. Phillips, 1971.

Haviland, Virginia. **Favorite Fairy Tales Told in Japan.** New York: Little, Brown, 1967.

Hearn, Lafcadio. **The Boy Who Drew Cats and Other Tales of Lafcadio Hearn.** New York: Macmillan, 1963.

Hodges, Margaret. **The Wave.** Boston: Houghton Mifflin, 1964.

Ishii, Momoko. **Issun Boshi the Inchling: An Old Tale of Japan.** New York: Walker, 1967.

Jameson, Cynthia, reteller. **One for the Price of Two.** New York: Parents' Magazine Press, 1972.

Kijima, Hajime. **Little White Hen.** New York: Harcourt, Brace and World, 1969.

Lifton, Betty Jean, reteller. **The Cock and the Ghost Cat.** New York: Atheneum, 1965.

———. **Kap and the Wicked Monkey.** New York: W. W. Norton, 1968.

———. **The Mud Snail Son.** New York: Atheneum, 1971.

———. **The One-Legged Ghost.** New York: Atheneum, 1969.

McAlpine, Helen, and William McAlpine, retellers. **Japanese Tales and Legends.** New York: Henry Z. Walck, 1959.

McDermott, Gerald, adapter. **The Stonecutter: A Japanese Folktale.** New York: Viking Press, 1975.

Marmur, Mildred. **Japanese Fairy Tales.** New York: Golden Press, 1960.

Matsui, Tadashi, reteller. **Oniroku and the Carpenter.** New York: Prentice-Hall, 1963.

Matsuno, Masako. **Taro and the Bamboo Shoot.** New York: Pantheon Books, 1974.

Matsutani, Miyoko. **The Crane Maiden.** New York: Parents' Magazine Press, 1968.

———. **The Fisherman under the Sea.** New York: Parents' Magazine Press, 1969.

———. **The Fox Wedding.** Chicago: Encyclopedia Britannica, 1963.

———. **How the Withered Trees Blossomed.** Philadelphia: J. B. Lippincott, 1969.

———. **The Witch's Magic Cloth.** New York: Parents' Magazine Press, 1969.

Mosel, Arlene, adapter. **The Funny Little Woman.** New York: E. P. Dutton, 1972.

Newton, Patricia, adapter. **The Five Sparrows: A Japanese Folktale.** New York: Atheneum, 1982.

Ozaki, Yei T. **The Japanese Fairy Book.** Rutland, Vermont: Charles E. Tuttle, 1970.

Pratt, Davis, and Elsa Kula. **Magic Animals of Japan.** Berkeley: Parnassus Press, 1967.

Sakade, Florence, editor. **Japanese Children's Favorite Stories.** Rutland, Vermont: Charles E. Tuttle, 1958.

———. **Little One-Inch and Other Japanese Children's Favorite Stories.** Rutland, Vermont: Charles E. Tuttle, 1958.

———. **Urashima Taro and Other Japanese Children's Stories.** Rutland, Vermont: Charles E. Tuttle, 1964.

Say, Allen, reteller. **Once under the Cherry Blossom Tree.** New York: Harper and Row, 1974.

Stamm, Claus, reteller. **The Dumplings and the Demons.** New York: Viking Press, 1964.

———. **Three Strong Women: A Tall Tale from Japan.** New York: Viking Press, 1962.

———. **The Very Special Badgers: A Tale of Magic from Japan.** New York: Viking Press, 1960.

Takeichi, Yasoo, reteller. **The Mighty Prince.** New York: Crown, 1971.

Titus, Eve. **The Two Stonecutters.** New York: Doubleday, 1967.

Uchida, Yoshiko. **The Dancing Kettle and Other Japanese Folk Tales.** New York: Harcourt, Brace, 1949.

———. **The Magic Listening Cap: More Folk Tales from Japan.** New York: Harcourt, Brace, 1955.

———. **Rokubei and the Thousand Rice Bowl.** New York: Charles Scribner's Sons, 1962.

———. **The Sea of Gold and Other Tales of Japan.** Boston: Gregg Press, 1965.

Yagawa, Sumiko, reteller. **The Crane Wife,** translated by Katherine Paterson. New York: William Morrow, 1981.

Yamaguchi, Tohr, reteller. **The Golden Crane.** New York: Holt, Rinehart and Winston, 1963.

Yashima, Taro. **Seashore Story.** New York: Viking Press, 1967.

Yasuda, Yuri. **Old Tales of Japan.** Rutland, Vermont: Charles E. Tuttle, 1953.

B. Modern Fantasy

Coatsworth, Elizabeth. **The Cat Who Went to Heaven.** New York: Macmillan, 1930.

Dobrin, Arnold. **Taro and the Sea Turtles.** New York: Coward, McCann and Geoghegan, 1966.

Hamada, Hirosuke. **The Tears of the Dragon.** New York: Parents' Magazine Press, 1967.

Kotzwinkle, William. **The Supreme, Superb, Exalted and Delightful, One and Only Magic Building.** New York: Farrar, Straus and Giroux, 1973. (Dedicated to Basho the poet and Hokusai the artist)

Lifton, Betty Jean. **The Dwarf Pine Tree.** New York: Atheneum, 1964.

———. **Joji and the Amanojaku.** New York: W. W. Norton, 1965.

———. **Joji and the Dragon.** New York: William Morrow, 1957.

———. **Joji and the Fog.** New York: William Morrow, 1959.

———. **The Rice-Cake Rabbit.** New York: W. W. Norton, 1966.

Winthrop, Elizabeth. **Journey to the Bright Kingdom.** New York: Holiday House, 1979.

Yamaguchi, Tohr. **Two Crabs and the Moonlight.** New York: Holt, Rinehart and Winston, 1965.

Yoda, Junichi. **The Rolling Rice Ball.** New York: Parents' Magazine Press, 1969.

C. Poetry

Atwood, Ann. **Fly with the Wind, Flow with the Water.** New York: Charles Scribner's Sons, 1979.

———. **Haiku: The Mood of the Earth.** New York: Charles Scribner's Sons, 1971.

———. **Haiku: Vision in Poetry and Photography.** New York: Charles Scribner's Sons, 1977.

———. **My Own Rhythm: An Approach to Haiku.** New York: Charles Scribner's Sons, 1973.

Baron, Virginia. **The Seasons of Time: Tanka Poetry of Ancient Japan.** New York: Dial Press, 1968.

Basho. **The Way of Silence: The Prose and Poetry of Basho.** New York: Dial Press, 1970.

Behn, Harry, translator. **Cricket Songs: Japanese Haiku.** New York: Harcourt, Brace and World, 1964.

———. **More Cricket Songs.** New York: Harcourt, Brace and World, 1964.

Caudill, Rebecca. **Come Along.** New York: Holt, Rinehart and Winston, 1969.

Fukuda, Hanako. **Wind in My Hand: The Story of Issa.** Chicago: Children's Press, 1970.

Howard, Coralie. **The First Book of Short Verse.** New York: Franklin Watts, 1964.

Issa. **A Few Flies and I: Haiku by Issa.** New York: Pantheon Books, 1969.

——— et al. **Don't Tell the Scarecrow and Other Japanese Poems.** New York: Four Winds Press, 1970.

Johnson, Hannah. **Hello, Small Sparrow.** New York: Lothrop, Lee and Shepard Books, 1971.

Lewis, Richard, editor. **In a Spring Garden.** New York: Dial Press, 1965.

———. **The Moment of Wonder: A Collection of Chinese and Japanese Poetry.** New York: Dial Press, 1964.

————. **Of This World: A Poet's Life in Poetry.** New York: Dial Press, 1968.

————. **There Are Two Lives: Poems by Children of Japan,** translated by Haruna Kimura. New York: Simon and Schuster, 1970.

Mizumura, Kazue. **Flower Moon Snow: A Book of Haiku.** New York: Thomas Y. Crowell, 1977.

D. Realistic Fiction: Contemporary and Historical

Bonham, Frank. **Mystery in Little Tokyo.** New York: E. P. Dutton, 1966.

Buck, Pearl. **The Big Wave.** New York: John Day, 1947.

Bunting, Eve. **Magic and the Night River.** New York: Harper and Row, 1978.

Creekmore, Raymond. **Fujio.** New York: Macmillan, 1951.

Gray, Elizabeth. **The Cheerful Heart.** New York: Viking Press, 1959.

Griese, Arnold. **The Wind Is Not a River.** New York: Thomas Y. Crowell, 1978.

Houston, Jeanne Wakatsuki, and James Houston. **Farewell to Manzanar.** Boston: Houghton Mifflin, 1973.

Means, Florence. **The Moved Outers.** Boston: Houghton Mifflin, 1945.

Namioka, Lensey. **The Samurai and the Long-Nosed Devils.** New York: David McKay, 1976. (16th-century Japan)

Paterson, Katherine. **The Master Puppeteer.** New York: Thomas Y. Crowell, 1975. (13-year-old boy in 18th-century Osaka)

————. **Of Nightingales That Weep.** New York: Thomas Y. Crowell, 1974. (Daughter of a samurai during the Gempei Wars, 1180–1185)

————. **The Sign of the Chrysanthemum.** New York: Thomas Y. Crowell, 1973. (Only son of a legendary samurai warrior searches for his father in feudal Japan)

Roy, Ronald. **A Thousand Pails of Water.** New York: Alfred A. Knopf, 1978.

Say, Allen. **The Bicycle Man.** Boston: Houghton Mifflin, 1982. (Based on author's childhood in Japan)

————. **The Ink-Keeper's Apprentice.** New York: Harper and Row, 1979.

Smith, Doris. **Salted Lemons.** New York: Four Winds Press, 1980.

Uchida, Yoshiko. **The Birthday Visitor.** New York: Charles Scribner's Sons, 1975.

————. **The Forever Christmas Tree.** New York: Charles Scribner's Sons, 1963.

———. **In-Between Miya.** New York: Charles Scribner's Sons, 1967.

———. **Journey Home.** New York: Atheneum, 1978.

———. **Journey to Topaz.** New York: Charles Scribner's Sons, 1971.

Yashima, Mitsu, and Taro Yashima. **Plenty to Watch.** New York: Viking Press, 1954.

Yashima, Taro. **Crow Boy.** New York: Viking Press, 1955.

———. **The Village Tree.** New York: Viking Press, 1953.

E. Nonfiction

Boardman, Gwenn. **Living in Tokyo.** Nashville: Thomas Nelson, 1970.

Buck, Pearl. **The People of Japan.** New York: Simon and Schuster, 1966.

Greene, Carol. **Enchantment of Japan.** Chicago: Children's Press, 1983.

Hoare, Sophy. **Japan: The Land and Its People.** London: MacDonald Educational, 1975.

Johnes, Raymond. **Japanese Art.** Spring Books, 1961.

Lifton, Betty. **Return to Hiroshima.** New York: Atheneum, 1970.

Maruki, Toshi. **Hiroshima No Pika** ("The Flash of Hiroshima"). New York: Lothrop, Lee and Shepard Books, 1982.

Nakamoto, Hiroko. **My Japan.** New York: McGraw-Hill, 1970.

Newman, Robert. **The Japanese: People of the Three Treasures.** New York: Atheneum, 1964.

Pitts, Forrest. **Japan.** Grand Rapids, Michigan: Fideler, 1979.

Ripley, Elizabeth. **Hokusai.** New York: J. B. Lippincott, 1968. (Biography of Japanese artist, 1760–1849)

Savage, Katherine. **The Story of World Religions.** New York: Henry Z. Walck, 1967.

Seeger, Elizabeth. **Eastern Religions.** New York: Thomas Y. Crowell, 1973.

Shirakigawa, Tomiko. **Children of Japan.** New York: Sterling, 1967.

Smith, Bradley. **Japan: A History in Art.** New York: Doubleday, 1964.

Sterling Publishing Company. **Japan in Pictures.** New York: Sterling, 1961.

Tobias, Tobi. **Isamu Noguchi: The Life of a Sculptor.** New York: Thomas Y. Crowell, 1974.

Vaughan, Josephine. **The Land and People of Japan.** New York: J. B. Lippincott, 1972.

Vining, Elizabeth Gray. **Return to Japan.** New York: J. B. Lippincott, 1960.

Walker, Richard. **Ancient Japan.** New York: Franklin Watts, 1975.

Group Story Sessions

During the first sessions of this Focus Unit on Japan, several stories were
selected from three collections of Japanese folktales compiled and retold
by Yoshiko Uchida: "The Golden Axe" in *The Magic Listening Cap,*
"The Old Man of the Flowers" and "Urashima Taro and the Princess of
the Sea" in *The Dancing Kettle,* and "The Sea of Gold" in *The Sea of
Gold and Other Tales from Japan.* Concomitant with these group sessions, each student was expected to select at least four Japanese tales to
read independently and to keep a written record of this outside reading in
a personal notebook. A model for the form and content of the individual
reading records was presented during the group sessions as significant
ideas and information were recorded along with story titles on large easel
paper hanging in the front of the classroom. In addition, the teacher's
questions used to guide the discussions during these group story sessions
were designed to serve as models for questioning techniques used in independent critical reading.

First Session

After listening to "The Golden Axe," the students were asked to respond
to the story itself and then to suggest which parts, if any, would seem to
reflect Japanese culture and geography. They observed that the themes—
honesty and kindness rewarded and greed and selfishness punished—could
be found in many other folktales from other countries. They speculated
that the presence of the water goddess in this tale could reflect a belief in
"nature gods." They also noted the importance of rice in this tale. At the
conclusion of the group session, the story title, the name of the reteller,
and pertinent comments were recorded on the easel paper.

Second Session

When the second tale, "The Old Man of the Flowers," was read aloud,
the students saw obvious similarities in terms of the themes (kindness
rewarded, greed punished), the importance of rice, the belief in supernatural powers, and the sudden rise to riches among poor peasants.
Several students commented that the cherry blossoms and dwarfed pine
trees mentioned in this tale were frequently seen in Japanese prints.

At this point, the teacher offered some background information about
Japanese folklore. These two stories are examples of *choja* tales, or stories
about a rich peasant. Usually these tales feature poor peasants who suddenly gain wealth or wealthy villagers who experience a decline in fortune.
In his book *Folk Legends of Japan* (1963), Richard M. Dorson describes
the characteristics of such stories: "the Buddhist element here, the con-

ception of change in the stream of life, from high station to low and from low to high, a conception to humble the lofty and reprove the faint hearted" (p. 178). He adds that in societies where there are such immense gaps between the poor and the rich and powerful, it is not surprising to find dreams of sudden wealth and security.

Dorson describes the different categories or types of Japanese tales and explains some of the background of tales about spirits: "For thirty-three years after bodily death, the 'reikon' (spirit, soul) of a deceased person hovers about its lifetime residence. . . . If death occurs when the 'shirei' (spirit) is troubled, inflamed, resentful or in any way disturbed, that angry spirit presents a fearful danger to any human being it encounters . . ." (p. 96). The students found it interesting to view the story "The Old Man of the Flowers" in this context. Several students suggested that the name of the murdered dog, Shiro, could be related to the word *shirei* because his death was the result of rage and resentment. Others noted that Shiro, as a spirit, possessed the power to reward the kindness of the old man and to punish the cruelty of the greedy neighbor.

One student had read independently a lovely illustrated version of this tale in *Japanese Fairy Tales* by Mildred Marmur, which she showed to the group. She was intrigued with the differences between these two retellings: "In my story, when the miser threw ashes at the prince, he realized that this was Shiro's revenge and asked for mercy. The prince let him go and the miser reformed!" Another student responded, "It seems that in your version, Shiro's biggest miracle was not the magic bowl but the changed man!"

Other students shared their discoveries of further examples of *choja* tales: "The Mountain Witch and the Pedlar" and "The Magic Mortar" (Yoshiko Uchida, in *The Magic Listening Cap*), "The Dancing Kettle" (Yoshiko Uchida, in *The Dancing Kettle and Other Japanese Folk Tales*), and *The Five Sparrows* (Patricia Newton). The girl who had selected *The Five Sparrows* read aloud the moral of this tale, which she had found in the summary on the book jacket flap: "Yet rewards, this story says, go not to deeds but to the feelings behind deeds." This statement and other information were added to the growing list of notes on the easel paper.

Third Session

Two additional tales by Yoshiko Uchida were read aloud next: "Urashima Taro and the Princess of the Sea" (in *The Dancing Kettle and Other Japanese Folk Tales*) and "The Sea of Gold" (in *The Sea of Gold and Other Tales of Japan*). By this time the students had begun to consult a large wall map of Japan and to make connections between geographical features of Japan and its literature:

"I can see why so many stories were written about the sea."

"Fishing must be an important industry in Japan. A lot of the characters are fishermen, and in that story about the peddler and the witch, he sold fish."

"I read *The Wave* [Margaret Hodges]. It's about a fishing village that got wrecked by a tidal wave."

This led to discussion of the deep interest in the sea reflected in these tales. "Urashima Taro" and "The Sea of Gold" celebrate the mystery, beauty, and life-giving nature of the sea. Such tales suggest a belief in kingdoms under the sea and in sea gods with the power to reward or punish mortals. A student who had read *The Wave* commented, "This story seems to remind you that the sea can also be destructive and something to fear as well as a place to get food and earn a living."

The familiar patterns running through all four of the stories read aloud were identified: rewards for kindness and sudden reversals in fortune. There were several comments about the conclusion of the "Urashima Taro" story:

"That reminded me of Rip Van Winkle when he slept so many years and then came back."

"It was sad when he suddenly changed to an old man."

"I read that book *Seashore Story* [Taro Yashima] about the Urashima legend. The pictures are abstract like modern art and seem mysterious like the story. But those children in the book who hear the old legend asked about the ending, and the storyteller explained that Urashima stayed away too long and was punished because he forgot the people he loved."

"I think the reason he was punished was because he was curious and opened the box when he was warned *not* to—like Pandora."

Students who had read other illustrated versions of this story commented on the differences in the texts as well as in the illustrations. One girl was especially impressed with the detailed pictures in *Japanese Fairy Tales* by Mildred Marmur. She volunteered to bring in two Japanese dolls to display in the classroom. This prompted other offers: Japanese prints, a kimono, a painted fan, and a lacquer box. This exhibit was gradually expanded and eventually evolved into a more ambitious project, a classroom museum, which is described later in the chapter.

Following this third session, selected readings in textbooks and various supplementary sources were assigned to begin the process of using nonfiction material to study Japan—its history, economy, government, arts, way of life, and natural features. As these and additional nonfiction selections were explored throughout the unit, the students gradually integrated their growing background knowledge with their discoveries from the literature. They began to develop an understanding of the way a folk literature mirrors the culture from which it emerges.

Fourth Session

In this session, Lafcadio Hearn was introduced as the first Western writer to explain Japanese life to the Western world through retellings of old Japanese legends. (See Pearl Buck's introduction to *The Boy Who Drew Cats and Other Tales of Lafcadio Hearn.*) The student who had just read *The Wave* (Hodges) pulled it from her desk and read from the title page: "*The Wave,* adapted from Lafcadio Hearn's 'Gleanings in the Buddha Fields.' " Then two of Hearn's tales were read aloud and discussed: "The Boy Who Drew Cats" and "The Story of Kogi the Priest." The students noted that the tales reflected a deep respect for living creatures, the important role of the village temple and priests, and a great love of beauty revealed through artistic expression and appreciation. They observed that the mystical qualities of these two tales suggested a belief in the supernatural and demonstrated the influence of Shintoism, Japan's original religion involving the worship of the spirits of nature as well as ancestor worship. One boy felt that *The Stonecutter* by Gerald McDermott was a good example of this belief in spirits of nature: "The mountain spirit in this story had the power to reward or punish." Another student commented that in "The Boy Who Drew Cats" the priest's warning revealed his special powers to know the future and what dangers awaited the boy. He also commented on the importance of cats in Japan: "I read that cats are very respected and sometimes have special magical powers." In response, the teacher recommended the modern story *The Cat Who Went to Heaven* by Elizabeth Coatsworth as independent reading for those interested in a tale of an unusual cat who came to live with a poor Japanese artist. This Newbery Medal-winning story is a remarkable tale of compassion and love, and it alludes to "The Boy Who Drew Cats" as well as the Jataka tale by Virginia Haviland, "The Banyan Deer" (*Favorite Fairy Tales Told in India*), in which a self-sacrificing king deer offers to give his life to save a mother deer and her baby.

The discussion of "The Story of Kogi the Priest" continued as the children puzzled over this strange tale. One student tried to explain it in terms of the belief about a soul leaving the body and having a life of its own:

> "Maybe when he was sick, he was unconscious and his soul left his body and was taken down to the water world as a reward from the Dragon King. I think in the olden days people thought when you

dream, it's your soul doing the things and your body is sleeping. Maybe it's a lot like being unconscious because of sickness. Both the boy who drew the cats and Kogi were great artists who put a lot of themselves into their pictures. So—maybe the painting has a soul from the artist. So that's why those fish swam right off the page . . . or the silk, I guess."

The process of exploring these old tales required the students to stretch their minds and imaginations. They began to see the world from the viewpoint of people whose customs, superstitions, and beliefs are intricately interwoven with their long history, the geographical features of their country, and folk and formal religions, and to appreciate the rich and colorful tapestry of tradition and tale.

Little One-Inch by Barbara Brenner was read next to introduce the popular Japanese hero Issun Boshi (sometimes written as *Issoumbochi*), whose name means "small as a thumb" or "one-inch lad." The story also introduced three traditional Japanese demons: the *kappa, tengu,* and *oni.* Since several students had already read other retellings of this tale, they immediately made comparisons. For example, one comment was: "I really didn't like the way Ms. Brenner ended the story—with the girl getting as tiny as Issun Boshi. I read two other Issun Boshi stories, and they both ended with Issun Boshi getting to be a normal size and ending up being a famous person in Kyoto."

The students noted that Issun Boshi was similar to "Tom Thumb" in size and spirit. Other parallels with European tales were identified: "The Ogre Who Built a Bridge" by Yoshiko Uchida (1965) is a Japanese tale similar to "Rumpelstiltskin," and "Sima Who Wore the Big Hat" by Mildred Marmur resembles "Cinderella." One boy responded, "I guess Japan wasn't quite so isolated from the outside world as the textbook said because people must have brought in those story ideas—or maybe they took them out to Europe—depending on who started them." This was an interesting comment, for according to Stith Thompson (1977), "A good Chinese literary version of Cinderella has been reported from the ninth century after Christ" (p. 126).

At the conclusion of the fourth group session, one girl volunteered to share a book she had found in the Focus Unit collection, *Magic Animals of Japan* by Davis Pratt and Elsa Kula. The book includes twelve well-known legends of mythical creatures found in paintings, sculpture, and architecture throughout Japan as well as some background information about each of the magic animals. The students decided to record the names of these magic animals on a chart (mermaid, fox, cat, monkey, toad, badger, tengu, crane, dragon, rabbit, kappa, and tiger) and then to record additional titles of stories about these particular animals that the students selected for independent reading. The list gradually expanded as they continued to discover traditional and modern tales about these creatures. A few examples of the tales they found are: *The Rice-Cake Rabbit* by Betty Jean Lifton, *Kappa's Tug-of-War with Big Brown Horse: The Story of a Japanese Water Imp* by Dorothy Baruch, *The Very Special Badgers: A Tale of Magic from Japan* by Claus Stamm, *The Golden Crane* by Tohr Yamaguchi, *The Crane Maiden* by Miyoko Matsutani, "The Tengu's Magic Nose Fan" by Yoshiko Uchida (1965), "The Grateful Toad" by Garrett Bang, and *The Dragon Kite* by Nancy Luenn.

Because of the interest in these creatures, a creative writing project was suggested at this point in the Focus Unit sequence. Students were instructed to choose one of these traditional magic animals to use in writing an "original" Japanese folktale. When the stories were completed, each was illustrated and then read aloud to the group. The tales were bound together into a book entitled "The Second Book of Magic Animals of Japan."

By this time, many of the traditional tales had been read with the group or independently. The next series of story sessions featured modern tales, and the students were encouraged to select from the collection of modern fantasy, contemporary realistic fiction, or historical fiction for their next independent reading experience.

Fifth Session

The first modern literary fairy tale introduced in the group sessions was *A Japanese Fairy Tale* by Jane Hori Ike and Baruch Zimmerman, which is beautifully illustrated with delicate watercolors by author Ike. According to Charlotte Huck (1979), "The modern literary fairy tale utilizes the form of the old [traditional tales], but has an identifiable author" (p. 249). The students noted that the familiar words *adapted by, retold by, translated by,* or *collected by* were not used in reference to the authors of this tale. However, the book jacket flap read: "*A Japanese Fairy Tale* is based on an old story told to Mr. Zimmerman by his father."

The students were particularly impressed with the act of selflessness portrayed in this story and identified other tales with a similar theme: *The Dwarf Pine Tree* by Betty Jean Lifton, *Two Crabs and the Moonlight* by Tohr Yamaguchi, *The Cock and the Ghost Cat* by Lifton, and "The Grateful Statues" by Florence Sakade (1958). (The last story can also be found in *The Sea of Gold and Other Tales of Japan* by Yoshiko Uchida, under the title "New Year's Hats for the Statues.") One student who had looked up Buddhism in the encyclopedia explained that Buddhist teachings showed the way to overcome selfishness and sorrow and to achieve an ideal state of freedom, peace, and "perfect insight." He related that "self-control, generosity, mercy, and humility are very important if you want to gain self-knowledge and peace." His classmates responded to this new information with great interest, and they concluded that Buddhist thinking was a powerful force behind the literature of Japan. Because of their interest in Buddhism and their growing awareness of its significant role in the way of life in Japan, a class parent who had been actively involved in the local Zen Center was invited to come in to talk more about this ancient religion and to answer the many questions raised during the group session in which *A Japanese Fairy Tale* had been introduced.

Sixth Session

The second literary fairy tale read in the group session was *The Dragon Kite* by Nancy Luenn. This is the story of the thief Ishikawa, who dared to steal the gold dolphins from the roof of Nagoya Castle, built by the shogun for his son. After hearing this beautiful tale, several students immediately identified Ishikawa as a "Robin Hood type" because he stole from the rich to buy rice for the poor. One student saw similarities between Ishikawa and Tyl Uilenspiegel, a legendary hero from the Netherlands, because both enjoyed performing daring and cunning deeds, swindling the rich and powerful, and stealing for the benefit of the poor. They all admired the illustrations of Michael Hague and his detailed portrayal of the land and people of Japan. The question "How did Ishikawa change in the course of this story?" yielded these comments:

> "The kite maker taught him patience and self-control as well as the special skills needed to make his kite. He seemed almost like a Buddhist teacher!"

> "Ishikawa learned that if you really want to do an excellent job, it takes a long time and a lot of knowledge."

> "He learned that you have to keep trying."

> "He learned to hold his temper! When he finally got the gold fins, his friend just said, 'Well that was easy.' And Ishikawa didn't get mad or yell—even though he had spent *four* years getting ready! He just bowed low and didn't show any anger."

> "He had become wise. He gained the inner peace that is so important in the Buddhist religion."

Another question, "What can you learn about Japanese culture from this story?" generated comments about the gap between rich and poor; the importance of rice; the fearful power of the shogun's son; the belief in gods such as the red and silver dragon; the custom of bowing; the harsh and cruel justice inherent in execution by boiling oil as a punishment for theft; the clothing, buildings, and landscape shown in the illustrations; and the status and honor apparently attached to the profession of kite making. Some felt that the kite maker was as important a character as Ishikawa:

> "He reminded me of Kogi the Priest. Their art work was really a part of their religious life."

> "This is another example of the love of beauty in Japan and the great care and patience given to each detail in a painting or poem."

Seventh Session

When *Perfect Crane* by Anne Laurin was read aloud, it was immediately compared to *The Dragon Kite:*

> "Gami gave life and freedom to the crane—just like in *The Dragon Kite* when Ishikawa let the kite go."

> "It was the same in those stories about the boy who drew the cats and Kogi the Priest who drew fish. The things they painted came alive."

> "There must be some kind of mystical thing about an artist as a *creator.* In most of the stories we read, the supernatural is *natural,* so maybe there's also a belief that things in a picture can have a life of their own."

The importance of the crane in Japanese culture was also explored, and several students told about crane stories such as *The Golden Crane* by Tohr Yamaguchi and "The Cloth of a Thousand Feathers" by Garrett Bang. Information about the crane included in Davis Pratt and Elsa Kula's book, *Magic Animals of Japan,* was shared: " . . . the crane symbolizes peacefulness and good will and is supposed to bring good fortune."

Eighth Session

Sadako and the Thousand Paper Cranes by Eleanor Coerr, introduced in the next group session, is a remarkable story based on the life of a girl who lived in Japan from 1943–1955. She lived in Hiroshima when the atom bomb was dropped and died ten years later of leukemia caused by radiation from the bomb. The students were deeply touched by this tragic but inspiring story and its plea for world peace. Their full attention was focused on the courage of this child and the events which had led up to the day of the bomb.

Subsequent Sessions

Only in a subsequent group session were the students ready to take a more objective view of the story itself and note the way traditions from an ancient heritage could be found in this contemporary family. Of course, the crane legend and poems were of special interest as was the symbolism of the folded paper cranes in this moving story.

The paper cranes sparked interest in *origami,* the art of Japanese paper folding, and there were many requests to learn it. A student art teacher who happened to be working in the school at the time of this Focus Unit responded to these requests by arriving in the classroom the next morning wearing a beautiful kimono and carrying a box of colored paper squares. She bowed to the class and quietly beckoned each student to come to her to receive a few squares. As each student stood before her, she bowed. Soon they caught on and returned the courtesy. It was fascinating to observe this very lively group of youngsters gradually adjust themselves to an attitude of quiet and peace as they became immersed in the process of learning the skills of origami to create delicate birds and flowers. As they worked, the student teacher shared some of her special knowledge of various art forms of Japan and taught the class a number of Japanese words in the process.

Once the students had developed a degree of skill in origami, they were ready for a special project which involved the creation of greeting cards to send to friends and relatives wishing them peace and good fortune. On the front of each card were words for *peace* and *good luck* in many languages; on the inside, a folded paper crane was attached. Each student seemed to feel the symbolic significance of crane cards, the blending of ancient traditions with current events, and the message of hope and peace. A great deal of care, effort, and personal pride went into this creative process. Later, several students decided to make some crane peace posters for the classroom; others hung paper cranes from the ceiling as in *Sadako and the Thousand Paper Cranes.*

By this time in the Focus Unit sequence, the students were becoming familiar with the history, geography, and people of Japan as described in various nonfiction sources in the Focus Unit collection and reference books in the library. In addition, they had begun to read contemporary and historical realistic fiction to further enrich and complement their nonfiction reading. Several group sessions were used by the teacher to introduce and "sell" these realistic novels through a series of "book talks." Several students volunteered to discuss books they particularly wanted to recommend to their classmates. When each student had completed at least one of the realistic novels, the group sessions were devoted to discussing the significance and implications of each story and integrating the knowledge and insights gained from the fiction and nonfiction sources. An important dimension of all this independent reading was the development of the critical reading skills necessary for differentiating between fact and opinion and for making judgments about the author's viewpoint and purpose. These sessions helped the students to move toward synthesis and to pull together the ideas, concepts, and discoveries drawn from the diverse but related source materials selected for this unit.

Independent Projects

To provide opportunities for the expression of individual interests and talents and for in-depth study, a variety of ideas were suggested for a final independent project, and many of the students came up with additional ideas and plans on their own. A few projects are described here.

One boy created a dictionary of Japanese words which he found by searching through numerous books in the classroom collection. Gwenn Boardman's *Living in Tokyo* proved to be a rich resource for his purposes. His completed, hand-bound dictionary contained explanations for each word and appropriate illustrations and diagrams.

Several students were particularly interested in World War II and wrote reports of the events of this historical period by drawing from the textbooks and from relevant realistic fiction. After these students had shared their reports with the class, the teacher introduced *Hiroshima No Pika* by Toshi Maruki, a graphic portrayal of the effects of nuclear warfare. This is an extremely disturbing book and a difficult one to share with young people. The teacher waited on introducing it until the children had the background information and understanding necessary to confront the vivid description of nuclear warfare.

Some students researched various arts of Japan and prepared written reports. Others preferred to become more directly involved in creative expression through Japanese art forms. The products of these projects included several lovely books of original haiku illustrated with delicate watercolors, some wall hangings painted with Japanese landscapes, and an original play written and performed by three boys who called themselves "The Kabuki Company." Their play had been inspired by *The Rice-Cake Rabbit* by Betty Jean Lifton, a story about a rabbit who dreamed about becoming a samurai.

One student developed an interest in author-artist Taro Yashima. Using Yashima's books as biographical sources and through inference and synthesis, this student put together a word portrait of Yashima, his family, his childhood experiences in a Japanese village, and his philosophy of art and life.

Several students selected some of the Japanese picture books to share with younger children in their school. They arranged weekly half-hour sessions with a small group of first-graders and second-graders and read aloud stories they thought would appeal to this age group. They found that Betty Jean Lifton's series of books about Joji the scarecrow were especially well received. This inspired the older children to write a new series of stories about the adventures of Issun Boshi. These original tales reflected the literary background of the authors and were illustrated and bound into books which they shared with their young friends.

The Class Project

The culminating class project was the creation of a museum in the class-room to share the students' study of Japan with parents and the rest of the school. Displays were set up around the room to exhibit examples of Japanese painting, crafts, poetry, clothing, religious objects, architecture, and dolls, and there was an exhibit with miniature items to represent the types of manufactured goods Japan exports to foreign countries. Enlisting the help of parents and teachers with special skills, the students set up demonstrations to show the traditional cooking, music, dance, writing, flower arrangement, and games found in Japan. One parent volunteered to demonstrate a shortened version of the four-hour *Chanoyu,* or tea ceremony.

The small individual projects and this large class project offered oppor-tunities for each student to pursue an area of interest in Japanese culture or history and to take pride in achieving a degree of competence and understanding in that area. The students' enthusiastic and thoughtful involvement in their projects provided evidence that they had indeed begun to look at and appreciate another culture "from the inside out."

References

Haviland, Virginia. *Favorite Fairy Tales Told in India.* Boston: Little, Brown, 1973.

Huck, Charlotte. *Children's Literature in the Elementary School.* New York: Holt, Rinehart and Winston, 1979.

Thompson, Stith. *The Folktale.* Berkeley: University of California Press, 1977.

Yolen, Jane. *Touch Magic: Fantasy, Faerie and Folklore in the Literature of Childhood.* New York: Philomel Books, 1981.

12 Friendship: A Focus Unit for Grades One and Two

Children who can make inferences about a person's feelings and motives, who can see the world through the eyes of another, and who can anticipate the consequences of behavior are well equipped to understand social relationships in their own world and in the story world. The Friendship Focus Unit was designed to create a bridge between these two worlds and to assist children in developing social understandings and reading comprehension skills.

Research studies of children's social knowledge and narrative comprehension provided a background for the development of the Friendship Focus Unit. According to Nancy Stein (1978), "Knowledge about human social interaction . . . is important for story comprehension since stories are similar to the content and structure of social perceptions and human action sequences" (p. 7). Stein and others (e.g., Stein and Goldman 1981; Leander 1977; Stein and Glenn 1975) have demonstrated that when children make inferences about motives, feelings, and thoughts which are implicit in a story, the content of these inferences depends in large part on the children's knowledge of social situations and their ability to assume the perspective of another.

Research in the area of social development indicates that children differ significantly in their knowledge of peer relationships and their understanding of the dynamics involved in developing and maintaining friendships. Gottman et al. (1975) found that children who are well accepted by peers also exhibit greater social knowledge than those are are socially unaccepted or isolated. Various educational models have been developed to assist children in their social adjustment. For example, Oden and Asher (1977) used a technique called *coaching*, through which socially isolated children were provided with social skill training in order to help them gain in peer acceptance.

The Friendship Focus Unit was designed to help children expand their knowledge of social interactions as well as their narrative competence through exposure to stories with friendship themes. During the group

Note: Portions of this chapter originally appeared in "Children's Story Comprehension and Social Learning" by Joy F. Moss and Sherri Oden in *The Reading Teacher* (April 1983): 784–89. Reprinted with permission.

145

sessions in which these friendship stories were introduced, the children were encouraged to explore the structure and content of each story. In the process, they were guided toward a discovery of factors associated with establishing, building, and maintaining friendships. This provided a framework for comprehending the social interactions, motives, and problem-solving strategies of story characters. The ultimate goals for the Friendship Focus Unit included the development of critical reading and writing skills and the acquisition and application of understanding about human interaction in literature and reality.

Objectives

1. To improve story comprehension skills with special emphasis on:
   a. identifying the basic plot or central problem of a story.
   b. identifying logical relationships between story events.
   c. making inferences about motives, intentions, thoughts, and feelings of story characters.
   d. anticipating consequences of words and actions of story characters.
2. To improve story production skills with special emphasis on:
   a. descriptions of feelings, thoughts, and motives of story characters.
   b. creating logical relationships between story events.
3. To provide opportunity for independent reading.
4. To provide opportunity for creative expression.
5. To foster growth in social understandings and peer relationships.

Bibliography for the Friendship Focus Unit

I. Group Story Sessions

Brenner, Barbara. **Cunningham's Rooster.** New York: Parents' Magazine Press, 1975.

> Cunningham is a cat who writes music; Kenneth is a rooster who appreciates Cunningham's music and provides inspiration for his compositions. In this tale, the meaning of friendship is expressed through the emotions and actions of these delightful characters. The story has potential for musical or dramatic extensions.

Charlip, Remy. **Harlequin and the Gift of Many Colors.** New York: Parents' Magazine Press, 1973.

This beautifully illustrated story is set in fourteenth-century rural Italy at Carnival time. When Harlequin's friends discover that he has no costume to wear to the Carnival, they each cut a segment of their own costume to give their beloved friend. Harlequin's mother sews the multicolored bits of fabric together to create a magnificent patchwork costume. And Harlequin danced joyously at the Carnival, "clothed in the love of his friends."

Delton, Judy. **Two Good Friends.** New York: Crown, 1974.

Written for beginning readers, this story of Duck and Bear is a delightful example of maintaining a friendship by resolving differences and sharing special talents.

Edmondson, Madeleine. **The Witch's Egg.** New York: Seabury Press, 1974.

Agatha, an ill-tempered witch, discovers the meaning of friendship and love when she "hatches" an abandoned egg and begins to share her life with her "Witchbird."

Kessler, Leonard. **Here Comes the Strikeout.** New York: Harper and Row, 1965.

Bobby loves to play baseball but has never been able to hit the ball. His sense of frustration is intensified when the other boys tease him about his record of strikeouts. His friend Willy teaches him some techniques and encourages him to work hard and keep practicing. Willy's support and help contribute significantly to Bobby's growing self-confidence and competence and eventual success.

Lobel, Arnold. **Frog and Toad Are Friends.** New York: Harper and Row, 1970.

This book is about two friends whose relationship is characterized by caring, sensitivity, and thoughtfulness. The reciprocal nature of their friendship is reflected in their encounter with events and each other throughout the five short chapters of this "I Can Read" book.

Marshall, James. **What's the Matter with Carruthers?** Boston: Houghton Mifflin, 1972.

Emily Pig and Eugene Turtle are worried about the unusual behavior of their good friend Carruthers the bear. After many well-meaning attempts to lift his spirits, Emily suddenly understands what is the matter with Carruthers.

Steig, William. **Amos and Boris.** New York: Farrar, Straus and Giroux, 1971.

Through beautiful language and pictures, Steig creates a tender story of a tiny mouse and an enormous whale who develop a deep and lasting friendship.

Van Leeuwen, Jean. **Timothy's Flower.** New York: Random House, 1967.

This is a sensitive story of a quiet little boy in a busy city block. His love for a flower leads to new relationships and the discovery of a common bond with the one person he least expected would become his friend.

Venable, Alan. **The Checker Players.** Philadelphia: J. B. Lippincott, 1973.

Although the carpenter and tinker in this humorous story have very different life-styles, they discover that they can benefit from their differences and can work and play together as good friends.

II. Independent Reading

Armstrong, William. **The Tale of Tawny and Dingo.** New York: Harper and Row, 1979.

Artis, Vicky K. **Gray Duck Catches a Friend.** New York: G. P. Putnam's Sons, 1974.

Bartholic, Edward L. **Cricket and Sparrow.** Cleveland: William Collins, 1979.

Brown, Myra B. **Best Friends.** Chicago: Children's Press, 1967.

Child Study Children's Book Committee at Bank Street, editors. **Friends Are Like That! Stories to Read to Yourself.** New York: Thomas Y. Crowell, 1979.

Cohen, Miriam. **Will I Have a Friend?** New York: Collier Books, 1967.

Delaney, Ned. **Bert and Barney.** Boston: Houghton Mifflin, 1979.

Delton, Judy. **On a Picnic.** New York: Doubleday, 1979.

———. **Two Is Company.** New York: Crown Publishers, 1976.

Desbarats, Peter. **Gabrielle and Selena.** New York: Harcourt, Brace and World, 1968.

Duvoisin, Roger. **Periwinkle.** New York: Alfred A. Knopf, 1976.

———. **Snowy and Woody.** New York: Random House, 1979.

Erickson, Russell E. **Toad for Tuesday.** New York: Lothrop, Lee and Shepard Books, 1974.

———. **Warton and Morton.** New York: Lothrop, Lee and Shepard Books, 1976.

Gackenbach, Dick. **Hound and Bear.** New York: Seabury Press, 1976.

———. **More from Hound and Bear.** New York: Houghton Mifflin, 1979.

Gauch, Patricia L. **Christina Katerina and the Box.** New York: Coward, McCann and Geoghegan, 1971.

Goffstein, M. B. **Goldie, the Dollmaker.** New York: Farrar, Straus and Giroux, 1969.

Hill, Elizabeth S. **Evan's Corner.** New York: Holt, Rinehart and Winston, 1967.

Hoban, Russell. **A Bargain for Francis.** New York: Harper and Row, 1970.

———. **Best Friends for Francis.** New York: Harper and Row, 1969.

Hoffman, Phyllis. **Steffie and Me.** New York: Harper and Row, 1970.

Johnston, Tony. **Adventures of Mole and Troll.** New York: G. P. Putnam's Sons, 1972.

Kafka, Sherry. **I Need a Friend.** New York: G. P. Putnam's Sons, 1971.

Keats, Ezra J., and Pat Cherr. **My Dog Is Lost!** New York: Thomas Y. Crowell, 1960.

Keller, Beverly. **Fiona's Bee.** New York: Coward, McCann and Geoghegan, 1975.

Krasilovsky, Phyllis. **The Shy Little Girl.** Boston: Houghton Mifflin, 1970.

Lawrence, John. **The Giant of Grabbist.** New York: David White, 1969.

Lexau, Joan. **Benjie.** New York: Dial Press, 1964.

Lionni, Leo. **Tico and the Golden Wings.** New York: Pantheon Books, 1964.

Lobel, Arnold. **Frog and Toad Together.** New York: Harper and Row, 1972.

Lystad, Mary. **That New Boy.** New York: Crown, 1973.

Marshall, James. **George and Martha Encore.** Boston: Houghton Mifflin, 1977.

———. **Speedboat.** Boston: Houghton Mifflin, 1976.

Morrow, Suzanne S. **Inatuk's Friends.** Boston: Atlantic Monthly Press, 1968.

Norris, Gunilla B. **The Friendship Hedge.** New York: E. P. Dutton, 1973.

Oneal, Zibby. **Turtle and Snail.** New York: J. B. Lippincott, 1979.

Schick, Eleanor. **5A and 7B.** New York: Macmillan, 1967.

Schultz, Gwen. **The Blue Valentine.** New York: William Morrow, 1965.

Sharmat, Marjorie W. **Gladys Told Me to Meet Her Here.** New York: Harper and Row, 1970.

Slobodkin, Louis. **The Amiable Giant.** New York: Vanguard Press, 1955.

Steig, William. **The Amazing Bone.** New York: Farrar, Straus and Giroux, 1976.

Steptoe, John. **Stevie.** New York: Harper and Row, 1969.

Stevenson, James. **Fast Friends.** New York: Greenwillow Books, 1979.

Udry, Janice M. **Let's Be Enemies.** New York: Harper and Row, 1961.

Van Workom, Dorothy O. **Harry and Shellburt.** New York: Macmillan, 1977.

Viorst, Judith. **Rosie and Michael.** New York: Atheneum, 1974.

Wells, Rosemary. **Benjamin and Tulip.** New York: Dial Press, 1973.

Wildsmith, Brian. **The Lazy Bear.** New York: Franklin Watts, 1974.

Yolen, Jane. **Spider Jane.** New York: Coward, McCann and Geoghegan, 1978.

Zalben, Jane. **Lyle and Humus.** New York: Macmillan, 1974.

Zolotow, Charlotte. **Janey.** New York: Harper and Row, 1973.

————. **My Friend John.** New York: Harper and Row, 1968.

————. **A Tiger Called Thomas.** New York: Lothrop, Lee and Shepard Books, 1965.

Group Story Sessions

First Session

The book *Amos and Boris* by William Steig was used to introduce the Friendship Focus Unit. This is a sensitive story of a mouse and a whale who develop a close friendship as each learns to appreciate and respect the uniqueness of the other. Like Aesop's "The Lion and the Mouse," the theme of reciprocity or "kindness returned" is an integral part of this beautiful tale. After reading the story aloud, the teacher provided opportunity for spontaneous comments and then introduced questions about the narrative structure. For example, the questions "What were the problems in the story?" and "How were they solved?" were used to focus attention on the plot. In response, one child explained, "First Amos [the mouse] was about to drown and Boris [the whale] saved him, and then Boris got stranded on land and Amos helped get him back to the water. They each had a problem and the other solved it!" A question about setting, "Why do you think the author used two different places for the action in his story?" elicited this observation about the relationship between setting and plot in this narrative: "When they were at sea, the mouse needed help because that wasn't his *home,* but when they traded places and they were on land, Boris needed help because that wasn't *his* home! So the problem happened because of [being in] the wrong *place!*"

Questions about the characters in this story were intended to draw attention to the special relationship which developed between the tiny mouse and the enormous whale:

How did these characters differ?

How did they learn about each other?

How do you think they felt about each other?

How did they "show" their feelings?

What did they enjoy doing together?

These questions encouraged discussion about building friendships and provided practice in the use of vocabulary associated with social skills and friendship interactions. In response to a final question, "Can any of you think of a story which is similar to this one?" several children mentioned "The Lion and the Mouse." One child speculated, "I think Mr. Steig probably heard Aesop's fables when he was a kid and that's how he got the idea for *Amos and Boris.*"

Second Session

The Checker Players by Alan Venable, a story about two friends who must learn to deal with their differences in order to sustain their friendship and to enjoy each other's company, was read aloud next. Recognizing different interests might not be apparent to young readers. Stein and Goldman (1978) found evidence of developmental changes in the knowledge base for friendship interactions. In particular, they found that older children demonstrated "an increased awareness of the notion that shared interests facilitate the establishment of friendship and that the interests of others may differ from those of the self. Younger children may know that you play with a friend but are less aware of the need to match or establish common interests" (p. 22). Thus, a young listener or reader might not initially perceive the problem of individual differences presented in *The Checker Players*. The teacher's questions can help the children become aware of the problem so they can better comprehend the conflict inherent in the story and think about possible solutions.

Third Session

The third friendship book read aloud was Judy Delton's *Two Good Friends*. The two characters in this story, Duck and Bear, are portrayed as polar personality types; the way they resolve their differences and learn to complement each other leads to a very satisfactory ending to a charming story. (This book and two others about these characters were written for beginning readers and were popular choices for independent reading.) At this point, the children were asked to compare the three stories which they had heard during these first three story sessions. Below is an excerpt taken from their discussion:

> "Each book had two characters who were really different from each other."

> "Amos was little and Boris was big, and Duck was neat and Bear was messy . . ."

> "And Bear liked to bake and Duck liked to clean."

> "The carpenter and tinker [in *The Checker Players*] were the same way—one was neat and one was messy. They got mad at each other, but they were still friends."

> "Amos and Boris were good friends, too, even though they were so different."

> "They helped each other and so did Duck and Bear. Like when Bear baked the muffins for Duck and Duck cleaned his [Bear's] house. They *appreciated* each other."

> "The tinker and carpenter figured out that they could build a boat together and it would be better than doing it alone."

> "They *cooperated!*"

> "I think these stories are the same because it didn't matter that they [the characters] were sort of opposite. They still liked each other and liked to do stuff together."

Thus, the children focused on elements and processes of friendship interactions: discovering unique qualities of another, finding commonalities, sharing ideas and activities, learning to consider another's viewpoint, and developing feelings of responsibility, caring, and affection.

Fourth through Seventh Sessions

During the next four sessions, the children were introduced to: *Frog and Toad Are Friends* by Arnold Lobel, *Harlequin and the Gift of Many Colors* by Remy Charlip, *Here Comes the Strikeout* by Leonard Kessler, and *What's the Matter with Carruthers?* by James Marshall. Several of the discussion questions required inferential thinking about the effect of words or behavior of one character on the feelings of another and challenged the children to view events from the perspective of different characters in each of the seven stories. For example, the question "How do you think the carpenter felt when the tinker yelled at him?" elicited comments about the negative consequences of the angry words between these two characters in *The Checker Players*. By way of contrast, the children pointed to more positive actions and outcomes in other stories:

"Frog helped Toad solve his problem and Harlequin's friends helped him, too, so he'd be able to come to the Carnival."

"Emily and Eugene [*What's the Matter with Carruthers?*] spent a lot of time trying to get Carruthers to feel better, and they finally figured out what was the matter."

"And Willy [*Here Comes the Strikeout*] worked with Bobby until he was good at baseball and then he [Bobby] didn't feel like a *failure* any more."

"I think Willy felt good, too, when Bobby hit the ball!"

As the children discussed these last four stories, they recognized that behaviors reflecting attitudes of compassion and sensitivity were featured as significant dimensions of friendship interactions.

Subsequent Sessions

In subsequent sessions, as new stories were read aloud and discussed, the children demonstrated that they had begun to internalize questions about story structure and themes as they initiated their own story analyses. For example, *Cunningham's Rooster* by Barbara Brenner elicited these spontaneous comments:

"The two friends helped each other like in the other stories. Cunningham needed someone to listen to the songs he wrote, and Kenneth liked to listen."

"And Kenneth wanted to get out of the crowded barnyard, and Cunningham gave him a nice place to stay."

"You could tell that Cunningham really liked Kenneth because of how he acted when Kenneth was missing."

"When you're sad, sometimes you don't want to do anything. Cunningham just stayed in bed."

"I don't think Kenneth was being a good friend. He broke a promise, and he didn't seem to think how worried Cunningham would be. He just went off."

"But Cunningham was so glad to see him, he didn't yell at him and they stayed friends. But I think Cunningham should have said, 'Kenneth, how would *you* feel if I just went off and didn't tell you?' "

The children's responses to this story reflected their growing ability to identify the basic plot, to make inferences about feelings, and to go beyond the text with personal reactions to the interactions of the story characters.

The discussions were enriched by contributions from children who had discovered points of comparison with the stories they had read independently. For example, a discussion about *The Witch's Egg* by Madeleine Edmondson, read aloud in the ninth story session, included explanations of what happened in the story, why it happened, and how this story could be related to stories they had read independently:

> "At first Agatha [the witch] was really mean, and she didn't have any friends."

> "The only reason she decided to keep that egg was to show the birds that *she* could do a better job than *they* could!"

> "But then she really got to like the little bird—and she got happy and gentle. She really liked having a friend, and she was really different."

> "She was so sad when winter came and the bird had to fly south. She cried. I don't think witches are supposed to cry. You could tell she really loved that bird—just like Cunningham."

> "But that little bird really liked her, too, and so he came back to her . . . every summer."

> "It's like in *Spider Jane*. The spider was sad when her friend Burt had to go away. My friend Annie went away for two weeks, and I didn't have anyone to play with, and she sent me a postcard."

By the time the last book, *Timothy's Flower* by Jean Van Leeuwen, was read aloud, the children were ready to think about all the stories in the collection as a cohesive group bound by common themes. They identified these themes in the last group discussion:

> "Sometimes friends are really different like Duck and Bear . . . and that witch and the little bird . . ."

> "And Amos and Boris! And Spider Jane made friends with a fly! Spiders usually eat flies!"

> "I liked *Tawny and Dingo*. Those two [a sheep dog and a lamb] were really different, but they were such great friends!"

> "Sometimes the friends are more alike. In *Turtle and Snail* and *Fast Friends* . . . they're both about a turtle and snail who start out being friends because of their shells."

"And Timothy gets to be friends with that lady because they both like flowers."

"And all those friends liked to do things together and they helped each other."

"And they missed each other."

"And they liked to give presents to each other."

"And sometimes they got mad but they stayed friends and they tried to *understand* the other one."

In this excerpt, one sees the beginnings of an awareness of basic elements of developing and maintaining friendships as well as the significance of motives, feelings, and thoughts for social interactions.

Follow-up Activities: Creative Expression

While the children were listening to and reading the stories from the Friendship Focus Unit, they were also involved in a variety of group and independent projects which evolved naturally out of their reading experiences and which provided opportunities for creative expression.

For example, in the original discussion of *Amos and Boris,* the teacher called attention to the fact that the whale and the mouse could not remain together because of their different life needs. The question "Do any of you have a friend who lives far away?" was interjected to encourage the children to share personal experiences with separation from friends and the ways they managed to maintain these long-distance friendships. This discussion served as the stimulus for a long-term writing project in which the children wrote letters to pen pals, long-distance friends, or children in other classrooms. While practicing writing skills, the children gained experience in sharing themselves with another and, in turn, discovered what was interesting to and special about that person. Other projects associated with *Amos and Boris* involved the reconstruction of the plot or a favorite scene through drama, art, music, or dance. Several children chose to integrate their efforts: musicians created the sounds of the sea while dancers moved as waves surrounding the two children playing the parts of Amos and Boris. A mural committee painted a large seascape as background for detailed depictions of the main characters and the sequence of events in the story. Captions for each scene were worked into the waves to add to the total effect.

During the third story session, the children were asked to think about *Amos and Boris, The Checker Players,* and *Two Good Friends* and to decide what basic theme was common to all three tales. When they reached a consensus and formulated a theme statement, the teacher recorded it on a large chart. This was used as the starting point for a creative writing project. The children wrote original stories with the basic theme of friendship between two very different characters.

After listening to *What's the Matter with Carruthers?* the children made a list of ways to learn about the feelings, ideas, and interests of others. This formed the framework for a project in which each child had to discover the special interests, talents, favorite foods, and so forth of a particular person and to write a word portrait of that individual. One purpose of this assignment was to encourage the children to look outside themselves, to see another person with sharpened awareness and greater appreciation, and to begin to view the world through the eyes of another.

In another project, the children created a class book called "Helpful Hints for Being Friends." Each child contributed at least one page which included a "helpful hint" and an illustration. Here are a few examples of hints suggested by the children:

> Share your toys with a friend
>
> Read together
>
> Teach a friend how to tie his shoe
>
> Tell funny stories to make your friend laugh
>
> Ask a friend to come over and play
>
> Help your friend look for something that's lost
>
> Let your friend choose the game
>
> Make a picture for your friend

As an extension of this class project, several children created a series of vignettes to dramatize the hints in this book.

A final project for the Friendship Focus Unit involved the creation of original friendship stories based on a synthesis of the rich array of ideas, themes, and insights absorbed from group discussions, independent reading, and creative experiences associated with this unit. These stories were illustrated, bound into individual books with decorative cardboard covers, and added to the Friendship collection. In one of these imaginative stories, "The Elf Tale," a lonely, sad little elf is noticed by a happy little piece of cheese. "The little piece of cheese tried in every way to cheer up the little elf . . . but the little elf only turned his back." Eventually, the elf realizes that he has hurt the cheese's feelings and admits that he would like to play with the cheese. " 'Let's go play on the swing set,' said the little elf. 'OK,' said the little piece of cheese. And they made up." These original stories reflected the children's growing ability to create stories with well-developed plots and characters with feelings, motives, and intentions. In addition, the children's responses to the questions introduced during the story sessions demonstrated their ability to identify the basic plot of each story, to make inferences about the motives and feelings of the story characters, and to comprehend the social interactions in the stories.

References

Gottman, J. M., J. Gonso, and B. Rasmussen. "Social Interaction, Social Competence, and Friendship in Children." *Child Development* 46 (1975): 709–18.

Leonder, B. "Hatching Plots: Genesis of Storymaking." In *The Arts and Cognition,* edited by D. Perkins and B. Leonder. Baltimore: Johns Hopkins University Press, 1977.

Oden, S., and S. R. Asher. "Coaching Children in Social Skills for Friendship Making." *Child Development* 48 (1977): 495–506.

Stein, Nancy. "How Children Understand Stories: A Developmental Anaysis." University of Illinois Technical Report, No. 69. Champaign, Illinois: Center for the Study of Reading, March 1978.

Stein, Nancy, and C. G. Glenn. "An Analysis of Story Comprehension in Elementary School Children." In *New Directions in Discourse Processing,* vol. 2, edited by R. O. Freedle. Norwood, New Jersey: Ablex, 1979.

———. "An Analysis of Story Comprehension in Elementary School Children." Unpublished manuscript, Washington University, 1975.

Stein, N., and S. Goldman. "Children's Knowledge about Social Situations: From Causes to Consequences." In *The Development of Children's Friendships,* edited by S. R. Asher and J. M. Gottman. New York: Cambridge University Press, 1981.

13 Heroes and Heroines: A Focus Unit for Grades One and Two

The fact that a single individual can make a significant difference in the lives of others is a message inherent in a great many narratives written for children as well as adults. The Heroes and Heroines Focus Unit was structured around stories which transmit this message in diverse ways. These stories portray heroes and heroines who, in spite of limitations in size, age, strength, and experience or in spite of outward appearance, perform deeds which profoundly affect the lives of those around them. The stories in this Focus Unit collection were selected on the basis of similarities in theme, plot patterns, and character types; the children were encouraged to discover these literary connections.

Objectives

1. To focus attention on basic literary elements of plot, setting, character, theme, and style.
2. To set the stage for the discovery of recurring patterns which connect diverse stories.
3. To generate synthesis by formulating theme statements which could apply to all of the stories in this collection.
4. To focus attention on the qualities and inner resources of the hero and heroine characters in these stories and to explore the concept of heroism in a broader sense.
5. To provide a context for creative writing.
6. To provide a context for independent reading.
7. To instill in these young children a sense of their own potential to make a difference in the lives of others.

Bibliography for the Hero and Heroine Focus Unit

I. Group Story Sessions

Alan, Sandy. **The Plaid Peacock.** New York: Pantheon Books, 1965.

158

A peacock with a green plaid tail is teased by the other peafowl of the flock. He finds a friendly reception at the compound of Scottish Fusiliers when they discover that the plaid of his tail is the same as that of the regiment. One night the peacock risks his life to fly through a raging forest fire to warn the sleeping soldiers of the danger which threatens them. Thus, he is able to repay their kindness and to earn the respect of the flock as well.

Brett, Jan. **Fritz and the Beautiful Horses.** Boston: Houghton Mifflin, 1981.

Fritz is excluded from a group of beautiful horses who live inside a walled city. Although he is not beautiful, Fritz is a gentle, kind, and dependable pony. The citizens of the walled city learn to appreciate Fritz's special qualities when he rescues the children of the city. The lovely detailed illustrations have an old-world charm and invite a closer look.

Coombs, Patricia. **Molly Mullett.** New York: Lothrop, Lee and Shepard Books, 1975.

Molly, the delightful heroine of this modern fairy tale, triumphs over a wicked ogre who has terrorized the kingdom. Molly's father and even the king himself think of her as a "measly girl," and they are surprised and amazed when Molly is able to accomplish what even the king's bravest knights consider an impossible task.

Elkin, Benjamin, reteller. **The Wisest Man in the World: A Legend of Ancient Israel.** New York: Parents' Magazine Press, 1968.

When a bee enters the palace of the great King Solomon, the mighty monarch protects the tiny creature from his angry servants and allows the bee to fly away unharmed. The bee's promise to serve the king in return for this kindness is fulfilled one day during a visit from the Queen of Sheba. The proud and jealous queen has come to Solomon's court to make a fool of him before his own people. It is the bee who finally "saves the day" and helps the king in his moment of need. This legend can also be found in *Once upon a Time* by Rose Dobbs (New York: Random House, 1958), *Stories of King Solomon* by L. B. Freehof (Philadelphia: Jewish Publication Society of America, 1955), and *Favorite Stories Old and New* by S. M. Gruenberg (New York: Doubleday, 1955).

Francis, Frank. **Timimoto's Great Adventure.** New York: Holiday House, 1969.

Based on a traditional Japanese tale, this is the story of four-inch-tall Timimoto and his quest for adventure. He sails away from home in a rice bowl boat, with chopsticks for oars and a needle for his sword. After a long journey and a courageous battle with a huge frog, Timimoto finally arrives at the opposite shore. When he reaches the nearest town, he learns that a great ogre has been menacing the townspeople at night. Brave Timimoto manages to get rid of the dreaded ogre so the people can once again live in peace.

Geisel, Theodor Seuss (Dr. Seuss). **The King's Stilts.** New York: Random House, 1939.

King Birtram of the Kingdom of Binn loved to race around on his red stilts after a long day of work. Lord Droon's evil plan to deprive the king of his stilts and his favorite form of recreation sets into motion a sequence of events which almost leads to disaster. Fortunately, the king's loyal page, Eric, saves the day.

Green, Norma, reteller. **The Hole in the Dike.** New York: Thomas Y. Crowell, 1974.

First told by Mary Mapes Dodge over a hundred years ago, this is the story of Peter, the little Dutch boy who saved Holland from a flood when he discovered a tiny leak in the dike. This legend can also be found in *Hans Brinker or the Silver Skates* by M. M. Dodge (New York: Charles Scribner's Sons, 1915), *Favorite Stories Old and New* by S. M. Gruenberg (New York: Doubleday, 1955), *Tell It Again: Great Tales from around the World* by Margaret Hodges (New York: Dial Press, 1963), and *The World's Great Stories: Fifty-Five Legends That Live Forever* by Louis Untermeyer (New York: J. B. Lippincott, 1964).

La Fontaine, Jean de. **The Lion and the Rat.** New York: Franklin Watts, 1963.

This is a beautifully illustrated retelling of the old fable about the tiny rat who repays the kindness of the lion, Lord of the Jungle. This story is also found in *The Fables of Aesop,* retold by Joseph Jacobs (New York: Macmillan, 1964).

Van Woerkom, Dorothy. **Becky and the Bear.** New York: G. P. Putnam's Sons, 1975.

This story, based on an actual experience, takes place in colonial Maine after a long, hard winter. Becky's father and brother have gone hunting, and she is left home alone to stir the pudding and sand the floor. When a hungry bear appears at the door of the cabin and threatens the pigs in the barn, Becky thinks quickly and devises a clever plan to save the pigs and herself and to catch the bear.

Yolen, Jane. **The Emperor and the Kite.** Cleveland: World, 1967.

> Based on an ancient Chinese legend, this is the story of how the emperor's youngest daughter manages to help her father escape from a high tower where he has been imprisoned by three evil men.

II. Independent Reading

Alexander, Lloyd. **The King's Fountain.** New York: E. P. Dutton, 1971.

Ardizzone, Edward. **Tim to the Lighthouse.** New York: Henry Z. Walck, 1968.

Coville, Bruce, and Katherine Coville. **The Foolish Giant.** Philadelphia: J. B. Lippincott, 1978. (For beginning readers)

Daugherty, James. **Andy and the Lion.** New York: Viking Press, 1938.

Gauch, Patricia. **Aaron and the Green Mountain Boys.** New York: Coward, McCann and Geoghegan, 1972. (For beginning readers)

Grimm Brothers. **Tom Thumb.** New York: Atheneum, 1973.

Hodges, Margaret. **The Fire Bringer: A Paiute Indian Legend.** Boston: Little, Brown, 1972.

————. **The Wave.** Boston: Houghton Mifflin, 1964.

Lionni, Leo. **Swimmy.** New York: Pantheon Books, 1963.

Longstreth, Joseph. **Little Big Feather.** New York: Abelard-Schuman, 1956.

Moeri, Louise. **How the Rabbit Stole the Moon.** Boston: Houghton Mifflin, 1977.

Morrow, Barbara, reteller. **Well Done.** New York: Holt, Rinehart and Winston, 1974.

Peet, Bill. **The Ant and the Elephant.** Boston: Houghton Mifflin, 1972.

Prelutsky, Jack. **The Terrible Tiger.** New York: Macmillan, 1970.

Preston, Edna. **Too Little.** New York: Viking Press, 1969.

Rose, Anne. **Spider in the Sky.** New York: Harper and Row, 1978.

Steig, William. **Amos and Boris.** New York: Farrar, Straus and Giroux, 1971.

Wildsmith, Brian. **Little Wood Duck.** New York: Franklin Watts, 1973.

Group Story Sessions

First Session

The introductory session opened with a discussion of the terms *hero* and *heroine*. The children were asked to define these words and to offer relevant comments, descriptions, and examples. Initially, the children listed various contemporary heroes and heroines from popular television programs, movies, and comics. Then the dialogue moved in the direction of definition:

"A hero is strong and fights bad guys."

"A hero is like a superfriend who protects the people."

"The hero is the one who saves people from a fire or flood or something."

"A hero does good deeds."

"The hero is the one who saves the day!"

After all the children had an opportunity to contribute to this brainstorming process, consensus was reached regarding the distinguishing characteristics of the hero-figure, and these characteristics were recorded as a definition on a large chart: "A hero or heroine is someone who is very strong and brave and has superpowers and helps people. The hero saves the day."

Then, *The Lion and the Rat,* a fable by Jean de La Fontaine, was read aloud and discussed briefly. The questions used to generate the discussion were: "Is there a hero in this story? If so, who is it?" and "Why would this character be called a hero?" The children easily identified the tiny rat as the hero who managed to rescue the huge lion from a trap even when the other great beasts of the jungle felt that this was an impossible task.

Second Session

Before reading *The Hole in the Dike* by Norma Green, the teacher asked the children to look for clues in the illustrations which would suggest the setting for this story. As soon as the children recognized that this was a story about Holland, they were ready to discuss the word *dike* found in the title. Several of the children drew from their own knowledge to provide pertinent information about the important role of the dikes in Holland. This introductory discussion served to set the stage for story comprehension and, in particular, to focus attention on the critical contribution of the setting to the total meaning of the story. After the story was read aloud, the children again were asked to identify the hero. The next question, "Compare the rat in *The Lion and the Rat* to Peter in *The Hole in the Dike,*" elicited the following observations:

"The rat was small and so was Peter."

"The rat saved the lion, and Peter saved his town."

"They were both small, so everyone else was surprised about what they did."

"They both did something that was hard to do—and no one *told* them to."

The discussion changed course when one child introduced the perennial question, "Is it true?" This, of course, was the perfect opening for a brief explanation of the term *legend* and for providing the background to this particular legend of the Dutch boy "who symbolizes the perpetual struggle of Holland against the water," according to a statue in the little town of Spaarndam.

Third Session

Another legend, *The Wisest Man in the World* by Benjamin Elkin, was read aloud next. This legend of ancient Israel involves King Solomon and the Queen of Sheba. The group session again began with a discussion of the setting of the legend and included a discussion about King Solomon. Again, some of the children were able to draw from their own literary experience to offer relevant information about this great king. After the children had an opportunity to listen to the story and to look carefully at the detailed illustrations found in this particular edition, the following questions stimulated a comparative analysis of this legend and the fable *The Lion and the Rat:*

> Why did the king smile when the little bee offered to serve him in return for his freedom?
>
> In what way does this incident remind you of *The Lion and the Rat?*
>
> What did the lion and the king learn at the end of each story?
>
> How else is this story similar to *The Lion and the Rat?*

The children's comments demonstrated their grasp of the connections between these two tales in terms of characterization, plot pattern, and theme:

> "The lion is the king of the jungle, so he's really like King Solomon, and the bee and the rat are both so small—and not so important."
>
> "The lion and the king were both so big and proud, they thought it was funny when those little tiny creatures said they would help *them* some day."
>
> "But they both learned that even little creatures could do big things—like helping other people."

"In both stories the little creatures were freed by the other one [the lion and the king] and then later, when the other one was in trouble, the little creature helped him!"

"The lion and the king both got paid back for their kindness. It's the same kind of story!"

"I know another story sort of like that! It's about a whale that saves a mouse and then the mouse says, 'I'll do you a favor some day.' So the whale just laughs—but the little mouse really does!" [*Amos and Boris* by William Steig].

Just as this third session was drawing to a close, one child said, "But aren't you going to ask us who the hero is?" The others immediately responded, with obvious delight, "It's the bee!" At all subsequent sessions, this question and appropriate responses came from the children as soon as each story was completed. In addition, their spontaneous comments indicated that they had begun to internalize other key questions designed to generate comparisons among stories and to focus attention on basic narrative elements.

Fourth Session

The next story presented was *Timimoto's Great Adventure* by Frank Francis, a traditional Japanese tale. As soon as the children entered the story circle, they asked to see the illustrations so they could find clues about the setting of the story. Then, after listening to the tale of the four-inch-tall Timimoto who confronted an enormous ogre, the children spontaneously named Timimoto as the brave hero and then went on to compare this tale with those read previously:

"He saved the town from the mean ogre like when that Holland boy saved the town from a flood."

"Timimoto was really little and so was the rat and the bee—and Peter was just a little kid."

When asked to compare the conclusions of *Timimoto's Great Adventure* and *The Hole in the Dike,* one child observed:

"They didn't do those things just to get a reward or to get famous. Like Timimoto wouldn't even stay for the big party they wanted to give him. He just went back home! And Peter wasn't interested in being a big hero either."

In addition to the content, the children were also encouraged to focus on the language used to develop this tale. For example, they discussed the meaning of the phrase "he had the heart of a lion" and the author's choice of the word *lance* in reference to the chopstick Timimoto used to fight off a huge frog. One child, whose fund of knowledge was an especially rich one, explained, "A lance is what knights used in the olden days, so the author used that word to show that Timimoto is like a brave knight fighting a dragon." This led to a review of the phrases used by the author to highlight Timimoto's perception of the world around him:

" . . . a worm to him was the size of a snake."

". . . Timimoto found himself in quiet water where giant plants spread their leaves across the surface like islands."

"There—was a giant frog."

". . . the legs of the people were so large that they seemed like tree trunks."

Fifth Session

A modern story by Dr. Seuss (Theodor Seuss Geisel), *The King's Stilts*, was read during the fifth session. The children easily identified Eric, the king's page, as the hero of the story because he saved the kingdom. Since the plot of this story involves a rather complex chain of events, the first two questions were: "Explain what happened after Lord Droon stole the king's stilts" and "How did this deed lead to the problem with the dike trees?" Once the logical sequence of events was clarified, the children were asked, "Where do you think Dr. Seuss might have gotten the basic idea for this story?"

"He must have read *The Hole in the Dike.*"

"But he didn't really copy it. I mean his story is really different and it's all make-believe."

"But *The Hole in the Dike* wasn't true either, so it's just make-believe."

"Yeah, but it's not the *same*. It could have happened. And it was about regular people, but Dr. Seuss's story is about cartoon people."

"And there really is a Holland, but that kingdom in *The King's Stilts* is make-believe. Dr. Seuss probably read that legend and then made up his own story that was sort of like it and also *not* like it."

The next questions had the children focus on the character of Lord Droon:

What words would you use to describe him?

How is he the opposite of Eric?

In what way is he really important for the story?

After a discussion generated by these questions, the teacher introduced the word *villain*. To reinforce its meaning, the children were asked to think of villain-characters in other stories they had heard or read. Again, villains from popular television programs and movies were named along with such literary villains as the ogre in *Timimoto's Great Adventure,* the queen in *The Wisest Man in the World,* and the wolf in *The Three Little Pigs.* Attention was placed on the villain-character at this point in the dialogue to prepare for a more careful look at the role of the antagonist in a narrative and the interaction between antagonist and protagonist.

Sixth Session

The session began with the reading of another modern tale, *The Plaid Peacock* by Sandy Alan. After the children identified the plaid peacock as the hero, they were asked to explain the reasons for their choice. Their responses reflected their recognition of some important qualities associated with heroism:

> "He felt sorry for the soldiers more than himself so he went back to warn them even though he had to fly over that forest fire."

> "The fire hurt him, but he still kept going so he could warn them about the fire."

> "A hero thinks about *other* people and tries to help even when it's really hard or dangerous."

> "Like if someone dives in the water to save someone who's drowning even though it's really dangerous."

When asked to compare this story with those read in previous sessions, the children had little difficulty making connections:

> "In *The King's Stilts,* Eric saved the whole town from a flood, and the peacock saved the whole compound of soldiers from a fire."

> "And in *The Hole in the Dike,* Peter saved Holland."

> "It's also like *The Lion and the Rat* and that one about King Solomon and the bee because they all returned a favor. The soldiers were kind to the plaid peacock, and he wanted to do something nice for them sometime. And he really did!"

The next question, "Is there a villain in this story?" was more challenging. At first, most of the children decided that there was no villain. Then one child ventured this comment: "There weren't any really bad people like the ogre or Lord Droon. But still those other peacocks who teased the plaid peacock weren't being so nice! I mean they didn't make him feel so great!" At this point the teacher asked, "How would the story have been different if the rest of the flock had been kind to the plaid peacock and said nice things about his plaid tail?" This seemed to help them move toward an understanding of the role of antagonists in narratives:

> "He would be happy to stay home with his flock instead of going off by himself. So he probably wouldn't have found the compound."

> "They [the other peafowl] make him feel bad so that's why he left and found the soldiers and got to be friends."

> "And if they didn't get to be friends, he would never have gone to save them . . ."

> "So he wouldn't get to be a hero!"

> "Then the story would be all different."

> "I guess if they were nice to him, he wouldn't have a problem—and it would be kind of a boring story."

The Plaid Peacock has a number of words which were not part of the children's oral vocabularies. Although some of these words needed brief clarification during the oral presentation to ensure comprehension of the story, a more detailed study of word meanings was carried out as part of a language activity following this story session. Working in pairs, the children searched the text for "new and interesting words" which they recorded and defined, consulting dictionaries when necessary. After sharing their definitions in a subsequent group meeting, all the words were recorded on a wall chart. Each child selected one of these words to use in a sentence and to illustrate. The completed pages of "words-in-context" were compiled into a class book called "The Plaid Book of Words." Of course, the cover was decorated with a bright green plaid pattern.

Seventh Session

When the children heard *The Emperor and the Kite* by Jane Yolen, they immediately identified the tiny princess as the heroine (one child exclaimed, "Finally, we have a *heroine!*") and the men who kidnapped the emperor as the villains. Again, they were asked to think of the special qualities of this heroine and then to consider how the story would be different if there were no villains in it. The children recognized the courage, loyalty, and patience of the tiny princess. They were impressed that she did so much to help her father in spite of his neglect of her. They also recognized the important role of the villains:

"If those bad men never came, nothing would've changed!"

"If that emperor wasn't put in the tower, he would never find out how loyal his little daughter was and that she could be smart enough to rescue him!"

"When the villains come, the real action begins!"

The final questions for this session, "How did the emperor change at the end of this story?" and "What did he learn from his experience?" led the children to formulate theme statements which they were able to apply to other stories in this collection:

"The emperor started to pay attention to his tiniest daughter."

"He learned that even though she was tiny, she was more helpful than her big sisters and brothers."

"He learned to *respect* her because he saw how loyal she was."

"And he changed the way he ruled as emperor. After that he was very careful not to *neglect* people—even if they're little."

"He learned that even if you're small, you can do really good things."

"That's what *all* these stories are about! They're about little animals or people or kids who do big things."

"It just proves that little creatures can do great things."

This last statement was recorded on the chart, and the children were asked to consider it in relation to the stories read so far in the group sessions and to their own lives. After deciding that this could be a "hidden message" in each of these stories, the children eagerly shared their own experiences with inadequate recognition due to limitations of size and age. Gradually, they suggested attributes that others *should* focus their attention on, such as particular skills and inner strengths. One child expanded on the basic idea with this insightful comment:

"My aunt is very fat, and my cousins make fun of her, but they don't know she's really nice! It's like that little plaid peacock who went and saved the soldiers all by himself when none of the grown-ups did. But before, everyone teased him because he looked different, so they didn't know he was so nice and brave and everything."

Eighth Session

In response to the nature of the discussion stimulated by this comment, *Fritz and the Beautiful Horses* by Jan Brett was selected for the next story session because it highlighted the difference between "inside beauty" and "outside beauty." The children were able to translate their insights from the previous discussion into responses to this brief story about a pony who experiences rejection because of his appearance:

> "Even though Fritz didn't look like those beautiful horses, he was beautiful *inside* because he's gentle and dependable and kind and a hard worker."

> "You'd expect those other horses to be heroes because they look so great, but nobody expected Fritz to be a hero because he was funny looking."

Ninth and Tenth Sessions

The stories shared in the two final sessions were both about heroines. *Becky and the Bear* by Dorothy Van Woerkom describes the actual experience of an eight-year-old girl in colonial Maine, while *Molly Mullett* by Patricia Coombs is a modern fairy tale about a girl who rids the kingdom of a terrifying ogre. By this time, the children had begun to see how such factors as size, age, appearance, and sex can affect the way individuals are viewed by others, but that how people view themselves is far more important:

> "You shouldn't worry if people don't think you can do stuff because a lot of times you can!"

> "Like when Molly Mullett got that ogre even though her dad and the king said she was just a silly girl and couldn't do anything!"

> "Becky had the same problem. I bet her dad wouldn't let her go hunting with him just because she was a girl."

> "That's right! It wasn't her age because she said her brother got to use a gun when he was even younger!"

> "But in the end, she was the one who caught the bear! I liked that part."

> "I bet her dad will take her seriously now because she *proved* she was smart and brave."

> "It's the same as the story about the emperor and his tiny daughter!"

> "And Molly Mullett showed that king a thing or two!"

> "I think that in all the stories the characters showed that they could be *helpful* even if they're small or something. It seems like anyone can help other people. You don't have to be Superman!"

At this point, the children were asked to reconsider the definition of the words *hero* and *heroine* which had been recorded during the first story session. After a brief review of the protagonists in each of the stories read aloud, the children concluded that their original statements did not adequately define these terms. They suggested additions and revisions which were apparently influenced by insights they had gained during the discussions generated in the story sessions:

"A hero doesn't have to be big and strong or have superpowers. A hero can be an ordinary kid!"

"A hero is brave and uses his head!"

"And he's willing to do something that's dangerous or scary to help someone else."

"A hero isn't selfish."

"People who like to go off and have adventures a lot of times become heroes because they find people in trouble. Like if Timimoto just stayed home, he never would have found out about that ogre!"

"Molly Mullett was like that. She liked to have adventures and do sort of dangerous things. But she sure was brave."

"But I think *anyone* can be a hero or heroine—if you're really willing to help someone who needs you."

"I guess there are all different kinds of heroes. Like there's Superman-heroes and there's the adventure-heroes, and then there are the sort of ordinary heroes who're just regular people who do something brave and important to help other people!"

Creative Writing

The review of the qualities and characteristics of heroes and heroines during the final story session prepared the class for a creative writing project involving the production of original hero tales. First, each child drew a picture of the members of his or her own family (including pets), who would serve as the characters in the story. Next, one character was chosen to be the hero or heroine of the story. The third step involved building the plot: the child decided what problem would generate the conflict in the story and how the hero or heroine would manage to "save the day."

The children's stories reflected their grasp of the literary concepts explored in the story sessions. In particular, the heroes and heroines were developed in accordance with the children's concluding remarks and insights about heroes, heroines, and heroism. A few children had actually been involved in situations requiring heroic actions, and they built their stories around eyewitness accounts of these events. Most of the stories emerged from the children's imaginations and took shape as realistic narratives, fantasies, or humorous tales. The majority of the children chose themselves to be the hero or heroine in their stories. For them, the creative process proved to be especially pleasing as it afforded them opportunities to perform brave and daring deeds within the protective walls of the imagination. Eventually, each of these hero tales was illustrated, bound, read aloud during a group story session, and placed on display in the classroom along with the books selected for this Focus Unit.

Drama

After listening to the hero tales written by their classmates, the children identified several stories which they thought would be especially suitable for dramatization—stories with a great deal of action and interesting dialogue. Small drama groups were organized to present these stories. The children in one group chose to interpret their story through mime; in another group, the children created finger puppets to dramatize their story; while a third group planned a rather formal production, with a script, costumes, and props. One story was translated into a dance-drama, and another was recreated as a radio show with very effective sound effects. These productions evolved out of the cooperative efforts of children working together to solve problems as they experimented with various dramatic forms. In the process, they experienced the pleasures of creating and sharing, important features of dramatic activity in the classroom.

Independent Reading

Throughout the Hero and Heroine Focus Unit, the children were encouraged to select books from this collection for independent reading. A large chart entitled "Heroes and Heroines" was mounted on the wall behind the books. After reading a book, each child recorded the title and the name of the hero or heroine. The list grew as the children read the books in the classroom collection and other books which they had discovered on their own. Long after the Focus Unit had drawn to a close, the chart of hero-characters continued to serve as a stimulus for further independent reading and for discussion about heroes and heroines in both the story world and the real world. In their search for new hero-characters, many of the children moved into new areas of literary experience and made important discoveries about reading as an enjoyable activity.

14 Survival Tales: A Focus Unit for Grades Five and Six

In an attempt to identify the reasons behind the literary choices of seven- to twelve-year-old children, Norma Schlager (1978) studied the relationship between the reading preferences of children in middle childhood and the developmental characteristics of this age group as identified by Erik Erikson and Jean Piaget. Erikson used the term *reality orientation* to describe a seven- to twelve-year-old child's "keen desire to handle reality situations independently and to assess his or her own ability to cope and succeed in reality situations" (Schlager, p. 138). Other characteristics of this developmental period include the ability to plan logically and a growing "sense of industry and task orientation." That is, children are anxious to use their new skills and capacity for sustained involvement to master reality instead of being mastered by it. This period of middle childhood is also associated with a shift from egocentricity toward sociocenteredness.

In her study of children's reading preferences, Schlager found that among seven- to twelve-year-olds, the most popular books had main characters who demonstrated the developmental characteristics of this age group. "The research strongly supports the position that books which succeed are those that contain an identifiable stage of development, regardless of the literary quality so appropriately desired by the adult" (p. 141). Schlager found that readers in this age group are especially interested in main characters who are pitted against a reality in which they must struggle for survival without adult help.

In general, survival tales appeal to young readers in this age group because they identify with the main characters and appreciate their struggle to cope with conflict situations independent of adult help and authority. Heroes and heroines in the survival tales selected for this Focus Unit display the developmental characteristics of middle childhood described by Piaget and Erikson. The young reader can observe and learn from these characters as they grow toward independence, draw from inner resources, and gain insights about themselves and others in their struggle to survive, to overcome conflicts, and to understand reality.

172

Objectives

1. To introduce survival tales as a literary genre to children in grades five and six and to acquaint them with some of the remarkable and memorable individuals portrayed in these stories.
2. To expand reading interests and to stimulate independent reading.
3. To study narrative structure and character development in order to build comprehension and composing skills.
4. To provide a context for creative writing experiences in which skills of literary analysis are used as a natural resource in the process of producing narrative.

Bibliography for the Survival Tales Focus Unit

I. Group Story Sessions

Holman, Felice. **Slake's Limbo.** New York: Charles Scribner's Sons, 1974.

> Aremis Slake, a teenage misfit who has known only poverty, cruelty, and degradation, finds refuge in a cavelike room hidden in New York City's subway system. He makes this underground space his home for 121 days and survives by becoming an expert scavenger. When Aremis finally emerges from his hiding place, he is no longer the beaten creature who escaped into it. He has gained the self-confidence and self-respect to begin to take control of his life. He has discovered that not all people have evil intentions and that there *are* individuals who can be trusted.

Sperry, Armstrong. **Call It Courage.** New York: Macmillan, 1940. (A Newbery Medal Book)

> This is the legend of Mafatu, the son of the great chief of Hikueru, an island in the South Seas. Mafatu is called a coward because he is afraid of the sea, which took his mother when he was an infant. He knows that he must conquer his fear if he is to be accepted by his people, who worship courage. He sails to a distant island where he lives in solitude and learns about courage.

II. Independent Reading

Aaron, Chester. **An American Ghost.** New York: Harcourt Brace Jovanovich, 1973.

A frontier boy is trapped in a house with a mountain lion during a flood.

Aurembou, Renee. **Snowbound.** New York: Abelard-Schuman, 1965.

Four children are alone in their house when a severe blizzard isolates them from outside help.

Bond, Nancy. **The Voyage Begun.** New York: Atheneum, 1982.

This is a story of survival in the not-so-distant future when the energy supply is almost depleted.

Bradbury, Bianca. **Two on an Island.** Boston: Houghton Mifflin, 1965.

A brother and sister manage to survive for three days alone on an island.

Burnford, Sheila. **The Incredible Journey.** Boston: Little, Brown, 1961.

Three animals travel through the Canadian wilderness.

Byars, Betsy. **Trouble River.** New York: Viking Press, 1969.

This is a story of frontier survival and a daring escape from Indians.

Christopher, John. **The City of Gold and Lead.** New York: Macmillan, 1967. (Book II of a science fiction trilogy)

In a future time resembling medieval history, three boys become servants to the Masters to discover their secrets.

———. **The Pool of Fire.** New York: Macmillan, 1968. (Book III of a science fiction trilogy)

Three boys try to overcome the Tripods in hopes of attaining world peace.

———. **The White Mountains.** New York: Macmillan, 1967. (Book I of a science fiction trilogy)

Three boys attempt to escape from the Tripods, a machinelike race.

Cleaver, Vera, and Bill Cleaver. **Where the Lilies Bloom.** Philadelphia: J. B. Lippincott, 1969.

A fourteen-year-old girl attempts to raise her orphaned brothers and sisters.

Collier, James, and Christopher Collier. **The Bloody Country.** New York: Four Winds Press, 1976.

A family moves from Connecticut to Pennsylvania in the mid-1700s and struggles to build a home and live off the land. The story is based on an actual episode in early American history.

———. **Jump Ship to Freedom.** New York: Delacorte Press, 1981.

A fourteen-year-old slave struggles to gain freedom for himself and his mother from their Connecticut master in the mid-1700s.

Defoe, Daniel. **Robinson Crusoe.** New York: Charles Scribner's Sons, 1920.

The famous tale of shipwreck and survival on a desert island.

Degen, T. **Transport 7-41-R.** New York: Viking Press, 1974.

A thirteen-year-old German girl helps an old man conceal his wife's death from other evacuees aboard their train in 1946 so that he may fulfill his promise to bury her in Cologne.

Eckert, Allan. **Incident at Hawk's Hill.** Boston: Little, Brown, 1971.

A shy six-year-old boy, lost in the Canadian wilderness, is protected and sheltered by a female badger.

Engebrecht, P. A. **Under the Haystack.** Nashville: Thomas Nelson, 1973.

Abandoned by their parents, three sisters manage to stay together and run the family farm without adult help.

Farley, Walter. **The Black Stallion Legend.** New York: Random House, 1983.

Alex Ramsey, with his Black Stallion, struggles to survive a deep personal tragedy and a devastating natural disaster.

Fife, Dale. **Destination Unknown.** New York: E. P. Dutton, 1981.

A twelve-year-old boy is separated from his parents and stows away on a small Norwegian fishing boat during World War II.

Forman, James. **The Survivor.** New York: Farrar, Straus and Giroux, 1976.

In this story of a Jewish family from the Netherlands during the period of 1939–1945, only one family member survives the horror of the Nazi Holocaust.

George, Jean. **Julie of the Wolves.** New York: Harper and Row, 1972.

A thirteen-year-old Eskimo girl manages to survive alone on the North Slope of Alaska with the help of a pack of Arctic wolves who come to accept her as she learns to understand them and to love them as brothers.

———. **My Side of the Mountain.** New York: E. P. Dutton, 1959.

This is a first-person account of a city boy's self-imposed, year-long exile in the wilderness of the Catskill Mountains, where he masters the techniques of survival and learns to live off the land.

Hamilton, Virginia. **The Planet of Junior Brown.** New York: Macmillan, 1971.

Two black eighth-grade boys become friends and find the strength and resources for survival in an underground subculture which celebrates individual fulfillment and humane values.

Hautzig, Esther. **The Endless Steppe: Growing Up in Siberia.** New York: Thomas Y. Crowell, 1968.

This is an autobiographical account of five years of forced labor in Siberia during World War II.

Houston, James. **Tikta' Liktak: An Eskimo Legend.** New York: Harcourt, Brace and World, 1965.

A compelling tale of human strength and adaptability about Tikta' Liktak, who survives a winter alone on an ice floe.

Houston, Jeanne Wakatsuki, and James D. Houston. **Farewell to Manzanar.** Boston: Houghton Mifflin, 1973.

In this autobiographical account, a seven-year-old girl describes her life at the Manzanar internment camp, where she and her family were imprisoned along with 10,000 other Japanese Americans during World War II.

Jensen, Niels. **Days of Courage: A Medieval Adventure.** New York: Harcourt Brace Jovanovich, 1973.

The lone survivor in a Danish village during the great plague of medieval Europe attempts to rebuild his life.

Jones, Penelope. **Holding Together.** Scarsdale, New York: Bradbury Press, 1981.

A family struggles toward emotional survival after the death of the mother.

Karl, Jean. **Beloved Benjamin Is Waiting.** New York: E. P. Dutton, 1978.

A neglected girl survives alone in an abandoned house in a tale which blends contemporary realism and fantasy.

Kerr, Judith. **When Hitler Stole Pink Rabbit.** New York: Coward, McCann and Geoghegan, 1972.

In a story based on the author's own childhood experiences, Anna escapes from Germany in 1933 and struggles to learn the skills necessary to survive as a refugee. The story of Anna is continued in *The Other Way Round* (1975) and *A Small Person Far Away* (1978).

Konigsburg, E. L. **From the Mixed-up Files of Mrs. Basil E. Frankweiler.** New York: Atheneum, 1967.

A brother and sister hide and survive in the Metropolitan Museum of Art in New York City after running away from home.

Mazer, Harry. **Snowbound: A Story of Raw Survival.** New York: Delacorte Press, 1973.

Two teenagers are stranded for ten days in a desolate area of New York state in the midst of a severe snowstorm.

Moeri, Louise. **Save Queen of Sheba.** New York: E. P. Dutton, 1981.

A twelve-year-old boy and his little sister are the only survivors of a Sioux attack, and they must travel alone across the Oregon wilderness in search of other settlers.

Nostlinger, Christine. **Fly Away Home.** New York: Franklin Watts, 1975.

In this first-person account based on the author's experiences, a young girl must adapt to life in Vienna at the end of World War II and during the Soviet occupation.

O'Brien, Robert. **Z for Zachariah.** New York: Atheneum, 1975.

A science fiction tale of a fourteen-year-old girl who survives an atomic disaster and attempts to start her life anew.

O'Dell, Scott. **Island of the Blue Dolphins.** Boston: Houghton Mifflin, 1960.

A tale of courage and self-reliance based on the true experience of a young Indian girl who survives alone for eighteen years on an island far off the coast of California.

————. **Sarah Bishop.** Boston: Houghton Mifflin, 1980.

In this fictionalized biography, a young girl caught in the violence of the American Revolution escapes to the wilderness of northern Westchester County.

————. **Sing Down the Moon.** Boston: Houghton Mifflin, 1970.

A fourteen-year-old Navaho girl tells how Spanish slavers capture her and evict her tribe from its homeland in Arizona.

Orgel, Doris. **The Devil in Vienna.** New York: Dial Press, 1978.

In Vienna in 1938, a Jewish girl and the daughter of a Nazi officer are split apart by the Nazi reign of terror, but their friendship survives.

Phipson, Joan. **The Cats.** New York: Atheneum, 1976.

Two kidnapped brothers are trapped with their abductors in a wilderness hideout during a flood.

Reiss, Johanna. **The Upstairs Room.** New York: Thomas Y. Crowell, 1972.

In this first-person account of the author's experiences as a young girl in Holland during World War II, two young girls hide from the Germans in an upstairs room of a remote farmhouse.

Richter, Hans. **Friedrich.** New York: Holt, Rinehart and Winston, 1961.

Two boys, one Jewish and one a gentile, develop a friendship in Nazi Germany at a time when any relationship with a Jew represents a profound risk. The stark realism of this first-person account is powerful, as is the tragic ending.

Roy, Ron. **Avalanche!** New York: E. P. Dutton, 1981.

Two brothers are buried in an avalanche while skiing in Aspen, Colorado.

Sachs, Marilyn. **The Bears' House.** New York: Doubleday, 1971.

A nine-year-old neglected child, trying to manage without parents, creates a fantasy world which allows her to escape from responsibilities too great for her to assume.

———. **A Pocket Full of Seeds.** New York: Doubleday, 1973.

A Jewish girl whose family is taken away by the Nazis struggles to survive during the Nazi occupation of France. The story opens with a poem by Edna St. Vincent Millay describing a man who survives a flood and "makes for shore, with twisted face and pocket full of seeds."

Siegal, Aranka. **Upon the Head of the Goat: A Childhood in Hungary, 1939–1944.** New York: Farrar, Straus and Giroux, 1981.

A survivor of the Holocaust describes her childhood in Hungary during World War II.

Serraillier, Ian. **The Silver Sword.** New York: S. G. Philips, 1959.

Four children, traveling alone from Warsaw to Switzerland during World War II, must survive the chaotic upheaval and horror of this period.

Sleater, William. **House of Stairs.** New York: E. P. Dutton, 1974.

Five teenagers of the twenty-first century are subjected to mind-control experiments in a totalitarian world.

Southall, Ivan. **Ash Road.** New York: Greenwillow Books, 1965.

A group of children are left on their own to confront a raging Australian bush fire.

———. **Hill's End.** New York: Macmillan, 1962.

Seven children, cut off from adult help in an isolated Australian mining town, struggle to cope with the destruction caused by a natural disaster.

———. **To the Wild Sky.** New York: St. Martin's Press, 1967.

A group of children survive a plane crash on a barren Australian island.

Speare, Elizabeth. **The Sign of the Beaver.** Boston: Houghton Mifflin, 1983.

Thirteen-year-old Matt is left alone in the wilderness to guard his family's new cabin while his father travels back to Quincy to get his mother and sister. This survival tale reveals the relationship between white settlers and Indians in the 1700s.

Steig, William. **Abel's Island.** New York: Farrar, Straus and Giroux, 1976.

A flood separates Abel and Amanda, a loving mouse couple. In this charming animal fantasy, Abel finds himself stranded for months on an uninhabited island where he faces the daily challenges of survival.

Sterling, Dorothy. **Freedom Train: The Story of Harriet Tubman.** New York: Doubleday, 1954.

A biography of the courageous woman called "Moses," who led her people out of slavery via the Underground Railroad.

Suhl, Yuri. **Uncle Misha's Partisans.** New York: Four Winds Press, 1973.

An orphaned twelve-year-old boy joins a band of Jewish partisans who live deep in a Ukranian forest and who are committed to fighting the Nazis.

Taylor, Mildred. **Roll of Thunder, Hear My Cry.** New York: Dial Press, 1976.

In this Newbery Award-winner, a black family living in Mississippi in the 1930s have the courage, pride, and love to help them survive the harsh realities of prejudice, ignorance, and cruelty.

Taylor, Theodore. **The Cay.** New York: Doubleday, 1969.

When their ship is torpedoed by the Germans during World War II, an old deckhand and a twelve-year-old passenger from Virginia survive on a raft and land on a barren Caribbean island.

Tolan, Stephanie. **The Liberation of Tansy Warner.** New York: Charles Scribner's Sons, 1980.

Tansy and her mother struggle to survive as individuals in a home dominated by strong personalities and demands for conformity. This is a contemporary, realistic portrayal of the search for self-worth and identity.

Voigt, Cynthia. **Homecoming.** New York: Atheneum, 1981.

Four children, abandoned by their mother, search for a home and an identity. The sequel is *Dicey's Song* (1983), winner of the 1983 Newbery Award.

Walsh, Jill Paton. **Fireweed.** Farrar, Straus and Giroux, 1969.

> Teenagers Bill and Julie meet during a London blitz in 1940 and join forces to cope with the problems of survival, loneliness, and fear. Their story is told in a first-person account by Bill years afterwards.

Wyss, Johann. **The Swiss Family Robinson.** New York: Grosset and Dunlap, 1949.

> Shipwrecked and marooned on an island in 1812, the Robinson family learn to make use of the flora and fauna on their island for survival.

Group Story Sessions

First Session

As an introduction to the broad scope of stories classified as survival tales, the teacher presented a series of brief book reviews to suggest the diversity of the books selected for this Focus Unit. The books reviewed included a representative sampling of the different types of survival tales which make up the collection. *Sarah Bishop* by Scott O'Dell and *Trouble River* by Betsy Byars were selected as examples of historical fiction. In a special subgroup within this broader category of historical fiction were stories about World War II: *Friedrich* by Hans Richter, *Farewell to Manzanar* by Jeanne Wakatsuki Houston and James D. Houston, and *Uncle Misha's Partisans* by Yuri Suhl. *The White Mountains* by John Christopher provided an example of science fiction, *Slake's Limbo* by Felice Holman introduced contemporary realism, and *Abel's Island* by William Steig represented fantasy. *Julie of the Wolves* by Jean George demonstrated the category of wilderness survival, and *Hill's End* by Ivan Southall illustrated tales labeled as "natural disaster survival." At the close of this first group session, the students were asked to select two books from the Survival Tales Focus Unit collection for independent reading. Each student was given a list of eight questions to use as a guide for the study of survival tales:

1. How would you categorize this survival tale?

2. What do you notice about the way this story is told? Identify the basic structure or plot pattern of the story.

3. What did you learn about the main character(s)? What techniques did the author use to portray the character(s)? What signs of growth or change in the character(s) did you notice?

4. What role does the setting play in the development of plot and characters?

5. What is the nature of the survival in this story?

6. What qualities of the main character(s) are critical for coping with conditions or events which threaten survival?

7. What is the central theme?

8. Compare this story with other survival tales.

Responses to these questions took three forms: the students were assigned to write a report about one of the books they had read independently, using the questions as the framework for the report; the teacher used the questions in a book conference with each student to discuss the other independent reading selection; and the group discussions of the survival tales read orally or silently were guided by the questions. Of course, the students were encouraged to reach beyond this list and to generate their own questions in the course of reading and thinking about the stories included in this unit.

Second through Sixth Sessions

Call It Courage by Armstrong Sperry was read aloud during the next few group sessions. The students used the eight questions listed above to guide their responses during the discussions which followed each segment read aloud. Relatively little teacher input was needed except for some initial clarification about the meaning of the questions themselves. Using this series of questions as a guide for comprehension and literary analysis in the group sessions prepared the students for the independent reading and writing assignments included in this Focus Unit.

The students identified *Call It Courage* as a hero legend with the familiar plot pattern found in traditional quest tales in which the hero leaves home to seek his or her fortune or identity, encounters various tests or trials, and finally returns home triumphant. They noted that the five chapter headings marked each phase of the quest: "Flight," "The Sea," "The Island," "Drums," and "Homeward." One student made a diagram of the quest sequence in a circular shape, beginning with the flight, moving through each of the tests of courage, and finally returning to the point of departure. Another student pointed out that the first two lines of the book are repeated at the very end and that this seemed to reinforce the circular pattern of the story.

Responding to the third set of questions about the main character, the students commented on the way the author built up a picture of Mafatu by presenting the critical incident in his past, the drowning of his mother, to explain his deep fear of the sea and by describing the reactions of others in his tribe, the older people, his peers, his stepmother and step-brothers, his father, and his one friend, Kana. The students identified Kana's words, "Mafatu is a coward" (p. 13), as the turning point in the story, the stimulus which Mafatu needed to begin his quest for courage and to prove himself worthy of living among his people. Then the students pointed out the particular incidents which marked the changes in Mafatu as he gained confidence, competence, and courage. They noted that after Mafatu escaped Moana, the sea god, his first courageous act on the island was psychological in nature: he violated a taboo. This set the stage for all subsequent acts of courage as he fought for physical survival. One student commented, "That first victory gave him the confidence in himself to fight the wild pig and that octopus and the shark and the other dangers." Another student added, "Each time he did a brave deed, he got more and more confident so that when he left the island he was *ready* to face the sea with courage instead of fear!"

Question four about the story setting focused attention on the aspects of the culture of the early Polynesians which initiated the events in the story. The students saw that courage was worshipped because it was necessary for survival. To become fishermen and warriors required fear-lessness. They compared this ancient culture with the contemporary one in which they lived. One student observed, "If Mafatu lived here, it wouldn't be a problem being afraid of the sea. He could still survive." This generated a discussion of the values which characterize our society. One student offered this insight: "In our society it's not so much the physical things that are needed for survival. I think if Mafatu lived here, he couldn't really make it unless he learned to read and write!"

The fifth question, "What is the nature of the survival in this story?" generated a discussion about the difference between physical survival and psychological survival. The students explored the way Mafatu achieved physical survival by using his skills and courage to get food; to build a fire, a shelter, and a canoe; to make clothing, tools, and weapons; and to defend himself against the wild animals and the savages who threatened his life. They discussed his growing sense of his own worth as a human being and his identity as a true Polynesian, "charged with the ancient fierceness of his race" (p. 80).

In analyzing the main character's coping qualities, question six, the students noted that it took a great act of will to embark on the quest in the first place. They felt that Mafatu's will power allowed him to attempt to master his fears. As his courage grew, he was able to draw from his own inner resources and to use his skills, knowledge, and capacity for quick thinking and for careful planning in order to survive. Several students went back to the text to find the skills employed in the struggle for survival. They reported their findings in the form of specific quotes from the story.

The students had no trouble identifying the central theme of the story. They observed that the title, *Call It Courage,* accurately expressed the theme. "The whole story is really about the nature of courage!"

By the time the reading and discussion of *Call It Courage* was completed in the group sessions, many of the students had completed at least one book of independent reading and were able to compare *Call It Courage* with other survival tales. For example, one student noted interesting similarities in *Island of the Blue Dolphins* by Scott O'Dell. She commented, "Karana also had to violate a taboo of her tribe which was that women weren't allowed to make weapons, and she was so surprised when she wasn't punished by some supernatural power. But as soon as she got rid of that fear, she could begin to do what she had to do to survive on the island like Mafatu."

At the conclusion of this final group session on *Call It Courage,* one boy suggested that a new question could be added to the list: "I found some symbolism in this story so maybe we should have a question about that. I think that the little dog Uri is supposed to symbolize love and loyalty and the albatross, Kivi, always seemed to be around to give direction and encouragement to keep going. I think Kivi would represent hope." Another student added, "It seems to me that love and hope would be important for survival. We should've included those when we talked about the courage and skills Mafatu needed for survival." These contributions prompted several students to suggest other symbols, such as the necklace of boar's teeth, the spear, and the "artfully built canoe." One student, referring to the homecoming scene at the end of the book, commented, "When his dad saw those things he knew that his son finally *deserved* his name, Mafatu, Stout Heart!"

Subsequent Sessions

The remaining group story sessions were devoted to sharing books read independently. In preparation for these large group meetings, the class was divided into small working groups according to the type of the survival tale chosen for independent reading. Thus, one group was made up of the students who had selected historical fiction, another group included those who had read stories of survival in the wilderness, and so on. Each group met to share and compare the stories they had read. One member served as a scribe and recorded interesting insights and observations, common patterns and themes.

The records from each small group were used as the starting point for discussion in the next three large group sessions. A major focus of these sessions was the exploration of the meaning of survival for the various characters in the diverse tales. Several examples of observations and insights which emerged from these discussions are included here.

Students who had read *Farewell to Manzanar* by Jeanne Wakatsuki Houston and James D. Houston and Scott O'Dell's *Sarah Bishop* and *Sing Down the Moon* expressed feelings of shock and outrage when they discovered some of the realities of the tragic periods of American history portrayed in these tales of survival. *Farewell to Manzanar* is an autobiographical account of a native-born American child who lived behind barbed wire for three years in an internment camp along with 10,000 other Japanese Americans during World War II. The students who read this story recognized that in addition to the struggle for physical survival, these Japanese Americans had to endure the shame and degradation of forced detention and to maintain individual dignity and self-respect. One student suggested that the beautiful rock gardens which sprang up in the midst of the sterile prison camp seemed to symbolize the need for human expression and individual creativity. Another student noted that the motto *Shikata ga na* ("It cannot be helped"), repeated frequently in the camp, seemed to reflect a philosophy of acceptance which helped these people to cope with their confinement and to make the best of an inhumane situation. To support this idea, she quoted from the text, "In such a narrowed world, in order to survive, you learn to contain your rage and your despair, and you try to re-create, as well as you can, your normality, some sense of things continuing" (p. 72). Other students commented on the terrible scars left by this experience, especially the sense of shame, guilt, and unworthiness felt by so many of those who emerged from the camps. The students expressed feelings of empathy for author Jeanne Wakatsuki Houston and were especially moved by her descriptions of her life after leaving the camp: her attendance at an American junior high school, her encounters with hate, prejudice, and ignorance, and her struggle to prove herself worthy of acceptance as a human being in a hostile environment, a struggle in which she felt forced to betray her own heritage.

Sarah Bishop is a fictionalized biography of a young girl in New York during the American Revolution. After the battle for Brooklyn Heights, Sarah fled from the British into the wilderness of northern Westchester County, where she survived alone on Long Pond. The students who read this book compared it with such other stories of wilderness survival as *Island of the Blue Dolphins* by Scott O'Dell and *My Side of the Mountain* by Jean George. They identified the fierce independence and resourcefulness of the main character in each story as critical factors in coping with the basic problems of physical survival. However, they saw a major difference in Sarah's story: her struggle to cope with the natural environment was compounded by her fear of a hostile and violent human environment, especially those people ("the rebels and redcoats") responsible for killing her father and her brother.

In *Sing Down the Moon,* a fourteen-year-old Navaho girl describes life in the 1860s, the threat of Spanish slavers, and the forced migration of her people from their homeland in Arizona to Fort Sumner, New Mexico. Shocked by this example of man's inhumanity to man, the students who read this book were especially impressed by the courage and stoicism of the Navaho people in the face of inhumane treatment and were upset by the cruelty associated with white people's conquest of American Indians. The students focused on the two main characters, Bright Morning and Tall Boy, who managed to survive physically and emotionally and to emerge from their ordeal with the strength and will to begin a new life.

Readers of *Roll of Thunder, Hear My Cry* by Mildred Taylor and *Jump Ship to Freedom* by James and Christopher Collier saw further evidence of the strength of the human spirit to survive in the face of degradation and deprivation and, in particular, recognized the cruelty generated by the institution of slavery in the United States. Again, they realized that the struggle for physical survival was integrally bound up with the drive to maintain independence, dignity, and pride. These two stories were compared with *The Endless Steppe: Growing Up in Siberia* by Esther Hautzig, an autobiographical account of the author's childhood in Siberia, where she and her family spent five years in forced labor during World War II. Like the others, this is a story of family solidarity and love and a portrayal of the triumph of the human spirit and humane values in an inhumane world. It is a story of a family rising above the daily struggle for survival, enduring hardships, deprivation, and degradation, and maintaining their dignity and self-respect. Several students observed that the survival of this family was in large part due to their steadfast determination to carry on an intellectually and socially stimulating life in spite of the cruel conditions imposed on them and to preserve the moral and ethical standards which defined them as human beings in an inhumane environment. One student commented:

> "In all three stories the families are very close and have a strong sense of right and wrong. And they have a very hopeful and positive outlook about the future. I think that's a very important part of surviving. I mean, you can't give up hope!"

Ivan Southall's books *Hill's End* and *Ash Road,* gripping tales of human courage and survival, were especially popular as choices for the independent reading assignment. Each story is about a small group of children cut off from adult help and struggling to survive a natural disaster. The students recognized the growth and maturation of the individual characters in response to crises and pointed to specific episodes in the texts which illustrated a growing capacity for cooperation, an increased understanding of others and the meaning of interdependence, and discoveries of inner resources and strengths. Readers of *Ash Road* debated the moral dilemma posed in this story; their responses reflected a wide range of opinion and moral judgment. However, they did agree that Graham, the character directly responsible for the raging bush fire which destroyed land, homes, and lives, would survive emotionally as a result of his decision at the end of the book to confess his role in the tragic accident rather than to spend the rest of his life running from the truth.

Three students who had read *The Planet of Junior Brown* by Virginia Hamilton and had puzzled together over its meaning shared their conclusions about the author's message during a group "sharing-comparing" session. This unusual and thought-provoking novel is about the friendship between two black eighth-grade boys: Junior Brown, a 300-pound musician, who is being suffocated by an overprotective, neurotic mother, and Buddy Clark, a homeless street boy with a brilliant mathematical mind, who lives in the deserted tenements of New York City. The school janitor becomes their friend and adviser and offers them a secret place in a basement room where they can be themselves and be together, safely removed from the harsh conventions and selfish narrow-mindedness of the adult world. The focal point of this haven is a magnificent model of the solar system which includes one planet made by Buddy and named for Junior Brown. But Buddy has another secret life: for years he has been a leader in a complex network of secret underground shelters, called "planets," for homeless street children. In this subculture he is known as "Tomorrow Billy" and assumes responsibility for these children, helping them to become strong, moral, and caring individuals in an underground world of cooperation, friendship, and love.

The three students who read this story decided that it held a message about the future of the human race. One student referred to the janitor's comment, "The human race is bound to come one time," and Buddy's response, "Maybe it's already come . . . and you don't know where to find it" (p. 159). He went on to describe the final scene of the book in which the school janitor, Mr. Pool, is invited into the underground community of homeless children and Buddy explains the foundation of their world: "the highest law for us is to live for one another." Mr. Pool recognizes that *this* is the human race for which he had been waiting, a humane and compassionate world of whole human beings who integrate individual freedom and responsibility. A student's concluding remark about this story expressed an idea which could well be applied to survival tales in general:

"It seems to me that survival means a lot more than just staying alive. It means staying *human*—which has to do with freedom and love and self-respect and caring about others and things like that."

Slake's Limbo by Felice Holman, another novel about survival in an underground world, was read aloud and discussed during the last group story sessions for this Focus Unit. The eight questions introduced at the beginning of the unit were used by the students as a framework for responding to this story and for comparing it to the other survival tales. *Slake's Limbo* is the story of thirteen-year-old Aremis Slake, who escapes from the cruelty and humiliation which mark his existence and takes refuge for 121 days in a cavelike room hidden in the New York City subway system. The students recognized that the story setting—the realities of existence on inner-city streets and in homes where poverty is a basic fact of life—produced the character Aremis Slake, intimidated and defeated, who sees himself only as "a worthless lump." Although in the first part of the book Aremis behaves like a hunted animal, he gradually takes charge of his life and begins to discover his own inner resources and capabilities. He also learns to recognize the positive qualities and good intentions of other human beings he encounters in his emotional journey toward self-respect and self-confidence.

The students found evidence of this emotional growth in Slake's struggle for physical survival. One student observed, "When Slake finally came out of the cave, he was different. He didn't seem like a *victim* anymore. He wasn't running away. He seemed to be ready to take part in the world, the real world above ground." Another student read aloud the last lines of the book to support his observation:

"He turned and started up the stairs and out of the subway. Slake did not know exactly where he was going, but the general direction was up." (P. 123)

Several students noted parallels between Slake and the character Jeanne in *Farewell to Manzanar*. Both children carried feelings of worthlessness shaped by the treatment and attitudes of others. Slake is treated as a misfit and learns to view himself as one. One student read an excerpt from *Farewell to Manzanar* to show the similarity of Jeanne's response:

"As I came to understand what Manzanar had meant, it gradually filled me with shame for being a person guilty of something enormous enough to deserve that kind of treatment. In order to please my accusers, I tried, for the first years after our release, to become someone acceptable." (P. 133)

This student noted that in contrast to Slake, who withdrew into himself, Jeanne overcame her shame and moved outward, striving to gain social acceptance from her peers. Students also observed that both characters gradually gained self-knowledge and self-respect, which in turn formed the foundation for personal growth and a more healthy adjustment to the realities of their lives.

After several other survival tales were brought into the discussion for comparative analysis, there was a gradual movement toward synthesis as recurring themes were identified. For example, one student remarked, "Most of these characters will always have scars from their experiences, but most of them managed to survive, both physically and emotionally." Another added, "And those characters, afterwards, wouldn't really be children again. I mean, they knew they could make it on their own. So they looked at things in a different way and could feel independent." A girl who had read *The Bears' House* by Marilyn Sachs observed, "But in the book I read, the character wasn't *ready* to get along without adult help. She just couldn't handle it—the reality—so she escaped into a fantasy world which was how she wanted things to be. When we were listening to *Slake's Limbo,* I thought at first he was going to be like Fran Ellen [in *The Bears' House*] when he escaped into that cave. But he was older—he was ready to grow up!" Another child who had read *The Bears' House* said, "Fran Ellen wanted to be a child; she wanted to be loved and to sit on someone's lap. She really tried hard to take care of her baby sister, and she was pretty courageous but, I agree, she just wasn't ready to take on such a big load." This character provided an interesting contrast to those characters who had been sucessful in their struggle to survive, to master reality, to be independent. The contrast helped to sharpen the students' picture of the "successful survivor." The image that emerged from the concluding discussion was a picture of an individual in middle childhood with the determination and self-confidence needed to face the realities of life. These are the basic developmental characteristics described by Piaget and Erikson and used by Norma Schlager in her study of children's reading preferences.

Creative Writing

The eight questions presented at the beginning of the Survival Tales Focus Unit to assist comprehension of written narrative were used again to help students prepare to produce an original survival tale. Prior to writing, the students were asked to think about the structure and content of their story. A brief review of the genre categories, literary techniques and patterns, and basic plots of the survival tales already read and discussed served to stimulate their thinking about form and content for their own story. For example, several of the students, having observed that many of the survival tales were written as first-person accounts, decided to use the first-person viewpoint for their own story. Others identified literary techniques such as flashbacks and foreshadowing and wanted to use them to develop their narratives. One student was especially interested in the journal format used in *My Side of the Mountain* by Jean George, while another preferred the legendary quality of *Call It Courage* by Armstrong Sperry. Most of the students chose to write contemporary realism, although some decided on historical realism and a few settled on science fiction or fantasy for their narratives. Following this review and brainstorming session, the students were ready to begin constructing an outline of their story using the eight questions to guide their thinking about the basic ingredients of narrative and to check for possible gaps in their story-plan. Once this rough sketch was completed, the students had a solid base on which to build their story, adding descriptive details, dialogue, and interesting events according to their unique vision and imagination.

Each student had at least two conferences with the teacher to read and discuss his or her story. The first conference was held at a midpoint in the creative process; the second, at the completion of the story. In addition, each student was paired with a classmate so that the two could share their writing at any point in the process—when one wanted to celebrate a new idea or to get some help with a problem. These writing conferences with the teacher and peers provided the feedback necessary to produce cohesive and comprehensible narratives. The primary purpose of these conferences was to teach a basic writing strategy: reading. As a writer reads and rereads what is on the page, she or he asks, "Does this make sense? Does it express the meaning I had intended?" In the writing conference, the student reads his or her work to a teacher or classmate who, in turn, questions those parts of the text found confusing or difficult to understand. Gradually, the student learns to assume this role of critical reader of his or her own work, to detect problem areas where the meaning is unclear, and to make the revisions necessary to produce a cohesive text which conveys the intended meaning. During the writing conferences, the immediate feedback from a listener/reader served to develop and reinforce the writer's awareness that written texts must be directed to a potential audience. This "audience-awareness" is essential during the writing-rereading-rewriting cycle to guide the writer toward producing texts which can be comprehended by other readers.

When the students completed their original survival tales and shared them with the group, they found that their efforts were appropriately rewarded by the enthusiastic feedback of an appreciative audience. Although the group meetings for sharing these stories concluded the Survival Tales Focus Unit sequence, the students continued to read and recommend survival tales written by professional writers as well as classmates.

Reference

Norma Schlager. "Predicting Children's Choices in Literature: A Developmental Approach." In *Children's Literature in Education* 9 (1978): 136–42.

15 Giants: A Focus Unit
for Grades Two and Three

Literature is full of tales about enormous creatures. There are giants in the Bible, in ancient mythologies, and in the folklore of most of the peoples of the world. These giant tales, handed down from generation to generation, and carried across land and sea, are an integral part of our children's literary heritage. The Giant Focus Unit was initially created as a vehicle for passing on this heritage to our children by introducing them to traditional tales about well-known giants and the heroes who challenged them.

These tales are part of our oral tradition, having traveled through time and space by word of mouth and, eventually, having been collected and recorded in written form. Through this Focus Unit, the children were exposed to several different versions of each of these ancient tales to help them become aware of this oral tradition. Gradually, the children discovered that each version is actually a "retelling" or "adaptation" or "variant" of an old tale which had originally been told orally. They were guided toward an understanding that each version represented a personal interpretation of an ancient tale by an unknown writer or artist from a particular culture.

Modern stories about giants were also included in this Focus Unit. Each of these stories was introduced as the original creation of a specific, known author. However, the children soon realized that these authors had been influenced or inspired by tales from the oral tradition. A comparison of traditional and modern tales was initiated to help the children begin to grasp the idea that traditional literature is the base from which modern literature evolves. The children's growing knowledge of traditional tales would serve as the groundwork for their understanding and appreciation of modern tales.

Objectives

1. To introduce children to tales from the oral tradition, their literary heritage.
2. To compare selected traditional tales and discover recurring patterns and motifs.

3. To compare traditional and modern tales and to discover the threads which bind the new to the old.

4. To contribute to children's understanding of human interaction through a study of motives and behaviors of characters in the story world.

5. To provide a context for independent reading and to foster growth of reading interests.

6. To develop and practice creative writing skills.

Bibliography for the Giant Focus Unit

I. Group Story Sessions

A. Traditional Tales

de Paolo, Tomie. **Finn M'Coul: The Giant of Knockmany Hill.** New York: Holiday House, 1981.

Grimm Brothers. **The Brave Little Tailor.** New York: Larousse, 1979.

Johnson, D. William, adapter. **Jack and the Beanstalk.** Boston: Little, Brown, 1976.

Lawrence, John. **The Giant of Grabbist.** New York: David White, 1968.

Manning-Sanders, Ruth. "Jack the Giant Killer." In **A Book of Giants.** New York: E. P. Dutton, 1962.

Werth, Kurt, and Mabel Watts. **Molly and the Giant.** New York: Parents' Magazine Press, 1973.

B. Modern Tales

Briggs, Raymond. **Jim and the Beanstalk.** New York: Coward, McCann and Geoghegan, 1970.

Cunliffe, John. **The Giant Who Swallowed the Wind.** London: André Deutsch, 1972.

Slobodkin, Louis. **The Amiable Giant.** New York: Vanguard Press, 1955.

Thurber, James. **The Great Quillow.** New York: Harcourt, Brace, 1944.

Yorinks, Arthur. **Sid and Sol.** New York: Farrar, Straus and Giroux, 1977.

II. Independent Reading

A. Traditional Tales

Ambrus, Victor, reteller. **The Valiant Little Tailor.** New York: Oxford University Press, 1980.

Asbjörnsen, Peter C., and Jörgen Moe. "The Giant Who Had No Heart in His Body." In **East of the Sun and West of the Moon.** New York: Macmillan, 1963.

Briggs, Katherine, and Ruth Tongue, editors. "The Giant of Grabbist and the 'Dorcas Jane,'" "The Giant of Grabbist and Hawkridge Church," "The Giant of Grabbist and the Whitstones," and "The Giant of Grabbist and the Stones of Battlegore." In **Folktales of England.** Chicago: University of Chicago Press, 1965.

Bunting, Eve. **The Two Giants.** Lexington, Massachusetts: Ginn, 1972.

Chase, Richard. "Jack in the Giants' New Ground." In **Jack Tales: Folktales from the Southern Appalachians.** Boston: Houghton Mifflin, 1943.

d'Aulaire, Ingri, and Edgar d'Aulaire. **Book of Greek Myths.** New York: Doubleday, 1962.

———. **Norse Gods and Giants.** New York: Doubleday, 1962.

de la Mare, Walter. **Jack and the Beanstalk.** New York: Alfred A. Knopf, 1959.

de Regniers, Beatrice Schenk. **David and Goliath.** New York: Viking Press, 1965.

———. "Jack the Giant-Killer," "Jack and the Beanstalk," "Giuanni and the Giant" (an Italian variant of "The Brave Little Tailor"), and "A Legend of Knockmany." In **The Giant Book.** New York: Atheneum, 1966.

Feagles, Anita. **Thor and the Giants.** New York: William R. Scott, 1968.

Feuerlecht, Roberta. **The Legends of Paul Bunyan.** New York: Macmillan, 1966.

Galdone, Paul. **Puss in Boots** (adapted from Perrault). New York: Seabury Press, 1976.

Grimm Brothers. **The Brave Little Tailor,** adapted by Aurand Harris. Glenview, Illinois: Scott, Foresman, 1971. (For beginning readers)

———. **The Brave Little Tailor,** retold by Kurt Werth. New York: Viking Press, 1965.

———. **The Valiant Little Tailor.** New York: Harvey House, 1967.

Haviland, Virginia. **Favorite Fairy Tales Told in England.** Boston: Little, Brown, 1959.

Hill, Kay. **More Glooscap Stories: Legends of the Wabanaki Indians.** New York: Dodd, Mead, 1970.

Hillert, Margaret. **The Magic Beans.** Chicago: Follett, 1966. (For beginning readers)

Jacobs, Joseph. **Jack the Giant Killer.** New York: Henry Z. Walck, 1971.

————— . "The Legend of Knockmany." In **Celtic Fairy Tales.** London: Frederick Muller, 1958.

Kitt, Tamara. **The Boy Who Fooled the Giant.** New York: Grosset and Dunlap, 1963. (For beginning readers)

Lang, Andrew. "Puss in Boots" and "Jack the Giant Killer." In **The Blue Fairy Book.** New York: Random House, 1959.

Littledale, Freya. **Seven at One Blow.** New York: Scholastic Book Services, 1976. (For beginning readers)

Lurie, Alison, reteller. "Molly Whuppie." In **Clever Gretchen and Other Forgotten Folktales.** New York: Thomas Y. Crowell, 1980.

Lyons, Grant. "The Giant and the Rabbit." In **Tales People Tell in Mexico.** New York: Julian Messner, 1972.

McCormick, Dell. **Paul Bunyan Swings His Axe.** New York: Scholastic Book Services, 1963.

McDermott, Beverly. **The Golem: A Jewish Legend.** Philadelphia: J. B. Lippincott, 1976.

Manning-Sanders, Ruth. "Jack and the Beanstalk," "Fin M'Coul and Cucullin," "Jack the Giant Killer," and "The Brave Little Tailor." In **A Book of Giants.** New York: E. P. Dutton, 1963.

Mayne, William. "Jack the Giant Killer," "Jack and the Beanstalk," and "Clever Oonagh." In **A Book of Giants.** New York: Penguin Books, 1968.

Price, Christine. **Sixty at a Blow: A Tall Tale from Turkey.** New York: E. P. Dutton, 1968.

Rounds, Glen. **Ol' Paul, the Mighty Logger.** New York: Holiday House, 1949.

Spicer, Dorothy. **13 Giants.** New York: Coward-McCann, 1966.

Stobbs, William. **Jack and the Beanstalk.** New York: Delacorte Press, 1965.

Stontenberg, Adrien. **American Tall Tales.** New York: Viking Press, 1966.

Sutcliff, Rosemary. **The High Deeds of Finn MacCool.** New York: E. P. Dutton, 1967.

Voight, Virginia. **Close to the Rising Sun: Algonquian Indian Legends.** Champaign, Illinois: Garrard, 1972.

Williams, Jay. **Seven at One Blow.** New York: Parents' Magazine Press, 1972.

Zemach, Harve, adapter. **Salt,** by Alexei Afanasev. Chicago: Follett, 1965.

B. Modern Tales

Bolliger, Max. **The Giants' Feast.** Reading, Massachusetts: Addison-Wesley, 1976.

Coville, Bruce, and Katherine Coville. **The Foolish Giant.** Philadelphia: J. B. Lippincott, 1978. (For beginning readers)

Dahlstrom, Tore. **Bread for the Giant.** New York: Golden Press, 1966.

Harrison, David. **A Book of Giant Stories.** London: Jonathan Cape, 1972.

Herrmann, Frank. **The Giant Alexander in America.** New York: McGraw-Hill, 1968. (Series)

Houghton, Eric. **A Giant Can Do Anything.** London: André Deutsch, 1975.

Hughes, Ted. **The Iron Giant.** New York: Harper and Row, 1968.

Kahl, Virginia. **Giants, Indeed!** New York: Charles Scribner's Sons, 1974.

Polushkin, Marie. **The Little Hen and the Giant.** New York: Harper and Row, 1977.

Sarnoff, Jane, and Reynold Ruffins. **Giants! A Riddle Book.** New York: Charles Scribner's Sons, 1977.

Wallace, Daisy. **Giant Poems.** New York: Holiday House, 1978.

Wilde, Oscar. **The Selfish Giant.** New York: Harlan Quist Books, 1967.

Yolen, Jane. **The Giants' Farm.** New York: Seabury Press, 1977. (For beginning readers)

C. Background Information

Larkin, David. **Giants.** New York: Harry Abrams, 1979.

McHargue, Georgess. **The Impossible People: A History Natural and Unnatural of Beings Terrible and Wonderful.** New York: Holt, Rinehart and Winston, 1972.

Group Story Sessions

Traditional giant tales were introduced first in the story sessions for the Giant Focus Unit to provide a background for the modern stories about giants. One version of each of these traditional tales was selected for the group session; other versions were made available for independent reading. The children were invited to share their personal reading experiences during the group discussions to generate a comparison of different retellings or variants of a particular tale.

First Session

The Brave Little Tailor by the Brothers Grimm was the first of the
traditional tales introduced. The children were asked if they recognized
the name *Grimm* on the cover of this illustrated edition. Several were
able to name other Grimm tales they had heard or read, and a few
children were aware that the name referred to two brothers from Germany. The teacher provided further information about the Brothers
Grimm, who had collected and recorded many tales from the oral tradition of Germany. The title page of this book listed the names of the
illustrator and translator. The concept of *translation* was a new one for
these children but important for their eventual understanding of the nature
of the oral tradition.

After reading the story aloud, the teacher introduced a series of questions intended to assess comprehension and to focus attention on the
narrative sequence and the logical relationships among the events in this
tale:

> What words did the tailor embroider on his belt? What did the
> words mean? Why did he do this?
>
> Why did the tailor leave his workshop? What did the tailor take
> with him on his journey? How did he use these items to outwit the
> first giant he met along the way?
>
> How did the tailor manage to escape from the giants' cave?
>
> Why was the tailor introduced to the king as a "mighty warrior"?
>
> Why did the king give the tailor three dangerous tasks to perform?

These questions highlighted major episodes in the story and required the
children to think inferentially in order to grasp the implied meanings in
the narrative.

A final question, "Are there any parts of this story which remind you
of other tales you've read or heard?" was intended to draw attention to
recurring patterns or motifs which can be found in folktales and fairy
tales. Most of the children recognized the ending as a typical one in which
the central character marries the king's daughter and eventually becomes
king himself. This question was inserted at this early point in the Focus
Unit sequence to set the stage for an ongoing search for recurring patterns
in subsequent story sessions.

This first session ended with a brief look at several other versions of
this story in fairy-tale collections and in single editions. The children were
invited to choose one to read independently during their regularly scheduled quiet reading period. These and the other books selected for independent reading varied in terms of readability levels in order to meet the

diverse needs of these young readers. For example, *The Boy Who Fooled the Giant* by Tamara Kitt is tailored especially for beginning readers, while Kurt Werth's version of the Grimm tale *The Brave Little Tailor* requires greater reading skill.

In preparation for subsequent sessions, the children were asked to begin to select versions of other giant tales to read on their own. In this way, a group discussion of a particular tale could be enriched by contributions from individuals who had read variants of that tale.

Second Session

Since the children were familiar with the popular English fairy tale *Jack and the Beanstalk,* a new adaptation by D. William Johnson was chosen for the group session. This version has a medieval setting and includes background information about Jack's family. In Johnson's story, Jack discovers that a giant had killed his father, a rich knight, and had usurped his castles and treasures. Jack begins his quest to restore his inheritance; he eventually kills the giant and rights the wrong done to his family. The children's spontaneous responses to this adaptation reflected their own sense of morality and justice. For example, one child commented: "I like that story better than the one I heard before. In the other story, Jack just stole all that stuff from the giant for no reason. It didn't seem fair, because the giant wasn't bothering anybody. But in this story, Jack did the right thing because he just took back what had belonged to his father in the first place!" A child who had read the version by Walter de la Mare added: "I read a story like this one. In my story, Jack meets a stranger in that country at the top of the beanstalk and the stranger tells Jack that the ogre in the castle had stolen those treasures!" Another child had read William Stobbs's *Jack and the Beanstalk* and found a similar episode in which Jack discovers the circumstances of his father's death. Most of the other children agreed that Jack had the right to take the treasures from the giant because they had originally belonged to his father.

When asked to compare *Jack and the Beanstalk* and *The Brave Little Tailor,* the children responded with observations which reflected their awareness of common fairy-tale motifs:

> "The endings are the same. Jack got rich and married a princess, too."

> "And Jack is small like the tailor—I mean, compared to the giant. But they both outsmart the giant!"

> "But this story has more magic things in it like the beans and the harp and the hen. And he got help from a fairy, but the tailor didn't get any help."

Third Session

"Jack the Giant Killer" in Ruth Manning-Sanders's *A Book of Giants* was read aloud next. This tale includes the six adventures and brave deeds of Jack, who lived during the reign of King Arthur. The children were asked to compare this story with the previous ones in terms of the heroes, giants, use of magic, and story endings. They noted that this Jack was as bold and clever as the heroes in the previous tales, and that he too used his brains to outwit most of the giants. However, he resorted to magic to get rid of the last giant. The children also noted that the giants in all three stories seemed to be rather easily fooled, which, of course, was fortunate for the heroes. The endings were similar, too; Jack married the duke's daughter and lived happily ever after. Several children found another link: Jack was given a belt embroidered with words about his deeds just like the one the tailor had fashioned for himself. One child pointed to an important difference between the embroidered belts: "The little tailor made the belt when he had only killed some flies, but that sort of got him *started* on his adventures. Jack was given his belt *after* he had already killed a giant. But both were really pretty brave and smart."

Fourth Session

Many stories have been written about Fin M'Coul, a popular Irish giant who is known for the Giants' Causeway, the highway he built between Ireland and Scotland. In the fourth story session, Tomie de Paolo's *Fin M'Coul: The Giant of Knockmany Hill* was read aloud. In this tale, Fin's wife, Oonagh, helps him outwit his enemy, the fierce Cucullin, the biggest of all the giants in Ireland. This story generated spontaneous observations indicating that the children had initiated their own comparative analysis of this group of giant tales and had begun to search for recurring patterns and critical differences. For example, one child commented, "That trick with the cheese Fin used to fool Cucullin is just like in *The Brave Little Tailor*." A second child identified another motif: "Oonagh used her brains to get rid of that mean giant just like in the other stories." However, the children were more impressed with the way this tale departed from the basic "brave hero versus terrible giant" formula of the three previous narratives:

> "This story is really different because it's about a nice giant and a mean giant. In the other stories, all the giants were bad."

> "And in this story the giants seemed like regular people instead of evil creatures. Fin had a job and nice wife, and they lived in a nice house instead of a cave."

These observations opened the way for further questions about these interesting story characters. For example, the question "Why did Fin build his house on top of Knockmany Hill?" drew attention to Fin's fear of Cucullin and his attempt to avoid a confrontation with that giant. When asked to compare these giants, one child responded, "I really liked Fin. He wasn't very brave but he was friendly and honest." Another child continued, "Cucullin was just a big bully who liked to show off how strong he was, so he just went around beating up on everyone." A third child applied this insight to his own personal experience: "There's a kid on my street who's just like that. He's always going around beating up the little kids. He should pick on someone his own size!" A fourth child related this back to Cucullin: "That's like Cucullin. He wasn't so brave! He only went to fight Fin because he thought Fin was much weaker and smaller!"

Finally, the children were asked to compare this story to other versions they had read independently. Several children had read *The Bigger Giant* by Nancy Green. They noted that Fin's wife was a tiny woman instead of a giant herself, and they thought this factor added humor to the episode in which she confronts Cucullin: "It was so funny when she kept scolding that huge giant. 'You did it you bad little man. You woke up the baby!'"

Fifth Session

The Giant of Grabbist, from the folklore of England, is a peaceful, benevolent giant known for his kind and helpful deeds in the village of Exmoor in Somerset. An illustrated retelling of this old legend by John Lawrence was introduced during the fifth session of the Giant Focus Unit. In this story, the Giant of Grabbist rescues a small fishing boat, the *Dorcas Jane,* during a terrible storm and saves Joshua and Uncle Elijah from drowning. Because this story differed significantly from the previous tales, several questions were introduced to focus on the characters portrayed in the narrative:

> How did the villagers feel when they first heard the news about the Giant of Grabbist coming to their village of Exmoor?
>
> What made them change their minds about this giant?
>
> How did the Giant of Grabbist feel about the villagers? Why did he count the fishing boats?
>
> When was the first time he smiled? the second time? the third time?
>
> In what way is this story like the Aesop fable "The Lion and the Mouse"?
>
> Can you think of other stories about "kindness returned"?

In the discussion generated by these questions, the children focused on the relationship between the giant and the villagers. The children recognized that this story was about a friendship that developed between the giant and the villagers and that acts of kindness and caring were reciprocated. The children also expressed an interest in the way the giant showed what he was feeling and thinking through his actions instead of words. A question such as "Why did the giant count the fishing boats?" was used to stimulate the search for implied meanings through inferential thinking. This higher-level thinking was reflected in the response of the child who explained, "The giant counted the boats to see if any were missing in the storm. That showed how much he cared about the fishermen and he worried about them like a mother!" Another child added this analogy: "It's like when we have a fire drill and the teacher counts all the kids to make sure everybody's safe!"

The questions about the villagers generated further analogies between story characters and people in real life:

> "The people were afraid of the giant at first because he looked scary. But then when they got to know him, they found out how nice he was."

> "Everybody was afraid at first because they figured he'd be mean just because he's a giant. They expect a giant to be bad."

> "That happens a lot of times—like when you first meet someone, you may not like them, but then you find out that they're really nice and everything."

> "That's what it means when people say, 'You can't tell a book by its cover.'"

A discussion of the basic theme was generated by this exploration of human interaction and, more specifically, by the question comparing this story and "The Lion and the Mouse." The children saw that both stories are about kindness and reciprocity, and they named other stories with a similar theme. For example, several children recalled *Amos and Boris* by William Steig:

> "Boris was a gigantic whale who seemed like a giant to little Amos [the mouse]. He saved Amos from drowning just like the Giant of Grabbist saved the fisherman."

> "And then later Amos saved Boris after that big storm. So they really helped each other like when the villagers made that big sweater for the giant to keep him warm."

This discussion was concluded by comparing *The Giant of Grabbist* with the giant tales read in previous story sessions. One child's statement seemed to sum up the various comments of other members of the group:

"Those other stories are all about contests, and the winner had to use his brains to beat someone who's much bigger and stronger. But this story is about friends instead of enemies and about being helpful instead of tricky!"

Sixth Session

Molly Whuppie is a heroine in a tale told in England, Scotland, and Ireland. Through courage and cunning, she outwits a giant and gains a fortune and a husband. After *Molly and the Giant* by Kurt Werth and Mabel Watts was read aloud, the children were anxious to share their observations about familiar patterns they had discovered while listening to this story:

"This story is like the first three when a giant gets outwitted. But this time it's a girl who's the brave hero . . ."

"You mean *heroine!* I thought it was good that a girl was the important character for a change and did all the exciting stuff."

"And she does three tasks for the king just like in *The Brave Little Tailor.*"

"It's really like *Jack and the Beanstalk,* too, because she steals three treasures from the giant."

"And she marries the king's son and lives happily ever after like in the other stories."

One of the children had read "Molly Whuppie" in Virginia Haviland's *Favorite Fairy Tales Told in England.* She added this observation:

"This story is the same except it's from England instead of Ireland. The giant says, 'Fee-fi-fo-fum, I smell the blood of some earthly one' like in *Jack and the Beanstalk.*"

During this story session, the teacher refrained from interjecting any questions in order to give the children a chance to generate their own discussion of this story and its relationship to the other traditional tales heard in the group sessions or read independently. The children demonstrated their ability to compare stories and find recurring patterns and themes, as set forth in the second objective for this Focus Unit.

Subsequent Sessions

The next series of story sessions focused on modern fairy tales about giants. *The Amiable Giant* by Louis Slobodkin was the first of these modern tales introduced to the group. Before reading it aloud, the teacher asked the children to define the word *amiable.* Since none of them responded with an accurate definition, they were asked to try to figure out its meaning as they listened to the story. Following the story, all the children were able to explain the word as it applied to the giant in the tale. One child commented that this giant was similar to the Giant of Grabbist. This contribution led to further comparisons:

> "In both stories the villagers were afraid at first until they found out that the giant was friendly."

> "But they're different, because in this story the villagers don't find out until the end, so the whole story is about that!"

> "But in *The Giant of Grabbist,* they find out right away, so the story is all about what happens when you have a nice giant around!"

After discussing the plot and individual characters in this story, the children were asked to explain why it could be identified as a "modern fairy tale."

> "Mr. Slobodkin made it up himself. It doesn't say he "retold" it or anything. He's the real author so it's *modern!*"

> "But he wrote it like a regular fairy tale with a giant and a wicked wizard."

> "And the villagers think of a plan to get rid of the villain."

> "They outwit the wizard like in those other stories."

Several children had selected *The Foolish Giant* by Bruce and Katherine Coville for independent reading. After briefly summarizing this story for the benefit of those who had not read it, they explained how it was similar to *The Amiable Giant:*

> "Harry [the giant] was friendly and gentle, too, and he just wanted to do nice things for people like the Amiable Giant."

> "And there was a wicked wizard in this story, too, but Harry was the one who got rid of him and saved the people from his mean tricks."

Their enthusiastic response to this story for beginning readers prompted other children to select it to read independently. Fostering interest in reading is a basic objective of every Focus Unit. As children share the stories they have enjoyed reading, their classmates become motivated to read the stories too. Excitement about books can be contagious in a classroom!

The Giant Who Swallowed the Wind by John Cunliffe was the next modern tale shared with the group. Several questions were introduced to focus attention on the major characters and to elicit comparison with *The Amiable Giant:*

What made the people decide that this giant was not really bad or cruel?

In what way is this story similar to *The Amiable Giant* in terms of the problem and the conclusion?

Compare the character of Bob Miller in this story with Gwendolyn in *The Amiable Giant*. How did they manage to save their towns from starvation?

In what way does the giant in this story differ from the Amiable Giant? How are they similar?

Other questions were used to highlight the significant role of setting on the development of the plot in a story:

Why is the wind so important to these people living in a "land of windmills"?

What happened when the giant swallowed the wind?

Why did the giant play this trick on the "little men"?

The modern tale of *Jim and the Beanstalk* by Raymond Briggs was read aloud next, and the children thoroughly enjoyed this humorous sequel to *Jack and the Beanstalk*. The giant in this very modern tale is the aging son of the original giant whose treasures were stolen by Jack in years past. The children, of course, recognized that Briggs had used the traditional tale as the basis for his own story and had created humor by adding contemporary touches and by portraying the giant as a benign character to whom Jim brings three items (reading glasses, false teeth, and a wig) instead of stealing treasures from him.

Sid and Sol by Arthur Yorinks is another humorous, contemporary tale about an enormous giant, Sol, who threatened the whole world and about an unlikely hero, Sid, who confronted the giant and caused his downfall. The children were quick to comment on the familiar plot structure of this story:

"It's sort of like in *Jack the Giant Killer*. Sid is such a little guy but he's so brave, and he outsmarts the giant like Jack did."

"And Sol is such a *typical* giant—always showing off how big and strong he is, like Cucullin!"

"It sure is a good thing all those giants were so stupid, or people like Jack and the tailor would never have become heroes!"

The last of the modern tales to be read aloud during the group sessions was *The Great Quillow* by James Thurber. By this time, the children had enough of a background to generate their own analysis of this story and to compare it to other tales in the Giant Focus Unit. Their responses reflected their appreciation of the wonderful humor of the language and the superb character portrayals created by this gifted author.

After a rather detailed discussion of this delightful narrative, the children considered it in light of the other modern and traditional giant tales. Some examples of their observations are included here:

> "This is the only one of the modern stories which is about a really mean giant except for *Sid and Sol*."

> "Most of the giants in the modern stories really wanted to be friendly and helpful. Like the Amiable Giant was lonely because everyone was afraid of him, but he wanted to make friends."

> "The giant in *The Foolish Giant* is the same way, but he keeps busting stuff because he's so big and clumsy. But he doesn't mean to. He just can't help it."

> "Hunder [*The Great Quillow*] is just the opposite. He went around smashing houses and everything just to show off, like Cucullin or Sol!"

> "*The Great Quillow* is more like a lot of the old tales of giants. The giant is really big and terrifying and the hero is small and cunning! His plan to get rid of the giant and save the town was really smart."

> "And in a lot of other stories the hero isn't really taken seriously at first. Like that toymaker [*The Great Quillow*]. Everyone just teased him, and they didn't think he ever did anything important."

> "And nobody really paid attention to Gwendolyn [*The Amiable Giant*] at first."

> "Or Sid. Nobody believed he'd ever be able to get rid of that giant!"

> "It seems that most of the old stories are about contests between a giant who is sort of stupid and gullible and a little hero who has to fight with his brains!"

> "Except the Giant of Grabbist. He was really nice. Everyone liked him. Maybe that man who wrote *The Amiable Giant* got some ideas from that story."

> "I think people like Mr. Thurber probably read a lot of old tales and that's how he learned how to write such a good story."

> "Maybe that's why a lot of the new stories are sort of like the old ones."

These excerpts from the concluding dialogue of the story sessions for the Giant Focus Unit suggest the children's movement toward synthesis and their growing ability to identify some of the links which unite traditional and modern tales into a cohesive literary structure.

Follow-up Activities

Creative writing evolved naturally out of this cumulative experience with giant stories. In preparation for the writing assignment, the children were asked to review some of the important features of the giant stories. For example, the question "What words would you use to describe the different kinds of giants you've met in these stories?" generated the following list of contrasts, recorded on a large wall chart in the story corner: good and evil; kind and cruel; helpful and destructive; generous and greedy; gentle and terrifying; lonely and loners; peaceful and fierce; friendly and mean. In addition, one child noted another significant difference: "Some of the giants were like regular human beings—like Fin M'Coul. But other ones were really like awful monsters!"

Next, the children were asked to compare the stories in terms of the plot or problem. They observed that in stories such as *The Great Quillow* and *Jack the Giant Killer*, a village or kingdom was threatened by a destructive, menacing giant. In contrast, in stories such as *The Giant of Grabbist, The Amiable Giant*, and *The Foolish Giant*, it was the giant who had a problem. Instead of being fierce and cruel, the giants in these tales were benign, gentle, friendly creatures in search of companionship.

Another narrative component reviewed in this preparatory session was setting. The children differentiated the "long ago, far away" tales from those with contemporary settings by finding clues such as clothing, houses, transportation, and the presence or absence of modern inventions (e.g., cars, telephones, and electric lights).

The children were asked to formulate theme-statements to summarize the messages or lessons associated with these tales. Some of these responses were:

"You can't always tell what someone is like by how they look."

"Someone can look scary on the outside but be nice on the inside."

"You have to get to know a person to find out what they're really like."

"Even if you're little, you can win over a giant or bully by thinking!"

"Some people are strong in muscles, and some people are strong in their brains."

"If you can't fight with muscles, you should use your brains."

"When you do something nice for someone, they might do something nice for you."

Finally, the children were asked to list some of the recurring patterns which they had discovered during their exploration of the giant tales.

Their list included trickery, magic objects, tasks or tests, supernatural helpers, patterns of three, kindness returned, magical spells, outwitting giants, and happy endings with riches and weddings.

This preparatory review session was used to set the stage for the creation of original giant tales. The children were encouraged to draw from this store of narrative components and patterns to plan their own stories. To prompt the children further, several questions were suggested:

> What kind of giant will be in your story?
>
> Who will the other characters be?
>
> What is the problem?
>
> How will the problem be solved?
>
> Will magic be used?
>
> Where will your story take place?
>
> How will it end?

By this time the children were ready and eager to work independently on their stories. Those who did not have adequate writing skills could choose to dictate their stories to a teacher or a student from the upper grades.

When the children's tales were completed, several group sessions were set aside so that each story could be read aloud and enjoyed by all. During the final group session, one child exclaimed, "Let's make a giant for our classroom!" The other children responded with great enthusiasm to this suggestion, thus setting into motion an entirely new group project which had not been part of the original plan for the Focus Unit. The children volunteered ideas for constructing a three-dimensional giant: what materials to use, where to obtain them, and so on. With the help of the art teacher, a "blueprint" was drawn up, working teams were selected, materials were collected, and the creation of a classroom giant was underway. The final product of this cooperative effort was an eight-foot giant with a papier-mâché head and a body made of chicken wire, boxes, and other assorted items. The children dressed him in clothing borrowed from several tall faculty members and named him Choris. Choris soon became an integral member of the class and the stimulus for further creative writing activities. The children began to talk about Choris as if he were a mysterious visitor. They speculated about his background, personality, interests, and reasons for coming to their school. These speculations were eventually translated into imaginative stories about the history of Choris and his many adventures in the classroom and in other areas of the school. Several children borrowed the story technique used in Hans Christian Andersen's "The Steadfast Tin Soldier," in which the toys came alive late at night when all was quiet. Story patterns borrowed from the giant tales were also incorporated into their narratives. Each story was illustrated and bound into a small book to be used for independent reading in the classroom.

Choris became the center of a "Giant Exhibit." He was surrounded by the children's stories and a variety of paintings and poems produced by individuals and small groups. In addition, the exhibit included the collection of library books used in this Focus Unit. This attractive display of books and creative efforts was a source of pride for the children, who enjoyed sharing the material with each visitor to the classroom.

Independent Activities

During their quiet reading periods, the children enjoyed rereading stories introduced in the group sessions or reading the other books in the Giant Focus Unit collection. A number of children found giant tales at home or at their local libraries and brought them to school to add to the collection. As the children's own stories were completed and placed in the display area, these too were selected for independent reading. Several children chose to read about giants in Georgess McHargue's *The Impossible People* and David Larkin's *Giants*.

Suggestions for other independent activities were printed on 5 × 8-inch cards and stored in a decorated box in the display area. For example, one suggestion card, designed to stimulate poetry writing, presented a list of words used to describe the giant characters in the stories read in the group sessions. The card was an invitation to draw words from this list to create a "word picture" of a giant and to create a painting to correspond to the verbal description. Another suggestion card offered ideas for constructing puppets to represent the "stock characters" for traditional giant tales. A third card suggested the creation of murals or diaramas to depict scenes from favorite giant tales. Many of the children selected the "Giant Riddle" card, which challenged them to write riddles about the characters or plots in the giant stories. A few examples were included on the suggestion card to help the children get started. Each child illustrated his or her own riddle and added it to a loose-leaf notebook designated as "The Giant Riddle Book." This proved to be a source of great enjoyment for all. In addition, the children responded to the riddles by reviewing the stories again and again, focusing on general ideas or recalling specific details. This review tended to reinforce the literary background the children had acquired in the course of this cumulative Focus Unit.

Summary

The Giant Focus Unit extended over several months as a result of the children's enthusiastic response to the stories, discussions, creative writing assignments, and the various projects suggested for independent involvement. Throughout this period, the children were engaged in a wide range of language arts experiences designed to expand their literary background and their reading and writing skills. A key factor in the learning sequence was the general appeal of the subject matter. The children obviously enjoyed exploring the world of giants, and they were highly motivated to become involved in various reading and writing assignments, art projects, and creative dramatic activities, which were all interwoven into a total experience.

16 Dragons: A Focus Unit for Grades Three and Four

> Out of his mouth go burning torches,
> And sparks of fire leap forth.
> Out of his nostrils goeth smoke,
> As out of a seething pot and burning rushes. . . .
> If one lay at him with a sword, it will not hold;
> Nor the spear, the dart, nor the painted shaft.
> He esteemeth iron as straw,
> And brass as rotten wood. . . .
> He maketh the deep to boil like a pot,
> He maketh the sea like a seething mixture.
>
> (Description of Leviathan in
> Job 41:11–23)

The dragon is as old as recorded history and is found in the mythologies and folklore of nearly every tribe or civilization around the world. Students of dragon history have noted that descriptions of Tiamat (the dragon in the ancient Babylonian Creation Epic recorded 4000 years ago), the Chinese Dragon Kings (dating back to 2000 B.C.), and the dragon Leviathan in the Book of Job (40:25 to 41:26) have significantly influenced the features of traditional dragons in the centuries that followed.

Dragons of all shapes and sizes and dispositions have evolved out of the human mind and imagination and the inclination to personify the hopes and fears deeply entrenched in the human psyche. Many volumes have been written by students of dragon lore and by collectors and creators of dragon tales. This Focus Unit was designed to provide an introductory exposure to dragon lore and literature. Initially, the Focus Unit book display included only reference books about dragons, such as Peter Hogarth's *Dragons* and Georgess McHargue's *The Beasts of Never: A History Natural and Un-Natural of Monsters Mythical and Magical*. These and similar books are listed in the first section of the bibliography for this Focus Unit. The children were invited to explore these books and to learn as much as they could about dragons from the illustrations and by reading captions and text. These reference books were used to set the stage for the children's involvement in the Dragon Focus Unit and to contribute to their literary background. These texts also served as valuable resources for the teacher in the preparation and planning stages of the development of this Focus Unit.

The preliminary exposure to the dragons and dragon slayers described in these texts generated interest and provoked curiosity and questions. The first story session was timed appropriately to provide an outlet for the growing excitement about these mythical creatures. At this point, diverse books of dragon tales were added to the reference books on the display table to complete the Focus Unit collection. The students were expected to choose at least three traditional tales and two modern tales for independent reading. The stories read aloud in the group sessions were selected as samples of the broad spectrum of dragon tales from the ancient world, from classical Greece and Rome, from the Middle Ages, from traditional folklore, and from modern literary tales and fantasies.

Objectives

1. To introduce students to dragon lore and literature, including some particularly famous dragons and dragon slayers in literary history.

2. To explore literature featuring two distinctive species of dragons, the Western or European dragon and the Eastern or Oriental dragon.

3. To provide a context for discovering the significance of the dragon in human experience and as an expression of universal hopes and fears.

4. To provide experience with different literary genres and to draw attention to distinguishing features of these genres.

5. To provide opportunities for in-depth study projects designed to challenge those students with exceptional interests and capabilities who are ready for advanced reading, research, and writing experiences.

6. To generate creative expression through writing, painting, and drama.

7. To generate new areas of interest for independent reading.

Bibliography for the Dragon Focus Unit

I. Background

Aylesworth, Thomas. **The Story of Dragons and Other Monsters.** New York: McGraw-Hill, 1980.

Barber, Richard, and Anne Riches. **A Dictionary of Fabulous Beasts.** New York: Macmillan, 1971.

Beisner, Monika, and Alison Lurie. **Fabulous Beasts.** New York: Farrar, Straus and Giroux, 1981.

Epstein, Perle. **Monsters: Their Histories, Homes and Habits.** New York: Doubleday, 1973.

Headon, Deirdre. **Mythical Beasts.** New York: G. P. Putnam's Sons, 1981.

Hogarth, Peter. **Dragons.** New York: Viking Press, 1979.

Huxley, Francis. **The Dragon: Nature of Spirit, Spirit of Nature.** New York: Macmillan, 1979.

Lum, Peter. **Fabulous Beasts.** New York: Pantheon Books, 1951.

McGowen, Tom. **Encyclopedia of Legendary Creatures.** Chicago: Rand McNally, 1981.

McHargue, Georgess. **The Beasts of Never: A History Natural and Un-Natural of Monsters Mythical and Magical.** Indianapolis: Bobbs-Merrill, 1968.

Palmer, Robin. **Dragons, Unicorns, and Other Magical Beasts.** New York: Henry Z. Walck, 1966.

Wise, William. **Monsters of the Middle Ages.** New York: G. P. Putnam's Sons, 1971. (For beginning readers)

II. Group Story Sessions

A. References for Oral Presentations

"Daniel and the Dragon of Babylonia." Sources used for an oral retelling were:

Hogarth, Peter. **Dragons.** New York: Viking Press, 1979.

McHargue, Georgess. **The Beasts of Never.** Indianapolis: Bobbs-Merrill, 1968.

Spicer, Dorothy. **13 Dragons.** New York: Coward, McCann and Geoghegan, 1974.

Zacharias, Alfred. **The Babylonian Dragon and Other Tales.** Muhlenberg Press, 1961.

"Leviathan." Sources used for an oral retelling were:

Book of Job, 40:25 to 41:26.

Hogarth, Peter. **Dragons.** New York: Viking Press, 1979.

McHargue, Georgess. **The Beasts of Never.** Indianapolis: Bobbs-Merrill, 1968.

"Tiamat." Sources used for an oral retelling were:

Aylesworth, Thomas. **The Story of Dragons and Other Monsters.** New York: McGraw-Hill, 1980.

Hogarth, Peter. **Dragons.** New York: Viking Press, 1979.

Huxley, Francis. **The Dragon.** New York: Macmillan, 1979.

McHargue, Georgess. **The Beasts of Never.** Indianapolis: Bobbs-Merrill, 1968.

B. Stories Read Aloud

Brown, Michael, editor. "Thor and the Midgard Serpent." In **A Cavalcade of Sea Legends**. New York: Henry Z. Walck, 1971.

Thor, a popular Norse god, cannot resist the challenge presented by an encounter with the Midgard Serpent. The final outcome of the terrible struggle leaves Thor with a sense of anger and frustration.

Coolidge, Olivia. "Beowulf and the Fire Dragon." In **Legends of the North**. Boston: Houghton Mifflin, 1951.

A dragon guarding a great treasure is enraged by the theft of a single cup and threatens to destroy all in his path. Beowulf, with the help of his one loyal warrior, Wiglaf, slays the terrible monster, but the wound Beowulf receives in battle is fatal.

————. "Heracles." In **Greek Myths**. Boston: Houghton Mifflin, 1949.

Heracles must perform the twelve labors imposed on him by Hera. His second labor is to kill the Lernaean Hydra, a great serpent with nine heads, one of which is immortal. The eleventh labor involves the theft of the apples from the garden of the Hesperides, which is guarded by a dragon.

Cunliffe, John. "Sir Madoc and the Transmogrified Dragon." In **The Great Dragon Competition and Other Stories**. New York: André Deutsch, 1973.

A brave knight engages in extensive combat with a dragon who has the power to change his shape to whatever pleases him.

Domanska, Janina. **King Krakus and the Dragon**. New York: Greenwillow Books, 1979.

When a dragon threatens the town of Krakow, Dratevka, a shoemaker's apprentice, devises a plan to kill the monster.

Gardner, John. "Dragon, Dragon." In **Dragon, Dragon and Other Tales**. New York: Alfred A. Knopf, 1975.

The cobbler's youngest son slays the dragon which had plagued the kingdom and receives as his reward the princess and half the kingdom. This is a very modern and humorous story written in the tradition of the classic tales of dragons and heroes.

Godden, Rumer. **The Dragon of Og**. New York: Viking Press, 1981.

When Angus Og takes over the Castle of Tundergarth in the Scottish Lowlands, he refuses to continue an ancient custom which allowed the Dragon of Og to take two bullocks a month from his herd. Angus ignores the wise advice of those around him, and his stubborn pride nearly leads to tragedy.

Green, Roger, editor. "St. George and the Dragon." In **A Cavalcade of Dragons.** New York: Henry Z. Walck, 1970.

St. George rescues the king's daughter, the beautiful Princess Sabra, from the dragon, converts the king and all his subjects from their heathen beliefs, and baptizes them as Christians.

———. "Sigurd the Dragon Slayer." In **A Cavalcade of Dragons.** New York: Henry Z. Walck, 1970.

His evil guardian, Reginn, convinces Sigurd to go to battle against Fafnir, the dragon who guards Andvari's Treasure. With the help of Odin and the sword Gram, Sigurd survives, slays the dragon, and uncovers the truth about Fafnir and his brother, Reginn.

Holman, Felice, and Nanine Valen. "The Tarasque: The Terror of Nerluc" in **The Drac: French Tales of Dragons and Demons.** New York: Charles Scribner's Sons, 1975.

This is the legend of St. Martha, who saves the people of Nerluc by subduing the dreadful dragon Tarasque with a cross and holy water.

Manning-Sanders, Ruth. "Chien Tang." In **A Book of Dragons.** New York: E. P. Dutton, 1964.

Chien Tang, who lives in a well and whose duty it is to bring the rain, is punished by the Supreme Ruler of Heaven after losing his temper and causing torrents of rain to fall for nine years. However, when Chien Tang rescues the Dragon King's daughter, he is forgiven by the Supreme Ruler and released from his punishment.

———. "The Dragon of the Well." In **A Book of Dragons.** New York: E. P. Dutton, 1964.

When the king's youngest daughter says to him, "I love you like salt," he banishes her for what he interprets as an insult. She marries a poor man, Simonides, whose kindness to a dragon is richly rewarded. The princess is given a chance to teach her father the true meaning of her words.

———. "The Yellow Dragon." In **A Book of Dragons.** New York: E. P. Dutton, 1964.

Farmer Yin and his son, Wu, are protected by the Yellow Dragon from the destructive power of a great storm because of their kindness to the dragon in his disguise as a young stranger.

Nesbit, E. **The Last of the Dragons.** New York: McGraw-Hill, 1980.

The last dragon in Cornwall becomes the pet of the local princess and the prince who is to rescue her from the beast.

Price, Margaret, adapter. "Pegasus and Bellerophon." In **Myths and Enchantment Tales.** Chicago: Rand McNally, 1960.

Bellerophon, astride Pegasus the winged horse, slays the terrible Chimaera, but he is destroyed by his own pride. "Pride goeth before destruction and a haughty spirit before a fall."

————. "Perseus and Andromeda." In **Myths and Enchantment Tales.** Chicago: Rand McNally, 1960.

Returning from his quest to obtain the head of Medusa, Perseus rescues Andromeda from a sea monster and receives permission to marry her from her parents, the King and Queen of Ethiopia.

Spicer, Dorothy. "The Laidly Worm of Spindleston Heugh." In **13 Dragons.** New York: Coward, McCann and Geoghegan, 1974.

When May Margaret is transformed into a hideous Laidly Worm by her jealous stepmother, her faithful brother, Childy Wynd, returns from his adventures to rescue her from this horrible fate, break the spell, and turn the wicked witch-queen into a Laidly Toad.

Untermeyer, Louis. "Jason and the Golden Fleece." In **The Firebringer and Other Great Stories.** New York: M. Evans, 1968.

With the help of Medea, Jason captures the Golden Fleece, which is guarded by an enormous, immortal dragon.

Van Woerkom, Dorothy. **Alexandra the Rock-Eater: An Old Rumanian Tale Retold.** New York: Alfred A. Knopf, 1978.

Alexandra outwits a dragon and his mother in her quest to find enough food for her 100 children.

III. Independent Reading

Blitch, Fleming. **The Last Dragon.** Philadelphia: J. B. Lippincott, 1964.

Broun, Heywood. **The 51st Dragon.** New York: Prentice-Hall, 1968.

Brown, Michael, editor. **A Cavalcade of Sea Legends.** New York: Henry Z. Walck, 1971.

Cheney, Cora, reteller. "How to Become a Dragon." In **Tales from a Taiwan Kitchen.** New York: Dodd, Mead, 1976.

Child Study Association of America, compilers. **Castles and Dragons: Read-to-Yourself Fairy Tales.** New York: Thomas Y. Crowell, 1958.

Coolidge, Olivia. **Greek Myths.** Boston: Houghton Mifflin, 1949.

————. **Hercules and Other Tales from Greek Myths.** New York: Scholastic Book Services, 1960.

————. **Legends of the North.** Boston: Houghton Mifflin, 1951.

Cunliffe, John. **The Great Dragon Competition and Other Stories.** New York: André Deutsch, 1973.

Dalgliesh, Alice, adapter and reteller. **St. George and the Dragon.** New York: Charles Scribner's Sons, 1941.

d'Aulaire, Ingri, and Edgar d'Aulaire. **Book of Greek Myths.** New York: Doubleday, 1962.

———. **Norse Gods and Giants.** New York: Doubleday, 1967.

Delaney, Ned. **One Dragon to Another.** Boston: Houghton Mifflin, 1976.

de Paolo, Tomie. **The Knight and the Dragon.** New York: G. P. Putnam's Sons, 1980.

Dulieu, Jean. **Paulus and the Acornmen.** Cleveland: World, 1966.

———. **Paulus and the Dragon.** Trumansbury, New York: Crossing Press, 1978.

Elgin, Kathleen. **The First Book of Norse Legends.** New York: Franklin Watts, 1956.

Fenner, Phyllis. **Giants and Witches and a Dragon or Two.** New York: Alfred A. Knopf, 1943.

Flory, Jane. **The Lost and Found Princess.** Boston: Houghton Mifflin, 1979.

Froman, Elizabeth. **Mr. Drackle and His Dragons.** New York: Franklin Watts, 1971.

Gannett, Ruth. **The Dragons of Blueland.** New York: Random House, 1951.

———. **Elmer and the Dragon.** New York: Random House, 1950.

———. **My Father's Dragon.** New York: Random House, 1948.

Gardner, John. **Dragon, Dragon and Other Tales.** New York: Alfred A. Knopf, 1975.

Gaster, Theodor, translator and reteller. "The War of the Gods" and "The Snaring of the Dragon." In **The Oldest Stories in the World.** Boston: Beacon Press, 1952.

Grahame, Kenneth. **The Reluctant Dragon.** New York: Holiday House, 1938. New York: Holt, Rinehart and Winston, 1983 (illustrated edition).

Green, Roger, editor. **A Cavalcade of Dragons.** New York: Henry Z. Walck, 1970.

Gringhuis, Dirk. **Giants, Dragons, and Gods: Constellations and Their Folklore.** New York: Meredith Press, 1968.

Haviland, Virginia, reteller. "Assipattle and the Giant Sea Serpent." In **Favorite Fairy Tales Told in Scotland.** Boston: Little, Brown, 1963.

Hawthorne, Nathaniel, reteller. "The Three Golden Apples." In **A Wonder Book.** New York: Grosset and Dunlap, 1967.

Hoban, Russell. **Ace Dragon, Ltd.** London: Jonathan Cape, 1980.

Holl, Adelaide. **Sir Kevin of Devin.** New York: Lothrop, Lee and Shepard Books, 1963.

Holman, Felice, and Nanine Valen. **The Drac: French Tales of Dragons and Demons.** New York: Charles Scribner's Sons, 1975.

Hopf, Alice. **Biography of a Komodo Dragon.** New York: G. P. Putnam's Sons, 1981. (Nonfiction)

Hubbard, O. L. **Dragons, Dragons.** Chicago: Reilly and Lee, 1967.

Kendall, Carol, and Yao-wen Li, retellers. "The Serpent-Slayer." In **Sweet and Sour—Tales from China.** New York: Seabury Press, 1978.

Kingsley, Charles. **The Heroes.** New York: E. P. Dutton, 1965.

Konopka, Ursula, and Joseph Gugenmos. **Dragon Franz.** New York: Greenwillow Books, 1976.

Krahn, Fernando. **The Secret in the Dungeon.** Boston: Clarion Books, 1983.

Krensky, Stephen. **The Dragon Circle.** New York: Scholastic Book Services, 1977.

Laskowski, Jerzy. **The Dragon Liked Smoked Fish.** New York: Seabury Press, 1967.

Lifton, Betty Jean. **Joji and the Dragon.** New York: William Morrow, 1951.

Lloyd, Norris. **The Desperate Dragons.** New York: Hastings House, 1960.

McGowen, Tom. **Dragon Stew.** Chicago: Follett, 1969.

Mahood, Kenneth. **The Laughing Dragon.** New York: Charles Scribner's Sons, 1970.

Manning, Rosemary. **Dragon in Danger.** New York: Penguin Books, 1959.

Manning-Sanders, Ruth. **A Book of Dragons.** New York: E. P. Dutton, 1964.

Massie, Diane. **The Komodo Dragon's Jewels.** New York: Macmillan, 1975. (For beginning readers)

Morgan, Violet. **Sebastian and the Dragon.** New York: Scroll Press, 1970.

Nash, Ogden. **Custard the Dragon.** Boston: Little, Brown, 1936.

Nesbit, E. **The Complete Book of Dragons.** New York: Macmillan, 1972.

Nye, Robert. **Beowulf: A New Telling.** New York: Dell, 1968.

Price, Margaret, adapter. **Myths and Enchantment Tales.** Chicago: Rand McNally, 1960.

Reit, Seymour. **Benvenuto.** Reading, Massachusetts: Addison-Wesley, 1974.

Rinkoff, Barbara. **The Dragon's Handbook.** Camden, New Jersey: Thomas Nelson, 1966.

Rowe, Ann. **The Little Knight.** Chicago: Scott, Foresman, 1971.

Rudchenko, Ivan. **Ivanko and the Dragon.** New York: Atheneum, 1969.

Sakade, Florence, editor. "The Dragon's Tears." In **Urashima Taro and Other Japanese Children's Stories.** Rutland, Vermont: Charles E. Tuttle, 1959.

Scherman, Katherine, reteller. **The Sword of Siegfried.** New York: Random House, 1959.

Serraillier, Ian, reteller. **Beowulf the Warrior.** New York: Henry Z. Walck, 1961.

————. **The Clashing Rocks: The Story of Jason.** New York: Henry Z. Walck, 1964.

————. **The Gorgon's Head: The Story of Perseus.** New York: Henry Z. Walck, 1962.

————. **Hercules and His Labors.** New York: Henry Z. Walck, 1970.

Spicer, Dorothy. **13 Dragons.** New York: Coward, McCann and Geoghegan, 1974.

Squire, James, and Barbara Squire. **Greek Myths and Legends.** New York: Macmillan, 1967.

Sutcliff, Rosemary, reteller. **Beowulf.** New York: E. P. Dutton, 1962.

Tam China, Jurgen. **Dominique and the Dragon.** Harcourt, Brace and World, 1968.

Thayer, Jane. **The Popcorn Dragon.** New York: William Morrow, 1953.

Untermeyer, Louis. **The Firebringer and Other Great Stories.** New York: M. Evans, 1968.

Varga, Judy. **The Dragon Who Liked to Spit Fire.** New York: William Morrow, 1961.

White, Anne Terry. **The Golden Treasury of Myths and Legends.** New York: Golden Press, 1959.

Williams, Jay. **Everyone Knows What a Dragon Looks Like.** New York: Four Winds Press, 1976.

Wise, William. **Sir Howard the Coward.** New York: G. P. Putnam's Sons, 1967.

Yolen, Jane. **Dragon's Blood.** New York: Delacorte Press, 1982.

Zacharias, Alfred. **The Babylonian Dragon and Other Tales.** Muhlenberg Press, 1961.

Zarin, Jane. **The Return of the Dragon.** Boston: Houghton Mifflin, 1981.

IV. Poetry

Bennett, Rowena. "A Modern Dragon." In **Time for Poetry,** compiled by May Hill Arbuthnot. Chicago: Scott, Foresman, 1961.

Carroll, Lewis. "Jabberwocky." In **The Golden Treasury of Poetry,** selected by Louis Untermeyer. New York: Golden Press, 1959.

Holl, Adelaide. **Sir Kevin of Devin.** New York: Lothrop, Lee and Shepard Books, 1963.

Kuskin, Karla. "The Gold-Tinted Dragon." In **The Sound of Poetry** by Mary Austin and Queenie Mills. Boston: Allyn and Bacon, 1964.

Moore, Lilian. "Dragon Smoke." In **Poems Children Will Sit Still For,** compiled by Beatrice Schenk de Regniers et al. New York: Scholastic Book Services, 1969.

Nash, Ogden. **Custard the Dragon.** Boston: Little, Brown, 1936.

Smith, William Jay. "The Toaster." In **Humorous Poetry for Children,** edited by William Cole. Cleveland: World, 1955.

Untermeyer, Louis. "Leviathan." In **The Golden Treasury of Poetry,** selected by Louis Untermeyer. New York: Golden Press, 1959.

Group Story Sessions

First Session

The students were asked to share what they had discovered about dragons in the various reference books made available prior to this first group session. In addition to these individual and rather informal explorations, a more detailed study was carried out by a small "research committee" made up of volunteers interested in doing supplementary reading and record keeping. The following questions were used to guide their search:

1. What are some special characteristics of dragons? What can you learn about their appearance, habits, habitat, enemies, disposition, powers?

2. What are some superstitions about dragons' blood? teeth? eyes?

3. What are the important differences between Eastern and Western dragons?

4. Name some famous dragons.

5. Name some famous dragon slayers.

6. Explain what dragons had to do with ancient religious beliefs.

7. Explain the use of the dragon as a symbol.

By the end of the first group session, the various contributions from individuals and the research committee were pulled together, and the information was organized into broad subtopics determined by the group: 1) Western Dragons, 2) Eastern Dragons, 3) Famous Dragons and

Dragon Slayers, 4) Dragon Folktales, and 5) Dragons and Humans: The Dragon as a Symbol. Two students volunteered to record this material in a large loose-leaf notebook with sections for each category. Throughout the Focus Unit sequence, as the world of dragons was revealed through story, new pages were added to the notebook to include further information and insights as well as story summaries and illustrations. The "Dragon Notebook" was kept on the Focus Unit display table and used frequently as a reference and as a stimulus for informal discussion.

Second Series of Sessions

In the next group sessions, selected dragons from the ancient world were introduced. The children heard about Tiamat, the first dragon according to the Babylonian Creation Epic, about Leviathan in the Old Testament, and about the Babylonian Dragon slain by Daniel in the Apocryphal Book of Bel and the Dragon. Then, two stories from China, "Chien Tang" and "The Yellow Dragon" by Ruth Manning-Sanders, were read aloud. All five stories were discussed in terms of the dragon lore compiled during the initial group session. For example, most of the children recognized the remarkable differences in stories about Eastern and Western dragons. The different artistic treatments were also considered. Two students located in the reference books several paintings and drawings depicting these ancient tales. The children were particularly interested in the many different ways various artists had conceptualized these mythical creatures. Several students were inspired to create their own dragon paintings.

Third Series of Sessions

Classical dragon-slayer tales from Greek and Roman mythologies were selected for the next story sessions: "Jason and the Golden Fleece" by Louis Untermeyer, "Heracles" by Olivia Coolidge, and "Perseus and Andromeda" and "Pegasus and Bellerophon" by Margaret Price. By the time these myths were introduced in the group sessions, many of the children had read other versions of the same myths independently and found some interesting differences. For example, one student who had read "Jason and the Dragon of Colchis" in *A Cavalcade of Dragons* by Roger Green noted that this version provided very little background information: "When I was reading that story I had a lot of questions about what happened in the beginning of the story! But my questions were answered when I heard the story in *The Firebringer* [Louis Untermeyer] collection." Another child added, "In *Myths and Enchantment Tales* [Margaret Price], the story about Jason tells even more about what happened in the beginning and what happened in the end. The real ending is very sad." A student who had read Green's version noted, "In my version, Orpheus, one of the Argonauts, sang a song and played on his lyre and that put the dragon to sleep. But in this other version [Untermeyer], it's Medea who sings the lullaby to make the dragon go to sleep." After comparing different versions of each of these tales, the children were asked to compare the four tales read aloud to the group:

"In all four myths, the hero is sent off on a quest by someone who wants to get rid of him."

"Sometimes it was because of jealousy—like Proetus was jealous of Bellerophon so he planned to have King Iobates get rid of him, so the king sends Bellerophon out to kill the Chimaera because he figures that's a great way to get Bellerophon killed!"

"And Jason's Uncle Pelias gets him to go on a dangerous quest because he doesn't want Jason to get the throne!"

"But all the heroes handle the dragons without getting killed. They're all successful with their quests."

"But these stories have pretty sad endings *after* the hero has his victory."

"Another thing similar about these stories: the heroes get help from gods and goddesses who like them and reward them for being brave and courageous."

"But the heroes also get punished when they do something bad, like when Bellerophon got too proud and decided to ride Pegasus up to Mt. Olympus so Jupiter made him fall off."

"It's almost like that legend in Holland where there are those big strong dikes to hold back the water. But when there was one little crack, it almost caused the whole thing to fall. Bellerophon was so good, but he had that one little bad place inside that messed up everything."

At the conclusion of the discussions about these four myths, descriptions of the dragons and dragon slayers and of the quests were recorded in the appropriate section of the "Dragon Notebook."

Fourth Series of Sessions

Several examples of medieval tales were selected for the next series of group sessions: "Sigurd the Dragon Slayer" by Roger Green, "Beowulf and the Fire Dragon" by Olivia Coolidge, "Thor and the Midgard Serpent" by Michael Brown, "St. George and the Dragon" by Roger Green, "The Tarasque" by Felice Holman and Nanine Valen, and "The Laidly Worm of Spindleston Heugh" by Dorothy Spicer. Again, the children compared these stories with variants or other medieval tales they had read independently. Several had read fuller versions of the epic of Beowulf (Serraillier 1961; Sutcliff; and Nye) and presented some vivid accounts of Beowulf's encounters with Grendel. Robert Nye's book, *Beowulf: A New Telling,* was enthusiastically recommended and rapidly became a "best-seller" for independent reading. Others had read the section in Olivia Coolidge's *Legends of the North* titled "The Last of the Volsungs," which described events leading up to and following those included in "Sigurd the Dragon Slayer" selected for the group session. One student observed, "In the story I read [Coolidge], the *real* ending was very sad. In this one [Green], it only *seems* like a happy ending because you don't get the whole story about what happens next!" Another student added, "It's like the different versions of the legend about Jason. Some stop when it seems like a happy ending, and others tell the rest of the story—how he's not faithful to Medea and wrecks everything!"

A student who had read "How Finn MacCool Got His Wisdom Tooth" by Margaret Hodges (in *Tell It Again: Great Tales from around the World*) found an interesting connection with the legend of Sigurd: "Remember when Reginn gets Sigurd to roast the dragon's heart and, by mistake, Sigurd touches it and licks his finger and gets special knowledge? Well, the same thing happens to Finn. He's told to cook the Salmon of Knowledge for his teacher, but he touches it by mistake and burns his finger and puts it in his mouth, and then all of a sudden he has this super wisdom!" Another reader of the Finn legend noted its similarity to the myth of Perseus:

> "When Finn was born there was a prophecy that his grand-father, a king, would lose his own kingdom because of his grandson, so he threw the baby out the window. But Finn didn't get killed. He was saved by his other grandmother—his father's mother—who brought him up in secret. The same thing happened to the baby Perseus and his mom because of a prophecy that her father [King Acrisius of Argos] would be killed by his grandson, so he sent them off down the river! Prophecies were *really* important to them."

The story of Perseus was also compared with "St. George and the Dragon" by one student: "That scene where the princess is just waiting to be the dragon's dinner is like the part in the Perseus story when Andromeda is waiting to be sacrificed, too. But, fortunately, the hero comes just in time! But St. George doesn't end up marrying the princess; he just wants to get all the people to convert to the Christian religion!" This comment prompted discussion about the prominent role of Christian faith in these medieval stories and the power of sacred symbols, such as the cross and holy water, over evil, personified by the dragon. A student whose parents were reading the tales of King Arthur to him contributed some interesting background about knights and the Crusades.

The children looked for evidence of the spread of Christianity in the stories of this period:

"In 'The Laidly Worm,' when Childy Wynd threw those three drops of water at the wicked witch-queen, she shriveled up—and then he turned her into a toad. I think the water was supposed to be holy water like in baptism—and it has power against evil."

"That story is like a battle back and forth between good and evil. The witch-queen is evil and May Margaret and her brother, Childy Wynd, are good. When he goes back to rescue his sister, he makes a ship out of the Rowan Tree because it has power over evil. That's why the imps and devils she [the witch] sent couldn't harm Childy's ship!"

"I liked the Tarasque story best, because the one who gets the dragon is a *woman* for a change! This story is a lot like St. George. Martha wanted to teach the Christian religion and to do good deeds, and when she went to meet the Tarasque, she held up a cross and he froze—sort of like with Dracula! And then she sprinkled holy water, and then she led him back to the city, and he was tame, like a little lamb, just like in the St. George story."

"And she wore a white dress, which means purity—like when you get confirmed at church."

"I think we should add her to the list of heroes in our 'Dragon Notebook.' She's our first heroine!"

"All those stories were sort of like the good guys against the bad guys. The knights and saints and the regular people with Christian faith were all the good ones who were trying to get rid of the evil in the world. So they fought against dragons and devils and witches and sorcerers."

Fifth Series of Sessions

Following this exposure to dragons from the ancient world, classical Greece and Rome, and the Middle Ages, three examples of traditional folktales about dragons were introduced: *King Krakus and the Dragon* by Janina Domanska, *Alexandra the Rock-Eater: An Old Rumanian Tale Retold* by Dorothy Van Woerkom, and "The Dragon of the Well" by Ruth Manning-Sanders. The children were asked to compare these folktales with other familiar folktales or fairy tales and to contrast them with the myths and epic tales which had been introduced in the first part of this Focus Unit.

Initially, this question generated comparisons with specific stories which seemed to be closely connected to the three folktales read aloud. For example, they noticed that the method used by Dratevka, the apprentice shoemaker in *King Krakus and the Dragon,* was very similar to the plan devised by David in the Apocryphal story. *Alexandra the Rock-Eater* was identified as an interesting, illustrated variant of "Stan Bolovan" by those students who had read this folktale in Ruth Manning-Sanders's *The Book of Dragons.* Of course, they noticed that the major difference between these two retellings of this Romanian tale was that Van Woerkom chose a female character to outwit the dragon instead of the more typical hero. "The Dragon of the Well" was recognized as a Greek variant of a popular English tale, "Cap O' Rushes" (found in *Cap O' Rushes and Other Folk Tales* by Winifred Finlay and *Favorite Fairy Tales Told in England* by Virginia Haviland).

Several students were intrigued that the dragon in this story discriminated between kind and selfish people and responded with appropriate reward or punishment. One student identified similar personality traits in the Russian witch Baba Yaga (*Baba Yaga* by Ernest Small): "Baba Yaga only ate bad Russian children, *not* the good ones. And she helped Vasilisa [*Vasilisa the Beautiful* by Thomas Whitney] because she was so good and kind, and then she [Baba Yaga] punished the wicked stepmother and stepsisters who were so cruel to Vasilisa."

This comparative analysis of specific tales was followed by an examination of the more general patterns characteristic of folktales and fairy tales and of myths:

"The characters are typical: kings and queens and princesses."

"And folktales usually have people who are greedy and rich, like innkeepers and merchants, and people who are kind and hardworking, like shoemakers and farmers and woodcutters."

"And the good people usually get rewarded in fairy tales—and the bad people get punished."

"Or they get taught a lesson like the king in 'The Dragon of the Well.'"

"And there are usually patterns of three: like three princesses, three tasks."

"And the people who faced the dragons in these folktales were just regular people who had to use their brains to outwit the dragon or destroy it."

"They're [the folktales] different than the myths about those heroes with special powers of strength and magic. Those guys had really big battles with the dragons."

"In the folktales, the heroes aren't really dragon slayers like those knights and those Greek heroes. I mean they have to use other methods than the physical ones because they're just normal people."

"In the folktales, the heroes and heroines are usually poor people like the orphan shoemaker in the King Krakus story and like Simonides in "The Dragon of the Well" and Alexandra. But in the myths, the main characters are superheroes with special powers. In the Greek myths, they're related to the gods, and the gods help them. And the saints in those other stories get help from God because they have Christian faith."

"Another difference is the *detail*. Like in the Greek myths, the heroes have specific names, and you know all about their families and their background—like Heracles and Perseus and Jason. But in the folktales, the characters seem more like those generic packages in the grocery stores—with general labels like *farmer* or *king* or *shoemaker*. Sometimes they have a first name, but it's usually a common one like Ivan—remember when we read all those Russian folktales?"

"But they didn't have *family* names. I think they're supposed to be any farmer or any king—not specific people, like Perseus. There's only *one* Perseus!"

"Also, there's a lot more detail in the battles with the dragons in the myths—a lot of blood and wounds."

"And sometimes the *hero* gets killed—like Beowulf."

"That's another *big* difference. The fairy tales all end happily ever after—with happy families like Alexandra's or a big wedding. In the King Krakus story, the shoemaker and the princess didn't actually have a wedding—but you just figure they'll get married and live happily ever after! *Anyway,* in the myths, the endings are usually pretty sad. Heroes get killed and marriages break up—more like the real world, I guess. The fairy tale is more fantasy, sort of how you *wish* it could be."

Sixth Series of Sessions

A few examples of modern dragon tales were shared during the final series of group sessions. To prepare for listening, the children were asked to think about how these stories might be connected to traditional myths, legends, epics, and folktales about dragons. "Sir Madoc and the Transmogrified Dragon" by John Cunliffe was the first of the modern tales read aloud. The children recognized its close connection to medieval tales of brave knights riding off on their faithful horses to fight terrible dragons. Several students commented on the detailed description of the battle scene and the frightening nature of the dragon. Others noted the legendary quality of the tale:

> "It's like a legend because it tells about something that *supposedly* happened long ago, and it explains something *now*. Like this is the legend of how the River Dragon came to be."

> "Maybe the author got the idea when he saw a river that was running fast, like after a storm, and it made him think of a dragon, so he made up a story with the usual knight and dragon battle like the medieval ones."

"Dragon, Dragon" by John Gardner, the second modern tale, was compared with other folktales:

> "You can tell it's like a folktale because the hero is just a cobbler's son and not a knight or superhero."

> "And the 'three sons' in the story is typical. And it's the youngest one who is successful."

> "And he wins because he's not such a know-it-all like the first two brothers, and he's not too proud to take advice from the father. And he was the only one who was worried about the queen—so that shows he's kind."

> "And it's a *quest* tale! In the end, the hero returns and gets the princess and wealth."

> "But it's also very different from the normal folktales. Like usually dragons don't have *freezers* in their caves and don't have *conversations* with dragon slayers!"

> "I think the author didn't expect you to take it seriously. I think he wrote it to make you laugh. Like that silly old wizard and the cowardly knights are funny—so you figure it's not going to be scary like most dragon tales."

Several children who had read *The Desperate Dragons* by Norris Lloyd observed that the young heroes in both tales had unwittingly caused the dragons to laugh so hard that they became helpless.

The Last of the Dragons by E. Nesbit was read aloud next and identified as another humorous tale with the basic ingredients of the traditional fairy tale plus some nontraditional features:

> "As soon as you see the pictures, you know it's not going to be a regular fairy tale."

> "The princess doesn't want to be rescued. She likes to fence and wants to kill the dragon *herself!*"

"And the prince likes to study instead of fencing, and he rides a motorcar instead of a horse."

"And the dragon doesn't even *like* to eat princesses. He's really a tame dragon who's just looking for a little kindness and petrol!"

When asked to compare these three modern dragon tales, the children found that each author had used traditional forms and story motifs to create a new tale:

"The story about Sir Modoc seems closest to the old tales. It doesn't have the funny parts like in 'Dragon, Dragon' and *The Last of the Dragons.*"

"I think Mr. Cunliffe's dragon is more like the fierce old-fashioned dragons. And the dragons in the other two stories are more *new-fashioned.* Someone in *The Last of the Dragons* even said that dragons were out-of-date."

"It seems that maybe in modern times, people don't take dragons as seriously as they used to. In the olden times, they really believed in dragons. So that's why now the dragon stories are funnier, and a lot of the new dragons are funny and tame, and they're not really evil at all."

"But there are still a lot of other really terrible monsters in modern stories that are as bad as the old ones. Like *Jaws.* Maybe Jaws is sort of a modern dragon or sea serpent in an old-fashioned scary type of story.

Finally, *The Dragon of Og* by Rumer Godden was read aloud as an example of a tale created from an ancient legend by a master storyteller. The children especially enjoyed the references to dragon lore and the vivid account of the way of life in the Scottish Lowlands. They recognized that the first method used by Angus Og to get rid of the dragon was borrowed from the plan devised by Daniel and used again against the Dragon of Krakow; for the second attempt, Angus Og hired a knight in shining armor, reminiscent of the traditional medieval dragon-slaying hero. They noted that the author used her knowledge of dragon lore to construct the surprising and satisfying conclusion for this delightful tale.

The children appreciated the careful development of each of the main characters. After discussing the distinguishing features of Angus Og, Lady Matilda, Donald and Edith, the dragon, and Sir Robert, as well as the supporting cast of characters, many of the children expressed interest in dramatizing the story. These children were given the opportunity and necessary help to produce "Scenes from *The Dragon of Og,*" which was performed for their classmates and several neighboring classes.

Creative Expression

1. Drama

The production of "Scenes from *The Dragon of Og*" inspired other students to work together on informal dramatizations of favorite tales from the Dragon Focus Unit collection. One group did a mime portrayal of the confrontation between Jason and Medea and the dragon guarding the Golden Fleece. Another group, with assistance from the art teacher, created masks for a scene from "St. George and the Dragon." Dance-drama was the form used to dramatize the rescue of May Margaret from the curse condemning her to be the Laidly Worm. The children selected appropriate costumes and props from a large trunk containing a wonderful assortment of interesting items collected over the years from attics, basements, and garage sales.

2. Art

The wide variety of paintings, drawings, and illustrations of dragons found in the Focus Unit collection set the stage for a class project which involved the creation of a series of five dragon murals. After a brief review of the dragon tales read by the group or independently and of the five general categories into which these stories had been grouped (ancient, classical, medieval, folktale, and modern), five subcommittees were formed, each responsible for creating a mural to represent its category. First, each group painted an appropriate background for its category. Then, each member of the group chose a favorite hero, heroine, or dragon from a tale within that category to paint, cut out, and mount on the mural panel. The finished murals, displayed in sequence on the hall bulletin boards, presented an interesting total picture of the children's long-term study of dragons.

3. Poetry

Like the drama projects, the poetry projects were done on a volunteer basis. They provided additional challenges and opportunities for creative expression for those students with special interests, talents, and the motivation to become involved in diverse learning experiences. To set the stage for the creative process, the children were introduced to several examples of different types of dragon poems in the Focus Unit collection. Some students worked in pairs; others chose to work individually. The original poems produced by the young poets ranged from descriptive word portraits of famous dragons to vivid accounts of battle scenes between great fire-breathing dragons and brave knights with shining armor and flashing swords. One student wrote a very thoughtful and sensitive poem about a hero getting ready to face a dreaded dragon. Several children, inspired by William Jay Smith's "The Toaster" and Rowena Bennett's "A Modern Dragon," chose to experiment with metaphor and simile. Ogden Nash's *Custard the Dragon* stimulated others to create narrative poems about humorous dragon characters.

4. Creative Writing

A group session was scheduled to prepare for the creative writing project culminating the Dragon Focus Unit. "The Dragon Notebook" was used as a major resource to review the various types of stories explored by the group and by individuals: myths, legends, and epics; traditional folktales and fairy tales; modern fairy tales and longer fiction; tragic, comic, and romantic tales. This overview was designed to generate a framework for producing original dragon tales and to assist the children in making decisions about the nature of the tales they would write. Before leaving the group session to work independently, each child had determined what kind of story he or she planned to create. Once the writing was in progress, the teacher worked with students individually to discuss their emerging narratives. In these teacher-student conferences, the children read what they had written and received feedback to guide them toward syntactic and semantic accuracy and cohesion. A major goal of the conferences was to foster "a sense of audience" in these young writers. Their growing awareness of the public nature of their writing influenced them as they wrote. Knowing that their stories were to be bound into individual books and added to the class library for the reading enjoyment of others, the children were willing to revise and rewrite in order to produce a final draft which could be a source of personal pride and satisfaction.

References

Finlay, Winifred. *Cap O' Rushes and Other Folk Tales.* Eau Claire, Wisconsin: E. M. Hale, 1974.
Haviland, Virginia. *Favorite Fairy Tales Told in England,* retold by Joseph Jacobs. Boston: Little, Brown, 1959.
Small, Ernest. *Baba Yaga.* Boston: Houghton Mifflin, 1966.
Whitney, Thomas. *Vasilisa the Beautiful.* New York: Macmillan, 1968.

Appendix:
Professional References

Appendix:
Professional References

I. About Children's Books: Appreciation, Criticism, and Application

Bader, Barbara. *American Picturebooks from Noah's Ark to the Beast Within.* New York: Macmillan, 1976.

Bauer, Caroline. *This Way to Books.* New York: H. W. Wilson, 1983.

Bettelheim, Bruno. *The Uses of Enchantment: Meaning and Importance of Fairy Tales.* New York: Alfred A. Knopf, 1976.

Butler, Francelia. *Sharing Literature with Children: A Thematic Anthology.* New York: David McKay, 1977.

Carlson, Ruth. *Literature for Children: Enrichment Ideas.* Dubuque: William C. Brown, 1970.

Chambers, Aidan. *Introducing Books to Children.* London: Heinemann, 1973.

Chambers, Dewey. *Children's Literature in the Curriculum.* Chicago: Rand McNally, 1971.

Cianciolo, Patricia. *Illustrations in Children's Books.* Dubuque: William C. Brown, 1976.

Cullinan, Bernice. *Literature and the Child.* New York: Harcourt Brace Jovanovich, 1981.

Cullinan, Bernice, and Carolyn Carmichael. *Literature and Young Children.* Urbana, Illinois: National Council of Teachers of English, 1977.

Egoff, Sheila. *Thursday's Child: Trends and Patterns in Contemporary Children's Literature.* Chicago: American Library Association, 1981.

Georgiou, Constantine. *Children and Their Literature.* Englewood Cliffs, New Jersey: Prentice-Hall, 1969.

Hearne, Betsy. *Choosing Books for Children: A Commonsense Guide.* New York: Delacorte Press, 1981.

Hearne, Betsy, and Marilyn Kaye, editors. *Celebrating Children's Books: Essays on Children's Literature in Honor of Zena Sutherland.* New York: Lothrop, Lee and Shepard Books, 1981.

Hopkins, Lee Bennett. *The Best of Book Bonanza.* New York: Holt, Rinehart and Winston, 1980.

Huck, Charlotte. *Children's Literature in the Elementary School,* 3rd ed. New York: Holt, Rinehart and Winston, 1979.

Hunter, Mollie. *Talent Is Not Enough.* New York: Harper and Row, 1976.

Leonard, Charlotte. *Tied Together: Topics and Thoughts for Introducing Children's Books.* Metuchen, New Jersey: Scarecrow Press, 1980.

Lonsdale, Bernard, and Helen Mackintosh. *Children Experience Literature.* New York: Random House, 1973.

Meek, Margaret, et al. *The Cool Web: The Pattern of Children's Reading.* New York: Atheneum, 1978.

Meeker, Alice. *Enjoying Literature with Children.* New York: Odyssey Press, 1969.

Montebello, Mary. *Children's Literature in the Curriculum.* Dubuque: William C. Brown, 1972.

Moss, Joy F. "The Fable and Critical Thinking." *Language Arts* 57 (January 1980): 21–29.

———. "Paperbacks in the Classroom." *The Horn Book Magazine* 57 (February 1981): 98–103.

———. "Using the 'Focus Unit' to Enhance Children's Response to Literature." *Language Arts* 55 (April 1978): 482–88.

Paterson, Katherine. *Gates of Excellence: On Reading and Writing Books for Children.* New York: Elsevier/Nelson, 1981.

Roser, Nancy, and Margaret Frith. *Children's Choices: Teaching with Books Children Like.* Newark, Delaware: International Reading Association, 1983.

Sebesta, Sam L., and William Iverson. *Literature for Thursday's Child.* Palo Alto: Scientific Research Associates, 1975.

Sloan, Glenna Davis. *The Child as Critic: Teaching Literature in the Elementary School.* New York: Teachers College Press, 1975.

Smith, James, and Dorothy Park. *Word Music and Word Magic: Children's Literature Methods.* Boston: Allyn and Bacon, 1977.

Smith, Lillian. *The Unreluctant Years.* New York: Viking Press, 1967.

Stewig, John Warren, and Sam L. Sebesta, editors. *Using Literature in the Elementary Classroom.* Urbana, Illinois: National Council of Teachers of English, 1978.

Sutherland, Zena, Dianne Monson, and May H. Arbuthnot. *Children and Books,* 6th ed. Chicago: Scott, Foresman, 1981.

Trelease, Jim. *The Read-Aloud Handbook.* New York: Penguin Books, 1982.

Vandergrift, Kay. *Child and Story: The Literary Connection.* New York: Neal-Schuman, 1980.

White, Mary Lou. *Children's Literature: Criticism and Response.* Columbus, Ohio: Charles E. Merrill, 1976.

Yolen, Jane. *Touch Magic: Fantasy, Faerie and Folklore in the Literature of Childhood.* New York: Philomel Books, 1981.

II. Book Selection Aids

A. Books

Arbuthnot, May Hill, et al. *Children's Books Too Good to Miss.* Cleveland: Case Western Reserve University Press, 1971.

Baskin, Barbara, and Karen Harris, compilers. *Notes from a Different Drummer: A Guide to Juvenile Fiction Portraying the Handicapped.* New York: R. R. Bowker, 1977.

Brewton, John, Sara Brewton, and Meredith Blackburn III. *Index to Poetry for Children and Young People.* New York: H. W. Wilson, 1972.

Cathon, Laura, et al., editors. *Stories to Tell to Children: A Selected List.* Pittsburgh: University of Pittsburgh Press, 1974.

Child Study Association of America, Children's Book Committee. *Children's Books of the Year*. New York: Child Study Association of America. (Published annually)

Children's Books in Print. New York: R. R. Bowker. (Published annually)

Cianciolo, Patricia, editor. *Picture Books for Children*. Chicago: American Library Association, 1973.

Dill, Barbara, editor. *Children's Catalog*. New York: H. W. Wilson. (Published every five years)

Dryer, Sharon Spredermann. *The Bookfinder: A Guide to Children's Literature about the Needs and Problems of Youth Aged 2–15*. Circle Pines, Minnesota: American Guidance Service, 1977.

Fassler, Joan. *Helping Children Cope: Mastering Stress through Books and Stories*. New York: Free Press, 1978.

Fisher, Margery. *Who's Who in Children's Books: A Treasury of the Familiar Characters of Childhood*. New York: Holt, Rinehart and Winston, 1975.

Gillespie, John. *More Juniorplots*. New York: R. R. Bowker, 1977.

Gillespie, John T., and Diane Lembo. *Introducing Books: A Guide for the Middle Grades*. New York: R. R. Bowker, 1970.

———. *Juniorplots: A Book Talk Manual for Teachers and Librarians*. New York: R. R. Bowker, 1967.

Graves, Michael, et al. *Easy Reading: Book Series and Periodicals for Less Able Readers*. Newark, Delaware: International Reading Association, 1979.

Haviland, Virginia. *Children's Literature: A Guide to Reference Sources*. Washington, D.C.: Library of Congress, 1966, 1972, 1977.

Haviland, Virginia, and William Jay Smith, compilers. *Children and Poetry: A Selective, Annotated Bibliography*. Washington, D.C.: Library of Congress, 1970.

Hearne, Betsy. *Choosing Books for Children: A Commonsense Guide*. New York: Delacorte Press, 1981.

Iarusso, Marilyn, compiler. *Stories: A List of Stories to Tell and to Read Aloud*, 7th ed. New York: New York Public Library, 1977.

Kimmel, Mary Margaret, and Elizabeth Segal. *For Reading Out Loud!* New York: Delacorte Press, 1983.

Kingman, Lee, editor. *Newbery and Caldecott Medal Books: 1966–1975*. Boston: Horn Book, 1975.

Larrick, Nancy. *A Teacher's Guide to Children's Books*. Columbus, Ohio: Charles E. Merrill, 1960.

Lass-Woodin, Mary Jo, editor. *Books on American Indians and Eskimos: A Selection Guide for Children and Young Adults*. Chicago: American Library Association, 1977.

Lynn, Ruth N. *Fantasy for Children: An Annotated Checklist*. New York: R. R. Bowker, 1979.

Nicholsen, Margaret. *People in Books: A Selective Guide to Biographical Literature Arranged by Vocations and Other Fields of Reader Interest*. New York: H. W. Wilson, 1969.

Rudman, Masha K. *Children's Literature: An Issues Approach*. Lexington, Massachusetts: D. C. Heath, 1976.

Silverman, Judith, editor. *Index to Young Reader's Collective Biographies,* 2nd ed. New York: R. R. Bowker, 1975.

Spirt, Diana. *Introducing More Books: A Guide for the Middle Grades.* New York: R. R. Bowker, 1978.

Subject Guide to Children's Books in Print. New York: R. R. Bowker. (Published annually)

Sutherland, Zena, editor. *The Best in Children's Books: The University of Chicago Guide to Children's Literature, 1966–1972.* Chicago: University of Chicago Press, 1973.

Tway, Eileen, editor. *Reading Ladders for Human Relations.* Urbana, Illinois: National Council of Teachers of English, 1981.

White, Mary Lou, editor. *Adventuring with Books: A Booklist for Pre-K–Grade 8.* Urbana, Illinois: National Council of Teachers of English, 1981.

B. Journals

The Booklist (American Library Association)

The Bulletin of the Center for Children's Books (University of Chicago Press)

Cricket Magazine (Open Court Publishing)

Horn Book Magazine (Horn Book)

Language Arts (National Council of Teachers of English)

The New York Times Book Review (New York Times)

The Reading Teacher (International Reading Association)

School Library Journal (R. R. Bowker)

Top of the News (American Library Association)

The WEB (Ohio State University Center for Language, Literature and Reading)

III. Exploring Traditional Literature

Asimov, Isaac. *Words from the Myths.* Boston: Houghton Mifflin, 1961.

Barber, Richard. *A Companion to World Mythology.* New York: Delacorte Press, 1980.

Briggs, Katherine, editor. *A Dictionary of British Folk-Tales in the English Language.* Bloomington: Indiana University Press, 1970.

Bulfinch, Thomas. *Age of Fable: Or, Stories of Gods and Heroes.* Glendale, California: Heritage, 1958.

Carlson, Atelia, and Gilbert B. Croff. *World Folktales: A Scribner Resource Collection.* New York: Charles Scribner's Sons, 1980.

Carlson, Ruth, compiler and editor. *Folklore and Folktales around the World.* Newark, Delaware: International Reading Association, 1972.

Cook, Elizabeth. *The Ordinary and the Fabulous: An Introduction to Myths, Legends, and Fairy Tales for Teachers and Storytellers.* New York: Cambridge University Press, 1969.

Coughlan, Margaret. *Folklore from Africa to the United States.* Washington, D.C.: Library of Congress, 1976.

Dorson, Richard M., editor. Folktales of the World Series. Chicago: University of Chicago Press.

Eastman, Mary Huse. *Index to Fairy Tales, Myths and Legends.* Boston: F. W. Faxon, 1926, 1937, 1952.

Favat, Andre. *Child and Tale: The Origins of Interest.* Urbana, Illinois: National Council of Teachers of English, 1977.

Ireland, Norma. *Index to Fairy Tales, 1949–1972: Including Folklore, Legends and Myths in Collections.* Boston: F. W. Faxon, 1973.

Leach, Maria, and Jerome Fried, editors. *Funk and Wagnall's Standard Dictionary of Folklore, Mythology and Legend,* vols. I and II. New York: Funk and Wagnalls, 1949.

Lynn, Ruth Nadelman. *Fantasy for Children: An Annotated Checklist and Reference Guide.* New York: R. R. Bowker, 1983.

Luthi, Max. *Once upon a Time: On the Nature of Fairy Tales.* Bloomington: Indiana University Press, 1976.

MacDonald, Margaret Read. *Storyteller's Sourcebook.* Detroit: Gale Research, 1982.

McHargue, Georgess. *The Impossible People: A History Natural and Unnatural of Beings Terrible and Wonderful.* New York: Holt, Rinehart and Winston, 1972.

Opie, Iona, and Peter Opie. *The Classic Fairy Tales.* New York: Oxford University Press, 1974.

Propp, V. *Morphology of the Folktale.* Austin: University of Texas Press, 1968.

Sawyer, Ruth. *The Way of the Storyteller.* New York: Viking Press, 1942, 1962.

Thompson, Stith. *The Folktale.* Berkeley: University of California Press, 1977.

Travers, Pamela. *About the Sleeping Beauty.* New York: McGraw-Hill, 1975.

Ullom, Judith, compiler. *Folklore of the North American Indians: An Annotated Bibliography.* Washington, D.C.: Library of Congress, 1969.

Yolen, Jane. *Touch Magic: Fantasy, Faerie and Folklore in the Literature of Childhood.* New York: Philomel Books, 1981.

Ziegler, Elsie B. *Folklore: An Annotated Bibliography and Index to Single Editions.* Boston: F. W. Faxon, 1973.

IV. About Authors and Illustrators of Children's Books

Aldis, Dorothy. *Nothing Is Impossible: The Story of Beatrix Potter.* New York: Atheneum, 1969.

Blair, Gwenda. *Laura Ingalls Wilder.* New York: G. P. Putnam's Sons, 1981.

Blegvad, Erik. *Self-Portrait: Erik Blegvad.* Reading, Massachusetts: Addison-Wesley, 1979.

Block, Irving. *The Lives of Pearl Buck: A Tale of China and America.* New York: Thomas Y. Crowell, 1973.

Commire, Anne. *Something about the Author: Facts and Pictures about Contemporary Authors and Illustrators of Books for Young People.* Detroit: Gale Research Service. (1971 to present)

DeMontreville, Doris, and Elizabeth Crawford. *Fourth Book of Junior Authors and Illustrators.* New York: H. W. Wilson, 1978.

DeMontreville, Doris, and Donna Hill. *Third Book of Junior Authors.* New York: H. W. Wilson, 1972.

Doyle, Brian. *The Who's Who of Children's Literature.* New York: Schocken Books, 1969.

Fisher, Aileen, and Olive Rabe. *We Alcotts.* New York: Atheneum, 1968.

Fritz, Jean. *Homesick: My Own Story.* New York: G. P. Putnam's Sons, 1982.

Fuller, Muriel, editor. *More Junior Authors.* New York: H. W. Wilson, 1963.

Godden, Rumer. *Hans Christian Andersen: A Great Life in Brief.* New York: Alfred A. Knopf, 1955.

Hoffman, Miriam, and Eva Samuels, editors. *Authors and Illustrators of Children's Books: Writings on Their Lives and Works.* New York: R. R. Bowker, 1972.

Hopkins, Lee Bennett. *Books Are by People.* New York: Citation Press, 1969.

———. *More Books by More People.* New York: Citation Press, 1974.

Jones, Helen, editor. *Robert Lawson, Illustrator.* Boston: Little, Brown, 1972.

Kelen, Emery. *Mr. Nonsense: A Life of Edward Lear.* New York: W. W. Norton, 1973.

Kingman, Lee, editor. *The Illustrator's Notebook.* Boston: Horn Book, 1978.

———. *Illustrators of Children's Books: 1967–1976.* Boston: Horn Book, 1978.

Kirkpatrick, Daniel, editor. *Twentieth-Century Children's Writers.* New York: St. Martin's Press, 1978.

Kunitz, Stanley, and Howard Haycroft, editors. *The Junior Book of Authors,* 2nd ed. New York: H. W. Wilson, 1951.

Lane, Margaret. *The Tale of Beatrix Potter: A Biography.* New York: Frederick Warne, 1946.

Larkin, David, editor. *The Art of Nancy Ekholm Burkert.* New York: Harper and Row, 1977.

Lee, Betsy. *Judy Blume's Story.* Minneapolis: Dillon Press, 1981.

Lenski, Lois. *Journey into Childhood: The Autobiography of Lois Lenski.* Philadelphia: J. B. Lippincott, 1972.

Locher, Frances, editor. *Contemporary Authors.* Detroit: Gale Research Service. (1964 to present)

Mahony, Bertha, and Elinor Whitney. *Contemporary Illustrators of Children's Books.* Detroit: Gale Research Service, 1978.

Milne, Christopher. *The Enchanted Places.* New York: Penguin Books, 1974.

Proudfit, Isabel. *The Treasure Hunter: The Story of Robert Louis Stevenson.* New York: Julian Messner, 1939.

Richter, Hans Peter. *I Was There.* New York: Holt, Rinehart and Winston, 1972.

Singer, Isaac Bashevis. *A Day of Pleasure: Stories of a Boy Growing Up in Warsaw.* New York: Farrar, Straus and Giroux, 1969.

Ward, Martha E., and Dorothy A. Marquardt. *Authors of Books for Young People.* Metuchen, New Jersey: Scarecrow Press, 1971.

———. *Illustrators of Books for Young People.* Metuchen, New Jersey: Scarecrow Press, 1970.

Wilder, Laura Ingalls. *West from Home: Letters of Laura Ingalls Wilder, San Francisco, 1915,* edited by Roger MacBride. New York: Harper and Row, 1974.

Wintle, Justin, and Emma Fisher. *The Pied Pipers.* New York: Two Continents Publishing Group, 1975.

Wood, James. *The Lantern Bearer: A Life of Robert Louis Stevenson.* New York: Pantheon Books, 1965.

Zemach, Margot. *Self-Portrait: Margot Zemach.* Reading, Massachusetts: Addison-Wesley, 1978. (See other volumes of the "Self-Portrait Collection" about picture-book artists)

V. Collections of Poetry

Arbuthnot, May Hill. *Time for Poetry.* Chicago: Scott, Foresman, 1961.

Association for Childhood Education International, compiler. *Sung under the Silver Umbrella.* New York: Macmillan, 1935.

Behn, Harry, translator. *Cricket Songs: Japanese Haiku.* New York: Harcourt, Brace and World, 1964.

Blishen, Edward, compiler. *Oxford Book of Poetry for Children.* New York: Franklin Watts, 1963.

Ciardi, John. *The Reason for the Pelican.* Philadelphia: J. B. Lippincott, 1959.

Cole, William. *Humorous Poetry for Children.* Cleveland: World, 1955.

———. *Oh, What Nonsense!* New York: Viking Press, 1966.

de la Mare, Walter. *Come Hither.* New York: Alfred A. Knopf, 1957.

———. *Complete Poems of Walter de la Mare.* New York: Alfred A. Knopf, 1969.

Dunning, Stephen, et al., editors. *Reflections on a Gift of a Watermelon Pickle and Other Modern Verse.* New York: Lothrop, Lee and Shepard Books, 1967.

Frost, Robert. *Complete Poems of Robert Frost.* New York: Holt, Rinehart and Winston, 1958.

Fujikawa, Gyo, compiler. *A Child's Book of Poems.* New York: Grosset and Dunlap, 1969.

Hollowell, Lillian. *A Book of Children's Literature.* New York: Holt, Rinehart and Winston, 1966.

Hughes, Langston. *The Dream Keeper and Other Poems.* New York: Alfred A. Knopf, 1945.

Johnson, Edna, et al. *Anthology of Children's Literature.* Boston: Houghton Mifflin, 1970.

Kuskin, Karla. *Dogs and Dragons, Trees and Dreams.* New York: Harper and Row, 1980.

Larrick, Nancy. *Bring Me All Your Dreams.* New York: M. Evans, 1980.

———. *On City Streets: An Anthology of Poetry.* Philadelphia: J. B. Lippincott, 1968.

———. *Piping down the Valleys Wild: Poetry for the Young of All Ages.* New York: Delacorte Press, 1968.

Lear, Edward. *The Complete Nonsense Book.* New York: Dodd, Mead, 1912, 1958.

Lewis, Richard. *In a Spring Garden.* New York: Dial Press, 1965.

———. *Miracles: Poems by Children of the English Speaking World.* New York: Simon and Schuster, 1966.

———. *The Moment of Wonder: A Collection of Chinese and Japanese Poetry.* New York: Dial Press, 1954.

Livingston, Myra Cohn, editor. *Listen, Children, Listen.* New York: Atheneum, 1972.

———. *A Tune beyond Us: A Collection of Poems.* New York: Harcourt, Brace and World, 1968.

McCord, David. *One at a Time.* Boston: Little, Brown, 1966.

Milne, A. A. *When We Were Very Young.* New York: Dell, 1970.

Nash, Ogden. *Custard and Company,* compiled by Quentin Blake. Boston: Little, Brown, 1980.

O'Neill, Mary. *Hailstones and Halibut Bones.* New York: Doubleday, 1961.

Opie, Iona, and Peter Opie, editors. *The Oxford Book of Children's Verse.* New York: Oxford University Press, 1973.

———. *The Oxford Nursery Rhyme Book.* New York: Oxford University Press, 1955.

Prelutsky, Jack. *The Random House Book of Poetry for Children.* New York: Random House, 1983.

Read, Herbert, compiler. *This Way, Delight: A Book of Poetry for the Young.* New York: Pantheon Books, 1956.

The Real Mother Goose, illustrated by Blanche Fisher Wright. Chicago: Rand McNally, 1916.

Silverstein, Shel. *Where the Sidewalk Ends.* New York: Harper and Row, 1974.

Stevenson, Robert Louis. *A Child's Garden of Verses.* New York: Platt and Munk, 1977.

Untermeyer, Louis, compiler. *The Golden Treasury of Poetry.* New York: Golden Press, 1959.

The Tall Book of Mother Goose, illustrated by Feodor Rojankovsky. New York: Harper and Row, 1942.

Wallace, Daisy. *Fairy Poems.* New York: Holiday House, 1980.

———. *Giant Poems.* New York: Holiday House, 1978.

———. *Witch Poems.* New York: Holiday House, 1976.

Werner, Jane, editor. *The Golden Mother Goose.* New York: Simon and Schuster, 1948.

Wildsmith, Brian. *Brian Wildsmith's Mother Goose.* New York: Franklin Watts, 1965.

Withers, Carl, compiler. *A Rocket in My Pocket: The Rhymes and Chants of Young Americans.* New York: Holt, Rinehart and Winston, 1948.

Author

Joy F. Moss is Language Arts Resource Teacher and Reading Consultant at the Harley School, Rochester, New York, and is Adjunct Assistant Professor at the University of Rochester, where she has taught courses in reading and children's literature. She also serves as Director of the Community Teacher Center in Rochester. Recent publications have been on the topic of using children's literature in the classroom and have appeared in *Language Arts, The Reading Teacher,* and *The Horn Book Magazine.*

DATE DUE

RESERVE BOOK

DUE 2 HOURS FROM SIGN
OVERNIGHT LOAN DUE 8:00

GAYLORD